Afghanistan

From Terror to Freedom

Afghanistan

From Terror to Freedom

Apratim Mukarji

STERLING PUBLISHERS PRIVATE LIMITED

STERLING PUBLISHERS PRIVATE LIMITED
A-59 Okhla Industrial Area, Phase-II, New Delhi-110020.
Tel: 26387070, 26386209; Fax: 91-11-26383788
E-mail: ghai@nde.vsnl.net.in
www.sterlingpublishers.com

Afghanistan: From Terror to Freedom
© 2003, Apratim Mukarji
ISBN 81 207 2542 5

All rights are reserved. No part of this publication may be reproduced, stored in a retrieval system or transmitted, in any form or by any means, mechanical, photocopying, recording or otherwise, without prior written permission of the original publisher.

PRINTED IN INDIA

Published by Sterling Publishers Pvt. Ltd., New Delhi-110 020.
Laserset at Vikas Compographics, New Delhi-110020.
Printed at Rastra Rachna Printer, Delhi.

Contents

	Introduction	1
1.	Options Before Afghanistan	28
2.	Horror Called the Taleban	64
3.	The Dark Age Descends	100
4.	Terrorism at the Centre-Stage	153
5.	Two Days in September 2001	179
	Appendix 1 (a)	245
	Appendix 1 (b)	248
	Appendix 2	251
	Appendix 3	254
	Appendix 4	259
	Appendix 5 (a)	278
	Appendix 5 (b)	281
	Appendix 6	288
	Appendix 7	292
	Index	303

Introduction

It was early evening on 5 September 2002, a balmy weather prevailing in the midst of pomp and splendour. President Hamid Karzai, accompanied by his American bodyguards, was visiting Kandahar; first, to attend his brother's funeral, and then, grace a wedding. The presidential party had just got out of the Governor's House, with governor, the burly Gul Agha Sherzai, striding by his side and Karzai about to get into his limousine, when a man, apparently wearing the uniform of the new Afghan army, appeared right in front of the vehicle and opened fire. A bodyguard fired back at the man and both lay dead in an instant. Governor Gul Agha was slightly wounded in the neck; the president was whisked away before one could realise what was happening. One American serviceman was injured.

Abdel Rahman, the failed assassin, had joined the army barely a fortnight before, a former United States ambassador who was in the presidential party later told this author. Army recruitments go through screening, but this man, obviously a Taleban survivor, had managed to get through the checking process. One report later said that according to sources in Kandahar, two other gunmen, who had mingled successfully with the crowd at the wedding party where President Karzai went after the attempt, were also arrested.[1] The subsequent arrests indicated the extent of the conspiracy, since the conspirators had planned the back-up to the first assassin so that if the first attempt failed, Karzai would not be able to escape the second attempt.

About four hours earlier on the same Thursday, Kabul witnessed the most serious terrorist act since the fall of the Taleban (13 November 2001) and the installation of the interim administration (22 December 2001) and the assumption of office by the subsequent Transitional Islamic Government of Afghanistan (June 2002). A total of thirty-two people died and 150 others injured when two bombs exploded in quick succession in downtown Kabul. Most of the casualties were caused by the massive secondary blast, occurring outside the Ministry of Information and Culture. At least two cars were destroyed in the explosions and dozens of windowpanes in the Ministry were smashed. The blast was clearly the most serious terrorist attack in Kabul since sporadic violence had returned to Afghanistan.

For over a week before, smaller attacks were reported from the capital and southern and eastern Afghanistan. Starting with the 6 July 2002, assassination of Vice-President Haji Abdul Qadeer, the incidents (including the arrest of two persons in a Toyota Corolla containing semtex explosives on 29 July 2002 in Kabul, presumably a car-bomb meant for President Karzai) were gradually pointing towards a well-developed destabilisation campaign against the Karzai government. Even when targets were not discernible, the plotters were obviously hoping to recreate panic and tension in the country settling down to a restoration of normality after twenty-three years of constant warfare. That the elements inimical to the government had not been deterred by the detections and foiling of attempts was evident when the International Security Assistance Force (ISAF), the international force detailed to Afghanistan to

Introduction

maintain security in the capital, arrested two Pakistanis after a dynamite was detected in their fully loaded fuel tanker bound for a United States airbase at the Bagram airfield, north of Kabul.

Even as security is once again a concern in Afghanistan, one year after the sudden collapse of the evil Taleban government in Kabul and restoration of representative rule, the country continues to be depressingly devastated. Nobody had expected a quick recovery from the twenty-three years of depredation, but still the very realisation of what the country and its people had gone through over such a protracted period of time numbs the mind. In Kabul city, new houses are being constructed and new shops have come up, but in the country as a whole, there is little activity to show that the task of reconstructing the terribly bruised and battered Afghanistan has begun at last. Road construction has started in patches; no new factory is easily visible, and life has been resumed in shelled homes, bombed office buildings and along mined highways because there is no other option.

Afghanistan is, therefore, enveloped in greyness, a colour that represents destruction and depression; it is literally a grey country. It does not matter which way you look at it, whether from the sky or from the plains. (Louis Dupree, *Afghanistan*, ed. 1980, p.2: "Anyone flying over Afghanistan will be struck by the nakedness of the terrain. Bare rock dominates dramatically everywhere above 14,000 feet or 4,270 metres.") The unbroken grey confronts you wherever you look, at the mountains, at the city and village roads, on mud houses. It is the colour grey and dust which dominate the landscape. After a while, both elements seem to enter your body and you feel the greyness and the dust inside you. The mountains are bare, giving your eyes no relief at all from the all-pervading greyness. The famed caves appear to be extraterrestrial eyes fixed on giant misshapen faces. Even the permanent snowcaps offer little relief; they dazzle in the sun all right, but the soothing effect of snow on the Himalayas or the Alps is definitely missing.

But, like the Taleban, this omnipresent greyness is also a comparatively recent development. For justifiable reasons, the Afghans used to be proud of their pleasingly verdant valleys. All old photographs testify to the beauty that permeated this country in olden days. Fifty years ago, one could have driven straight from Kabul to the Panjsher Valley, passing through an unbroken flow of pleasant greenery dotted with flourishing orchards, with idyllic picnic spots literally strewn around. When one looks around at the equally unbroken devastation today, one can hardly give credence to the descriptions that elderly Afghans give of their country. Even frequent verifications of the extant photographs do not really help, because it is so difficult to connect the two.

The Bamiyan caves, for example. One does not see any sign of green anywhere near the caves today; yet the popular poster hung from hundreds of homes, restaurants and elsewhere shows how the Bamiyan valley looked like at one time, not many years ago; close to the caves lay tilled fields and groves of trees, a veritable jungle and then, closer to the camera, cultivated lands again punctuated with residential houses, and all dotted at intervals with luxurious lines of tall trees. In place of today's oppressive barrenness, it was green all around, a veritable feast for the eye.

Fortunately for Afghanistan, world opinion has taken cognisance of human depredation on the environment of the country, and on 12 September 2002, United Nations Environment Programme (UNEP) launched a scientific study of the environmental disaster. Scientific teams organised by the UNEP were deployed on the day to examine the impact of nearly three decades of armed conflict on the natural resources of Afghanistan.

Five four-men teams of both Afghan and international experts began to collect samples and examine sites around the country. Among other tasks, the teams were charged with identifying pollution hotspots and other health hazards, identifying strategies to protect and improve Afghanistan's natural resources, and training the country's own experts in environmental protection.

The experts' report, expected to be published in December 2002, will include recommendations for dealing with environmental threats, increasing Afghanistan's capacity for environmental management, creating jobs in the environmental sector, and implementing international environmental agreements.

"Although often forgotten when conflicts end and reconstruction begins, the natural environment is the foundation for all human society and civilisation," UNEP Executive Director Klaus Toepfer said.

"To succeed in the long term, the rebuilding of Afghanistan must, therefore, include efforts to revive and protect wildlife and ecosystem, clean up contaminated sites, and manage natural resources such as freshwater and forests more sustainably."[2]

Chairman of the UNEP Afghanistan Task Force Pekka Haavisto said, "Nearly three decades of conflict have ravaged the environment. Assessing and repairing the country's environment will prove vital to the long-term wellbeing of the Afghan people. Besides, protecting the environment will support sustainable development and enhance job creations in Afghanistan."[3]

The deflowering of Afghanistan, however, cannot be laid exclusively at the door of the modern man. According to Louis Dupree, "Nuristan and Paktiya are the most heavily forested areas in Afghanistan. The Panjsher Valley, as historical evidences attest (Le Strange G., *The Land of the Eastern Caliphate*, Cambridge, 1930, p.350), had large forests until they were destroyed by the greedy hand of man, who cut down and burned trees to smelt silver, copper and other ores during the heyday of the early Islamic period, before the thirteenth-century Mongol invasions. Man remained, but the forests never returned."[4]

Dupree adds, "Modern vegetation patterns in the eastern mountains consist mainly of thin grasses and stunted bushes. Actually, about 40 per cent of all Afghanistan is covered with sparse greenery."

While today's seemingly uninterrupted greyness apparently has something to do with the depredations that have visited the country during the past years of hostility, the state of natural vegetation at the beginning of those years speaks of not inconsiderable greenery. Thus, in the central, eastern and southern mountains and foothills, the forest zones of Nuristan and Paktiya at the elevation of 8-9,000 feet to 10-11,000 feet above the sea level contained conifer forests of pine, cedar, fir, larch and yew with broad-leaved trees like willow and poplar and ivy exclusively in Nuristan, bushes and broad-leaved forests of oak, including holly oak, with well-developed undergrowth, and some walnut, alder, ash, juniper, and in the Jalalabad region upto the height of 4-5,000 feet subtropical scrub and flowering plants and shrubs, including some palm trees around Jalalabad city, and on the valley floors and riverbanks plane trees, willow and mulberry thickets and substantive bush growth on uncultivated land.[5]

As for the northern mountains and foothills and the Turkestan plains, scrub of scattered trees, grasses, flowering plants, small bushes in clusters and oaks and conifers including junipers occurred at the 6-8,000 feet elevation in the west and at 6-10,000 height in the east and at higher levels willows and poplars, maple and hazel. Between 3-6,500 feet elevation, it was scrub of grasses, small bushes and pistachio trees; upto 3-3,500 feet meadows of reeds and grasses with occasional pistachio trees and on the valley floors and river banks, camel thorn (grass), plane trees, poplars, willows, mulberry trees in cultivated areas and reeds along the Amu Dariya.

If human habitation has led to large-scale deforestation, as has been the case in many developing countries, the overwhelming greyness of today's Afghanistan also has a lot to do with the intermittent warring and feuding, as noted above by the UNEP. The totally uprooted Shamali Plains is a stark example. Human Rights Watch, New York, records in its report "Crisis of Impunity", "In late July 1999, at peace talks held in Tashkent, the Six plus Two contact group issued the 'Tashkent Declaration', which called on all parties to resolve the conflict through 'peaceful political negotiation' and pledged 'not to provide military support to any Afghan party and to prevent the use of our territories for such purposes.' (Tashkent Declaration on Fundamental Principles for the Peaceful Settlement of the Conflict in Afghanistan, Tashkent, 19 July 1999.)"

"Almost immediately afterwards," the Human Rights Watch report continues, "both the Taleban and the United Front resumed fighting, with the Taleban focussing (their) efforts on territory held by (Commander Ahmad Shah) Massoud's forces north of Kabul. As (they) pushed north, the Taleban forced civilians from their homes and then set fire to houses and crops, and destroyed irrigation canals and wells, ostensibly to rout opposition sympathisers but effectively preventing the residents' return. In the Shamali region, men believed to be loyal to Massoud were arrested or shot, and women and children either fled or were taken to Jalalabad and Kabul. Over four days in August (1999), the United Nations estimated that over 20,000 people arrived in Kabul, bringing the total close to 40,000 in a two-week period. Thousands more fled to the Massoud-held Panjsher Valley."

The Shamali Plains today embodies the man-made greyness of Afghanistan. Mile after mile of devastation, minuscule remains of houses, stray walls standing forlorn amidst ruined homes, and almost the entire stretch a veritable minefield, though deactivating the landmines has been resumed on a visible scale.

In Kabul city, buildings destroyed during the intra-mujahideen internecine feuding and bloodletting of the 1992-96 (until the advent of the Taleban) period also serve to heighten the impression of greyness. A thoroughly disturbing illustration of the self-destructive tendencies of the Afghans, these buildings remain a grim reminder of Afghanistan's recent history.

To quote Human Rights Watch, "In June 1992, (Prof. Burhanuddin) Rabbani became President of Afghanistan, while (Gulbuddin) Hekmatyar continued to bombard Kabul with rockets. The United Nations reported that 1,800 civilians died in rocket attacks between May and August, and 500,000 people fled the city. In fighting between Hizb-i-Wahdat and another mujahideen faction, (Abdul Rasul) Sayyaf's Ittihad-i-Islami Bara-yi-Azadi Afghanistan, hundreds of civilians were abducted and 'disappeared' (Barnett R. Rubin, *The Fragmentation of Afghanistan*, pp.272-73). When most of the parties boycotted the shura (assembly) that was supposed to elect the next president – after Rabbani manipulated the process to place his supporters on the council – Rabbani was again elected president in December 1992, and fighting in Kabul intensified. In January 1994, Hekmatyar joined forces with Dostum to oust Rabbani and his defence minister, Massoud, launching full-scale civil war in Kabul. In 1994 alone, an estimated 25,000 were killed in Kabul, most of them

Introduction

civilians, in rocket and artillery attacks. One-third of the city was reduced to rubble, and much of the remainder sustained serious damage. (Amil Saikal, "The Rabbani Government 1992-96" in William Maley, ed. *Fundamentalism Reborn? Afghanistan and the Taliban*, New York, New York University Press, 1998, p.33). In September 1994, fighting between the two major Shia parties, Hizb-i-Wahdat and Harakat-i-Islami, left hundreds dead, most of them civilians. (In its Annual Human Rights Report for 1994, the United States State Department estimated that some 2,650 people, most of them civilians, were killed or injured in the fighting in the last two weeks of September 1994 alone. US Department of State, Country Reports of Human Rights Practices 1994, Washington DC, Government Printing Office, 1995, p.1,203.) Thousands of new refugees fled to Pakistan that year."[6]

It was on 22 December 2001, that a new dawn in the history of Afghanistan began with the installation of an interim government, headed by Chairman Hamid Karzai, under the provisions of the Bonn Agreement. On that day, the task of rebuilding the shattered country also commenced. Since the reconstruction of the terribly bruised country cannot be restricted to physical aspects alone, the question of the future identity of Afghanistan has also become crucial.

What kind of a country should the new Afghanistan be? What should be its identity? Afghanistan has just broken out of the horrific stigma of having been a religiously fanatic and politically and socially medieval country under the five-year rule of the Taleban, where the individual had been reduced to the status of a slave. More importantly, the experiences of the last five years had been preceded by eighteen years of political turmoil, the jihad (holy war) against the Soviet occupation and, with the advent of the mujahideen rule, the fratricidal war followed by the civil war between the Taleban and the

United Front. All through this, famine, drought and earthquake continued to visit the godforsaken country. Millions were rendered either refugees or internally displaced persons, and hundreds of thousands lost their lives, often following inhuman torture.

Afghanistan is the most mined country in the world today (according to the Mine Action Centre for Afghanistan, upto 300 people either get killed or wounded every month due to landmines) and its people became the largest refugee population in the world (in the 1980s, with the jihad raging against the Soviet occupation, the refugee population reached as high as six million or one-third of the total population,[7] and more than five million in the 1990s[8]); their children the most malnourished and their women the most suffering. All these chilling indicators make the task of rebuilding the country and its people all the more harder.

To understand the identity that the country is eventually likely to opt for, we can start with the United Nations framework for the rebuilding of the Afghanistan state, for it is through this instrument that the fundamentals of the new Afghan state are being established. The framework provides for:

- the establishment of an interim administration, a special independent commission for convening of the Emergency Loya Jirgah (traditional Grand Council) and a judicial commission (with UN aid) to rebuild the judicial system in accordance with Islamic principles, international standards, the rule of law and Afghan legal tradition;
- the interim administration would be composed of a chairman, five vice-chairmen and twenty-three other members and would be entrusted with the day-to-day conduct of the affairs of the Afghan state;
- the Emergency Loya Jirgah would be convened within six months of the establishment of the interim authority

and would be opened by former king Zahir Shah. It would decide on a transitional authority, including a broad-based transitional administration to lead Afghanistan until a fully representative government could be elected, not later than two years from the convening of the Loya Jirgah;
- upon the official transfer of power, all mujahideen, Afghan armed forces and armed groups in the country would come under the command and control of the interim authority and be reorganised according to the requirement of the new Afghan security and armed forces;
- the interim authority and the Emergency Loya Jirgah would act in accordance with the basic principles and provisions contained in international instruments on human rights and international humanitarian law to which Afghanistan was a party;
- the interim authority would cooperate with the international community in the fight against terrorism, drugs and organised crime;
- the interim bodies would ensure the participation of women as well equitable representation of all ethnic and religious communities in the interim administration and Emergency Loya Jirgah;
- the interim authority would not grant amnesty from prosecution to persons who had committed serious violations of international humanitarian law or crimes against humanity;
- the participants requested the assistance of the international community in helping the new Afghan authorities in the establishment and training of new Afghan security and armed forces;
- because time might be required to form the new Afghan security and armed forces, the participants in the UN talks on Afghanistan requested the UN Security Council to consider authorising the early deployment to

Afghanistan of a United Nations-mandated force. This force would assist in the maintenance of security for Kabul and its surrounding areas. Such a force could, as appropriate, be progressively expanded to other urban centres and other areas;
- the participants pledged to withdraw all military units from Kabul and other urban centres or other areas in which the UN-mandated force was deployed;
- the United Nations would advise the interim authority in establishing a politically neutral environment conducive to the holding of the Emergency Loya Jirgah in free and fair conditions; and
- the United Nations would have the right to investigate human rights violations and recommend corrective action.

Next to the installation of the interim authority in Kabul in December 2001, an international conference of donor countries in Tokyo in late-January 2002, pledged aid worth $4.5 billion, to be provided over a period of five years, for the reconstruction of the country. Of this amount, the donor countries (to be precise, the United States, the European Union, Japan and Saudi Arabia) said that they would make available an amount of $1.8 billion "in the next twelve months".

How has the nation fared since the heady days of taking Kabul over from the Taleban-al-Qaeda and the world community's large-hearted pledge of succour to enable it to get out of the rut and start rebuilding itself? A fair assessment was provided by the United Nations special envoy to Afghanistan Lakhdar Brahimi. "The peace process is on track," he said. "To be sure, it is a fragile peace, which must be handled with great care so that it does not unravel."[9]

Apart from the holding of the Emergency Loya Jirgah as one of the highlights of the period, Ambassador Brahimi noted that the country had also seen a resumption of primary education, the return of more than one million refugees and internally displaced persons, a modest but determined poppy eradication campaign as well as a successful locust control programme, and a series of nationwide vaccination campaigns that reached millions of children.

He, however, emphasised that despite these achievements, countless challenges and problems remained, with security being the foremost among them. The assassination of Vice-President Haji Abdul Qadeer served as a tragic reminder that "whatever successes we may have witnessed so far in Afghanistan, a single act of event can send fear down the spines of the most powerful people in Afghanistan, and has the potential to seriously destabilise the situation."

While the real key to the restoration of security lay in the creation of a national army and police force, Ambassador Brahimi urged that the International Security Assistance Force (ISAF), currently operating only in Kabul and which had been instrumental in stabilising the capital, be expanded to other parts of the country. Such an expansion would have an "enormous" impact on security and could be achieved with relatively few troops, at relatively little cost and with little danger.

Referring to the performance of the Islamic Transitional Government of Afghanistan and the UN Assistance Mission in Afghanistan (UNAMA), he said that the Afghan leadership would have to translate the priorities outlined by President Karzai into achievable objectives and that over the next eighteen months, the UN would help the government build national capacity and confidence in "governance systems" so that international assistance would flow more directly to the administration.

Ambassador Brahimi concluded by saying, "The challenge before us now is to prove to the people of Afghanistan that we will not disengage until we have made good on our promises to them, and that we will not allow setbacks to reverse our course. We owe this to the Afghan people and to regional and global security, for we all know too well that instability in that remote part of the world can have grave repercussion far beyond the borders of Afghanistan."

President Karzai, in his assessment of the situation in his country, told the UN General Assembly in September 2002 that the implementation of the Bonn Agreement and the peace process was completely "on track". Despite such achievements, however, (he said with an uncanny but predictable similarity to Ambassador Brahimi) Afghanistan was realistic about the countless challenges and problems it would have to confront, foremost of which was security. He appealed to the donor countries to follow up on their pledges for rebuilding the country, noting that actual contributions fell far short of $4.5 billion promised in Tokyo.

He also outlined his vision of Afghanistan. "My vision of Afghanistan," he told the General Assembly, "is of a modern state that builds on our Islamic values promoting justice, rule of law, human rights and freedom of commerce, and forming bridges between cultures and civilisations; a model of tolerance and prosperity based on the rich heritage of the Islamic civilisation."

He also emphasised that his country rejected outright both terrorism and religious fundamentalism. The threat posed by terrorist groups, he pointed out, required resolute commitment on the part of all nations "to fight this evil to the end" and pledged that Afghanistan "will never permit our soil to be used for any subversive activities against any of our neighbours and countries in the region and we expect the same."

While Afghanistan was a Muslim country, he said, and its people believed in the teaching of Islam, the country rejected any abuse and misuse of the holy name of Islam by extremist groups to justify violence, death and destruction.

As the above assessments show, ten months since the restoration of democracy and resumption of the peace process, Afghanistan today is surely and definitively on the way to peace and progress. However, there is an all-important impediment to genuine progress, and that is the absence of a political consensus in the country on governance.

This is not an assessment with which the present Afghan leadership concurs. Asked to comment on the absence of a political consensus as a factor that might deter Afghanistan's progress towards parliamentary democracy, Foreign Minister Dr Abdullah Abdullah told this author, "The political process is on, initiated by the steady implementation of the provisions of the Bonn Agreement. The Emergency Loya Jirgah has shown conclusively that the democratic process is also fully on. The Loya Jirgah was fully representative of the country and its people; and the very fact that it could be organised within six months of the installation of the interim administration spoke of the inner strength of the Afghan people to pursue the path of democracy to achieve development and progress. An experts' committee to draft a new constitution will be announced shortly, and after eighteen months, general election will be held to elect a parliament, paving the way for an elected government. There is absolutely no reason to doubt the eventual success of the political process."[10]

The ten months of democratisation of Afghanistan, however, also show that while the UN framework is being implemented in letter, it is lacking in spirit, which does not augur well for the traumatised country. The tussle between the two main ethnic communities, Pushtun and Tajik, continues though on a subdued scale and it is apparent to observers that the two communities are yet to begin to work for the country in a spirit of nationhood. Even though the United Front was obliged to forego some of its overwhelming importance in running the government in the Emergency Loya Jirgah in the interest of cooperation, the Pushtuns continue to be unhappy and unreconciled to the inescapable reality that for the first time in three hundred years, they are no longer ruling Afghanistan unilaterally. It would be in the interest of Afghanistan to ensure that this feeling of alienation is not allowed to fester for a longer period.

The initial selection and eventual election of Hamid Karzai as chairman of the interim authority and then as president of the Islamic Transitional Government of Afghanistan owed considerably to his ethnicity, Pushtun; though his ability to earn the confidence of the international community, especially the Americans, played a considerable role. Similarly, the choice of Haji Qadeer as a vice-president also owed a lot to his ethnicity, as did his eventual assassination on 6 July 2002. Just as his appointment to the vice-presidentship was calculated to soothe Pushtun feelings, his assassination may also have been linked to the necessity of removing this tall Pushtun figure from the government in order to reduce its image among the Pushtuns. Though, by all accounts, his murder had more to do with various other factors than his ethnicity.

The fact remains that while the Emergency Loya Jirgah was a remarkable achievement in the context in which it was held, there is a clear lack of understanding between the two main communities, and this requires immediate and deft handling.

Only a political dialogue, aiming to arrive at a political consensus on how to run the country, between the Pushtuns and the Tajiks, however, can bring this hiatus to an end. It should be recalled that throughout the period of the Taleban-United Front civil war, attempts were made from time to time to bring the two communities together at least for a working understanding and cooperation. Even though Commander

Ahmad Shah Massoud was perceived in some quarters to be incapable of accepting the Pushtuns as partners in governance, he nevertheless initiated moves at various periods of time to reach a pact with the Pushtuns, either through Gulbuddin Hekmatyar or through the Taleban.

It is, therefore, quite disquieting to see that no efforts are yet underway at the present juncture to make the beginning of a dialogue possible. As indications pile up, betraying Pakistan's anxiety to exploit this ethnic hiatus in Afghanistan, the political leadership of Afghanistan and the international community should lose no further time in addressing this major lacuna in the Afghan political process.

If the generation of a political consensus between the Pushtun and Tajik communities is a sine qua non for a sustainable progress of Afghanistan towards peace and development, an equally indispensable component should be a correct and adroit handling of the lubricant that had kept over the last few decades and now, in the post-Taleban period, continues to keep the wheels of the economy moving, the vast and all-pervading narcotics production and trade, in which more Afghans than one would care to identify participate.

Let us consider the following input from the United Nations: "A pre-assessment survey of opium poppy cultivation, conducted by the United Nations Drug Control Programme (UNDCP) from 1-10 February 2002, confirms earlier indications that cultivation has resumed at a 'relatively high level' throughout the country after the considerable decline recorded in 2001."[11]

The UNDCP said that its Country Office for Afghanistan and the Illicit Crop Monitoring Programme (ICMP) conducted a pre-assessment survey in 208 villages in forty-two districts in the traditional opium poppy growing areas of the southern and eastern Afghanistan in the provinces of Helmund,

Kandahar, Oruzgan, Nangarhar and Kunar. Those five provinces accounted for eighty-four per cent of the total opium poppy cultivation area in Afghanistan in 2000. The northern region of Afghanistan was not included in the survey because the colder climate in that area usually delays the opium poppy planting season and cultivation is not observed clearly in February.

"Based on the findings of this limited survey and assuming that poppy cultivation (was) also resumed in provinces not covered by the pre-assessment, it is estimated that opium poppy cultivation in Afghanistan could cover an area between 45,000 hectares and 65,000 hectares in 2002," the survey said. "This range of estimates compares to the levels of cultivation reached during the mid-1990s, but remains lower than those recorded in 1999 (about 95,000 hectares) and 2000 (about 82,000 hectares)."

The UNDCP pointed out that the interim administration (installed on 22 December 2001) banned opium poppy cultivation on 17 January 2002. "At that time, however, most opium poppy fields had already been sown. Although most farmers interviewed during the pre-assessment survey said (that) they were uncertain about being able to harvest opium this spring because of the ban, the high prices offered by local traders create a powerful incentive."[12]

The results of the survey were confirmed by the time the second Annual European Conference on Drug Trafficking and Law Enforcement opened in Paris on 26 September 2002. Drugscope, a British charity and organiser of the conference, estimated a staggering 1,400 per cent jump in Afghanistan's production of opium poppy since the fall of the Taleban government in November 2001. Chief Executive of Drugscope Roger Howard said, "If we are to stop the return to full-scale opium production, the international community must fulfil its commitment to help rebuild Afghan society, giving communities and individuals another option. Enforcement on its own is not the solution."

Druscope said on the occasion that "the total likely yield for 2002 will be between 1,900 and 2,700 tons, which amounts to a rise between 900 per cent and 1,400 per cent, in the space of only one year." It pointed out that "although this figure is still lower than the levels of production in 1999 or 2000, cultivation is back to a very significant level. It will also come as a blow to the countries which, in April 2002, agreed to take the international lead in assisting the Afghans develop their counter-narcotics capacity."

The charity invoked British Prime Minister Tony Blair's brave words uttered in October 2001, "We act also because the al-Qaeda network and the Taleban regime are funded by the drugs trade – ninety per cent of all heroin sold in Britain originates from Afghanistan (and stopping this) trade is again directly in our interests."

The Paris conference identified the problems facing the Afghan government in tackling the drugs trade as follows: poorly trained and ill-equipped staff; damaged buildings in poor condition, gaping holes in walls and ceilings; no furniture and no glass in the windows; no operational police equipment; lack of communications equipment; lack of transportation facilities; absence of scientific support capacity or a basic narcotic test; and lack of systems for the use of intelligence.

Interestingly, while British Foreign Secretary Jack Straw announced in July 2002, that almost a third of Afghanistan's poppy fields had been destroyed, an investigation by the BBC found there was little evidence that the crops were being eradicated. And the authoritative survey conducted since then confirmed that far from being eradicated, the crops were actually much larger than the previous year's. The BBC also quoted a military commander to the effect that better eradication of opium poppy crops would require an agreed plan, with alternative job opportunities offered to encourage farmers away from the lucrative cultivation of poppy. Farmers, on the other hand, took the stand that though they realised the dangers posed by heroin, the economic situation left them with no choice.

The BBC probe revealed that after the Taleban imposed a total ban on opium poppy cultivation under the United Nations directive, the crop was virtually eliminated. But, after the fall of the Taleban, farmers started planting the crop again, leaving the new government with the tough job of "destroying one of the few cash crops in this poor country".

Even assessing the success or failure of an eradication programme was considered too dangerous. The United Nations Office for Drugs Control and Crime Prevention said that it was too dangerous to send monitors to the main poppy growing areas in the southern and eastern Afghanistan.

On the other hand, farmers complained that the compensation money the government was expected to pay in lieu of planting and growing poppy never materialised. The BBC found that in some areas, government officials supposed to hand over the compensation money had not even turned up.

The probe also found out that the north-eastern province of Badakhshan, which was under the control of the United Front, had not even been touched as far as the poppy eradication programme was concerned.

CNN quoted president of the International Narcotics Control Board Hamid Ghodse on 27 February 2002, saying, "We are seriously concerned that illicit cultivation of opium poppy in Afghanistan is again increasing and we want to seek international cooperation to prevent Afghanistan (from) becoming the world's largest producer of opium." The

International Narcotics Control Board had called on the international community to provide adequate technical and financial assistance to Afghanistan so (that) it could implement international drug control treaties. It also urged the authorities in Afghanistan, now or in the future, to commit themselves to full compliance with international drug control treaties.

The news channel added that the interim administration had, like the Taleban before it, implemented a total ban on poppy cultivation. "But the extent of the problem facing the Karzai government is daunting," it said. "Despite the harvest in the crop year 2000/2001 being estimated at less than one tenth of the harvest in the previous crop year, the flow of illicit drugs from Afghanistan actually increased, highlighting the complexity of the trafficking industry in Central Asia and the vast reserve stockpiles in Afghanistan and neighbouring countries. In recent years, Afghanistan was the main source of illicit opium globally, with seventy per cent of (the) total production in 2000. As much as ninety per cent of heroin in European drug markets is believed to have originated in Afghanistan."

In a unique interpretation of the sudden soaring of opium poppy cultivation in the post-Taleban Afghanistan, an article by Michel Chossuovsky, entitled "Hidden agenda behind the 'War on Terrorism': US bombing of Afghanistan restores trade in narcotics", alleges that the United States-led bombing of Afghanistan was also aimed at the restoration of opium poppy cultivation in the country. "The annual proceeds of the Afghan Golden Crescent drug trade (between 100 and 200 billion dollars) represented approximately one third of the worldwide annual turnover of narcotics, estimated by the United Nations to be of the order of $500 billion," the article points out.[13]

"In many regards," says the article, "the trade in narcotics as well as the drug routes to the European and North American markets are considered to be 'strategic.' There are powerful financial interests behind the drug trade, which have a pervasive influence, behind the scenes, on the conduct of US foreign policy.

"These multi-billion dollar revenues of narcotics were deposited in the Western banking system. Most of the large international banks – together with their affiliates in the offshore banking havens – laundered large amounts of narco-dollars. In other words, Afghanistan, the poorest country on earth, was the source of tremendous financial wealth derived from the drug trade to financial institutions, business syndicates and organised crime. Part of the drug related revenues accrue to the CIA, which continues to protect both the Asian and Latin American drug trade. Visibly, only a very small percentage of these revenues stays in Afghanistan.

"Following the year 2000 ban on poppy production imposed by the Taleban government," the article says, "opium production collapsed by more than ninety per cent, leading to a dwindling drug trade and substantial losses to the interests underlying this multi-billion dollar trade including Western financial institutions. The (United Front) became the main political force involved in protecting the production and marketing of raw opium."

While oil and oil pipelines out of the Caspian Sea basin were undoubtedly a factor, the article concludes the bombing of Afghanistan also served to restore the multi-billion dollar drug trade, which is protected by the CIA. "Immediately following the installation of the US puppet government under Prime Minister (*sic*) Hamid Karzai, opium production soared, regaining its historic levels. According to the United Nations Drug Control Programme, opium cultivation increased by 657 per cent in 2002 (in relation to its 2001 level). In 2001, opium cultivation had fallen to an estimated 7,606 hectares. It is currently estimated by the UNDCP to be of the order of 45,000-65,000 hectares. In the immediate wake of September 11 (2001), the price of opium in Afghanistan increased threefold. By early 2002, the price (dollar/kg) was almost ten times higher than in the year 2000."

Be that as it may (at least, the statistics quoted in the article are authentic, though the interpretation is novel), writing in June 1999, Barnett R. Rubin noted that the drug and arms trade had brought international organised crime into the region. Though over ninety per cent of the opium was grown in the Taleban-controlled southern Afghanistan, increasing portions of it were smuggled northward, partly under the control of the Russian mafia. Russian organised crime groups had been involved in Afghanistan for years. "They are important as arms suppliers for (Commander Ahmad Shah) Massoud and as middlemen for opium exports. One major export route goes from territory controlled by Massoud and Rabbani in the north-east across the Tajikistan border, where some of it is transported by Russian troops and border guards to Osh, Kyrgyzstan, which has become a major transshipment point. The money involved in the drug and arms trades is undermining state institutions throughout Central Asia and is also affecting Russia."[14]

In retrospect, it seems that the Taleban could hoodwink the world and, especially the United States, with surprising ease about their narcotics policy. For two years, 1994-96, when they were establishing themselves as a power in Afghanistan, the United States showed a touching naiveté in trusting the Taleban for their formal position on narcotics. "During the first two years of the Taleban's ascendancy, 1994-96," writes John K. Cooley, "the US government indulged in excessive wishful thinking that they would curb or even end the plague of drugs from Afghanistan. This wishful respect for the

Taleban's supposedly good intentions was based in part upon their growing military power... The Taleban attitude toward drug cultivation, production and trafficking has proven to be a curious mix of religious principles, ambiguity and expediency. Following the capture of Kabul in 1996, Mullah Omar and other Taleban leaders realised that they might be able to exploit their very genuine, religious-based opposition to drugs to offset Western hostility, aroused by such practices as placing women in a kind of permanent purdah; floggings, stonings to death, amputation of fingers, hands and feet as punishment; and the public live burial (by bulldozing layers of rocks onto them) of men convicted by the Taleban courts of sodomy."[15]

Interestingly, while the Pakistani intelligence agency ISI and other government departments concerned with Afghanistan pursued the policy of ensuring that no Kabul government could gain enough strength to act independently of Islamabad, they also believed at the same time that the drug trade could only be controlled if there was internal and external peace and security in Afghanistan and if there was a strong central government in Kabul in a position to exercise authority over the whole country.[16]

The validity of this observation continues till today, even though the civil war was ended one year ago and there is relative peace in the country. Much earlier, perceptive observers of Afghanistan had reached a similar conclusion. Rubin's thesis as well as Ahmed Rashid's astute observations leave little scope for doubting the hypothesis that the question of establishing and sustaining peace and security in Afghanistan is linked uncomfortably intimately with that of controlling the contraband trade in drugs, arms and consumer goods.

The uppermost question of choosing the right option for the identity of the new Afghanistan is, therefore, equally vitally linked to this tortuous relationship between peace and security in Afghanistan and the massive illegal trade across the region involving Afghanistan, Pakistan and Central Asia.

Discussing the future of Afghanistan, Rashid says, "It seems that the only effective Afghan NGO (non-governmental organisation) is based on organised smuggling and the drug trade. Thus, the limited reconstruction which the Taleban (have) undertaken so far is entirely related to improving the efficiency of smuggling and drugs trafficking, such as repairing roads, setting up petrol pumps and inviting US businessmen to set up a mobile telephone network which will qualitatively speed up the movement of drugs and illicit trade. The benefits of this reconstruction all accrue to the transport and drugs mafia. No warlord is building schools, hospitals, water supply systems or anything remotely related to civic development."[17]

As Rubin and Rashid show convincingly, the unchecked free flowing illicit trade in consumer goods under the Afghan Transit Trade Agreement, drugs and arms with the concomitant growth in related service trades like transport, petrol pumps and hotels, that had spread all over the region during the war in Afghanistan, will continue to hamper the establishment and maintenance of peace and security in the resurgent Afghanistan, for the simple reason that so many stakes are involved in the continuity of the status quo.

The viability of this observation is already evident in the failure of the initial attempts to persuade Afghan farmers to switch over from opium poppy cultivation to cash crops. The United States is facilitating the Afghan Government's efforts in this regard, and the following statement by Philip T. Reeker, Deputy Spokesman, Department of State, on 5 April 2002, says it all:

"The United States strongly supports the Afghan Interim Authority's plan to implement its poppy ban and we look forward to working closely with the Authority to make it successful. On 16 January, the authority issued a decree banning the cultivation, processing and trafficking of opiates. The Authority subsequently announced on 4 April that it will implement, with international community funding, a compensation programme that offers cultivators approximately $1,200 per hectare of eradicated opium.

"The United States will support this partial compensation programme with short-term cash-for-work projects for labourers in poppy areas. The United States will also continue efforts to interdict the flow of opium into international markets by strengthening the law enforcement and judicial capacities of Afghanistan's neighbours.

"In the medium and long term, we will also support programmes aimed at developing alternative livelihoods and effective law enforcement in Afghanistan that will enable the country to replace the opium-based rural economy with legal ways to earn a living."

Ten months after the rescue of Afghanistan from the evil clutches of the Taleban regime, as Afghan economy continues to be as chaotic as before, the astonishing liquidity of foreign currency and the worthlessness of the afghani* can only be explained by the fact that the free flow of contraband cultivation and trade in opium is continuing, and that the dependence of the rural Afghanistan on this trade remains as deep and wide as before. The connection between the issue of establishing peace and security and ending this trade once and for all is all too obvious.

****

---

*   While the afghani traded at 1,000 to the US dollar or about twenty times the official exchange rate by the mid-1991, it stood at 43,000 to the US dollar by September 2002.

Endnotes

1. Davis, Anthony, "Recent violence obscures deeper threats for Afghanistan", www.janes.com/security international, 26 September 2002.
2. United Nations, http://www.un.org
3. ibid.
4. Dupree, Louis, *Afghanistan*, Princeton University Press, 1980, p.19.
5. ibid., p.20.
6. Human Rights Watch, "Crisis of Impunity: The role of Pakistan, Russia and Iran in Fuelling the Civil War", July 2001, Vol.13, No.3, New York.
7. Lama, Mahendra P., Professor of South Asian Economics, South Asia Centre, Jawaharlal Nehru University, New Delhi, "The Afghan Refugees", *The Hindu*, 5 February 2002.
8. World Migration Report 2000, p.106, quoting the United States Committee for Refugees 1999, World Refugee Survey, Washington DC.
9. United Nations special envoy for Afghanistan Lakhdar Brahimi's report to the UN Secretary-General, 19 July 2002.
10. Interview taken on 7 September 2002 in Kabul.
11. United Nations Information Service statement, datelined Vienna, dated 28 February 2002.
12. Posted on http://www.unis.unvienna.org
13. Posted on http://globalresearch.ca/articles/CHO205B.html
14. "The Political Economy of War and Peace in Afghanistan", see http://www.institute-for-afghan-studies.org, 21 June 1999.
15. Cooley, John K., *Unholy Wars: Afghanistan, America and International Terrorism,* Penguin Books India, 1999, 2000, p.148.
16. ibid., p.150.
17. Ahmed, Rashid, *Taliban, Islam, Oil and the New Great Game in Central Asia,* I. B.Taurus, 2000, p.213.

1
Options Before Afghanistan

On a late evening in June 2002, sipping green tea in his well-appointed office in the Foreign Ministry building in Kabul, the dapper and suitably articulate Foreign Minister Dr Abdullah Abdullah told this author, "Don't be surprised if, after a while, Afghanistan emerges as the most stable country in the region."[1]

Put in the context to which the remark belonged, it was little short of being audacious. It was not even full six months since the Bonn Agreement, signed under the aegis of the United Nations, had come into force and under which, as the second step forward, the transitional government had taken over from the interim administration, yielding place to the Northern Alliance, the Rome Group and various other combinations of Afghan ethnic and tribal affiliations.

But, within the short span of four months, February-July 2002, two assassinations had taken place, killing two important functionaries of the new dispensation in Kabul and heightening the sense of insecurity and instability within and about the country. Minister of Civil Aviation in the interim administration, Abdurrahman, was assassinated at the Kabul airport in full view of hundreds of people and after having been detained for several hours in February 2002. On 6 July 2002, Vice-President and Minister of Public Works of the Islamic Transitional Government of Afghanistan Haji Abdul Qadeer was assassinated while leaving his office, again in full view of the dozen or so security guards present at the entrance of the Ministry.

While the assassinations highlighted the continuing lack of security and stability in the country and, more significantly, the immediate dangers facing the Hamid Karzai administration,* the United Nations High Commissioner for Refugees sent the following report in early July 2002, which speaks for itself. While it welcomed the decision of the Transitional Government to send a special delegation to address the harassment of ethnic minorities in the northern and central parts of the country, it said that it had been "extremely concerned" about the escalating violence and worsening human rights situation in the region, especially in Faryab, Sar-i-Pul and Badghis provinces, and urged provincial authorities to protect the security and safety of the civilian population in the north.

"The situation in several parts of the two regions remains extremely tense," UNHCR spokesman Yusuf Hasan said at a press briefing in Kabul, noting that scores of attacks against ethnic minorities in Faryab, Balkh and Sar-i-Pul provinces had reportedly led to fatalities and destruction of property and that there was alongside an upsurge in robberies, rapes and murders.

---

*   Two months later, an unsuccessful attempt on President Karzai's life was made in Kandahar in the midst of a series of terrorist attacks including the killing of thirty-two civilians in a car-bomb explosion in Kabul.

According to the UNHCR, the renewed factional fighting was not only hampering the return of refugees but also causing fresh displacement. "Due to the precarious security situation," the spokesman said, "we have suspended the return of internally displaced persons from Herat to Faryab, Sar-i-Pul and Sholgara in Balkh province as well as to Samangan province."

He also reported that the security situation in Kahmard and Saighan in Bamiyan province was "rapidly" deteriorating, adding that in the last few days of June, there was intense fighting in Kahmard districts, resulting in the deaths of civilians, especially women and children. "The situation is extremely volatile, with reports of people fleeing to Saighan district as well as incidents of human rights violations in several villages in Kahmard districts such as Kakhul, Palenbagh, Dudaru and Khuhisan," he said.

While the security situation in widespread parts of Afghanistan in early July 2002 left much to be desired, the eruption of violence on ethnic lines and a high incidence of human rights violations was neither unexpected nor inexplicable. As we have seen at the beginning of this chapter, barely six months had elapsed since the fall of the Taleban-al-Qaeda rule. The country was expected to take much longer to recover from the traumas and travails of the war years; and nobody was willing to hazard a guess as to when ethnic warlords, nurtured on the exhilarating principle of total disobedience of the central authority and complete immunity from facing consequences, would be called to explain their conduct and rein in their natural flair for fighting.

In fact, in one of his earliest appeals to the international community for assistance in improving the security environment, the then chairman of the interim administration Hamid Karzai told the United Nations Security Council on 31 January 2002, "We hope you would authorise an extension and expansion of the mandate of this force (International Security Assistance Force). The extension of presence of multinational forces in Kabul and expanding their presence to other major cities will signal the ongoing commitment of the international community to peace and security in Afghanistan."

A week later, when Pushtun warlord Bacha Khan, appointed by the interim administration as the Governor of Paktia, tried to take the provincial capital Gardez over, and in the ensuing fierce fighting with the resisting local council at least forty-three persons were killed and dozens injured with considerable damage done to buildings, Karzai exploded, "We must finish warlordism in Afghanistan. But we can't disrupt the existing situation right now because of the continuing fight we have against terrorism." Incidentally, the local council was able to push Khan out for the time being.

Karzai further said, "I am mad, mad, mad about this. This proves our point that we must finish warlordism. A man that goes in and forces himself with the gun, it is just disgusting. To kill people in order to become governor – how can he do that? There's no way we can agree with that, absolutely no way." However, he explained that he had no choice but to appoint Bacha Khan as governor, pointing out that he needed the existing military and social structures of the provinces to remain undisturbed while the war against terrorism continued. "It had to go that way," he continued, "but we will punish him. We will tell him that taking a letter of appointment as governor does not mean you have a licence to kill."

Five months later, senior lawmakers in the United States, irrespective of their party affiliations, made a fervent plea to the Bush administration to play a more active role in Afghanistan by providing expanded security to the troubled country. "I fear that we may see this government (in Kabul) and our efforts unwind here if we don't make the appropriate investment of men and effort and resources," said Republican Senator Chuck Hagel, who was also a member of the Senate Foreign Relations Committee. "If we lose there, if this goes backward, this will be a huge defeat for us symbolically in that region, in the world, for our word, confidence in Americans all over the world. We cannot allow this to go down."

Matching the sentiment, Democratic Senator Evan Bayh said, "My own view is we went to war, we won the war; let's not lose it now. And I think we need to take stronger security steps."

"The assassination of Vice-President Haji Abdul Qadeer highlights the challenge that is still there in Afghanistan," said Senate Majority leader Tom Daschle. "We have a long way to go to accomplish our goals."

While the security situation continued to remain threatening, the US administration, however, stuck to its stand that it would not commit more US troops for peace enforcement tasks. At that moment, there were around 7,000 US troops stationed in the country with the specific job of ferreting out the Taleban-al-Qaeda remnants and neutralising them. The White House was dead set against increasing that number and maintained that the most effective way of tackling the security situation was to rapidly build up the new Afghan army and let it handle the situation.

However, we return to the comfortable office of the foreign minister, who had just spoken about the possibility that in not-too-distant-a-future his country might emerge as the most stable one in the region. Do not be surprised if such a thing ever happened, he had advised the author. Dr Abdullah was speaking a week after the first Loya Jirgah since the period of internecine warfare had ended; and this very fact was being displayed as a major achievement. The government, its leaders, the intelligentsia and the people were justifiably proud of the successful holding of the Emergency Loya Jirgah in a country which was, literally till the other day, irreversibly divided and had almost realised a death wish of self-destruction.

The Loya Jirgah itself went through phases of intense bickering, uncertainty and misgivings, and at least one important member of the government, Mohammad Younus Qanooni, held that the Grand Council had ended in an incomplete fashion for it had failed to elect a parliament, as it was required to do.

Many observers felt that Qanooni was being subjective in his assessment as at the moment he was registering his protest at being eased out of the powerful Interior Ministry and shoved into the docile Education Ministry. He had also threatened to form a political party; and this was also being interpreted as more of a political warning served to President Hamid Karzai than a serious move.

The point to note, however, is that the general assesssment, which was shared by both Afghan and non-Afghan elements, was that the Loya Jirgah had been reasonably successful. Dr Abdullah told this author, "The Loya Jirgah is a big achievement. Our aim was to give the basic rights to the men and women. The women are now enjoying their rights. While two million children have rejoined schools, half of them are girls. The biggest thing is that the real hope has been created for Afghanistan."

A senior official in the Ministry of Higher Education, Ahmad Zia Refhat said, "The Loya Jirgah was the venue for the people of Afghanistan to gather and take control into their own hands and say what they think for the first time in decades. It was the only way to legitimise the jurisdiction of the interim administration and the future government. Perhaps it could have achieved more, like establishing a parliament. If we are truly on the verge of applying democracy, parliament should play an important role. We can help the coming government reach its democratic goals. We accept that the interim government is newly established and accepted by the people. But whenever a new government or administration is formed, there is a tendency for it to become corrupt or dictatorial if it has no rivals or checks on its powers. During the Loya Jirgah, some people said a parliament should not be established because this or that group or faction would use it to oppose the government. But opposition is good for a government. Establishing a parliament would also be a way to create a battle of ideas between representatives of different parties and factions instead of battles with guns."

The reason for the extensive quotation (there will be more to follow) from a government official's comments is to show that the Afghans, irrespective of their stations in life, are liable to speak out their minds, surely a sign that democracy should take roots in such a society despite the history of traditional divides on ethnic grounds. In fact, the concept of the Grand Council itself rests on the assumption and actual practice to the effect that the people who gather together speak out freely and that from such an open-to-all churning of ideas emerge the principal ideas and decisions that the gathering collectively throws up. The point to note is that being a tribal society, the concept of democracy at the grass-root level is not alien to the country even though the fiefdoms run by local chieftains, throwing to the winds the fundamental rights of the people, understandably characterise the Afghan society as anachronistically feudal and inherently autocratic.

Examining the concept and practice of parliamentary democracy in Afghanistan, the eminent scholar of the country Louis Dupree writes, "With the exception of the Seventh ('liberal') Parliament (1949-52), the preceding seven (six?) shura had been largely 'rubber-stamp' institutions. Members came largely from the second line of power, sent to Kabul by the local power elites to maintain the façade of constitutional parliamentarianism. The 1965 elections, however, began a new era in Afghan politics, a genuine attempt to create a constitutional monarchy with at least a theoretical emphasis on parliamentary procedures. Many in the rural areas were at first sceptical of the *democracy-yi-naw*, but eventually many new faces appeared for election. Some younger, educated types, returned to their village homes and successfully challenged incumbents. In Kabul and other larger urban centres, many newcomers appeared and were elected. Most proved to be liberal, leftist or religiously conservative and became the chief architects of the investigation activities of the Wolesi Jirgah (Lower House of the People).

"The key feature of the Twelfth Parliament, however, was the rapid realisation by its members that it did have power – legitimate, constitutional power – and because the executive remained relatively inactive (and unprotected, because of the lack of responsible political parties), Parliament seized more and more power but did little constructive with it."[2]

When one reads Dupree's analysis of Afghanistan of the mid-1960s, one wonders if it could at all be applied to today's Afghanistan. The apparent dichotomy is, however, quite explicable, for the most significant aspect about today's Afghanistan, arising out of the rubble of the long years of no-holds-barred warfare, is that the roots for building a secular, tolerant, modern and democratic country lie within the confines of its recent history. Such a statement might even seem blunt, especially in the context of the five years of the Taleban rule. During those years, the country and its people had come to be identified in the popular perception with all the negative aspects of human endeavour, such as extreme religious bigotry, state brutality, complete denial of human rights and mediaeval treatment meted out to women and children. Whichever way one looks at it, one perforce comes to the conclusion that the five years of the Taleban rule, September 1996-September 2001, were an anachronism. The logical way for the country to begin to rebuild itself would, therefore, be to completely ignore the Taleban period and pick up the thread of secularism and modern parliamentary democracy, both of which showed signs of being unfolded in the period characterised by the 1964 Constitution.

Unerringly, to their credit, this is exactly what the new leaders of the country are doing. The debate over the Emergency Loya Jirgah carries ample proof that the country has learned (or re-learned) the value of open debate, the right of the people to question the motives and actions of the government and, above all, their right to dissent. Analyses of the two Grand Councils, the first giving birth to the 1964 Constitution and the second legitimising the Interim Government and the establishment of the Transitional Government, lend substantive support to the above assertion.

Keeping in mind the fact that the traditional Pushtun majority versus other ethnic minorities issue resurfaced in various forms during and after the war against the Taleban and al-Qaeda, it is important to note that the issue was actually decided once and for all by the Loya Jirgah discussing the 1964 Constitution. Dupree notes, "In the legal terminology of the Constitution, 'Afghan' refers to all citizens of Afghanistan, but to most citizens the word means the Pushtun ethnic group, which makes up probably less than fifty per cent of the population. The minority groups, therefore, insisted on a definition which would, once and for all time, declare all native peoples, not only Pushtun, to be Afghan. No satisfactory definition could be reached, even after four hours of heated debate, so the presiding officer reminded the Loya Jirgah that a committee had been appointed on the first day to consider the problem. He then appointed two additional members from the floor to assist in the committee's deliberations and then closed off the debate. The ad hoc committee suggested the following sentence be added to Article 1, Paragraph 3, 'the word Afghan shall apply to each such individual'. The Loya Jirgah approved the definition."[3]

Similarly, the Afghans chose deliberately and consciously to opt for a secular, and not a theocratic, state all those thirty-eight years ago. To quote Dupree, "Article 69, another extremely important article, brought on a long discussion of legal and philosophical points. This Article reads, 'Excepting the conditions for which specific provisions have been made in this Constitution, a law is a resolution passed by both Houses (of Parliament) and signed by the King. In the area where no such law exists, the provisions of the Hanafi jurisprudence of the Shari'a shall be considered as law. Immediately after the reading of Article 69, several religious leaders demanded to know why the Hanafi Shari'a had been placed in a secondary position to secular laws. The secretary patiently explained (ironically, to his own father, a respected religious leader) that Article 64, Paragraph 2 ("There shall be no law repugnant to the basic principles of the sacred religion of Islam...") covered repugnancy to Islam for all time. Only a few of the more traditionalist mullahs voted against Article 69, a great triumph for the new breed of liberal religious thinkers in Afghanistan."

"The writers of (the) 1964 Constitution used Islam as a weapon against the traditionalists," Dupree explains. "The implacable attitude of former Prime Minister Sardar Mohammad Daoud toward the conservative religious leaders helped to smother potential opposition from these quarters during the constitutional jirgah. Prime Minister Daoud had not hesitated to use his military base of power to smash any opposition, secular or religious, to his modernisation plans. Religious leaders at the Loya Jirgah remembered this, and for the most part, limited their comments to technical points."

Dupree adds, "Islamic modernists in Afghanistan accept the principle that ijtihad (legal decision based on knowledge and reason) holds precedence over the hardening of the legal arteries which occurred in Islam about a thousand years ago, when qiyas 'aqli (logical deduction by analogy) and qiyas shar'i (legal deduction by analogy) made it possible for a Muslim judge to reach a verdict (opinion or zann) in a case (qadiya) without considering changed social conditions or legal decisions other than the analogs.

"Modernist Islamic thinkers in Afghanistan consider themselves the intellectual heirs of the ninth and tenth centuries AD Baghdadi scholars. They believe Islamic jurisprudence must operate at two levels: the basic dogma (the ideals or essence) and attendant laws and interpretations based on actual cases in order to translate the ideals into reality. To accomplish these goals, the writers of the Constitution also drafted laws to reorganise the country along completely secular lines."

"It is noteworthy," continues Dupree, "that Article 102* enjoins the courts to consider cases in the light of the 'Constitution and the laws of the state', and mentions the

---

* The courts in the cases under their consideration shall apply the provisions of this Constitution and the laws of the state. Whenever no provision exists in this Constitution or the laws for a case under consideration, the courts shall, by following the basis principles of the Hanafi jurisprudence of the Sharia of Islam and within the limitations set forth in this Constitution, render a decision that in their opinion secures justice in the best possible way.

Hanafi Shari'a as a last resort. In effect, Article 102 (with Article 69, which deals with legislation) makes Afghanistan essentially a secular state, even while paying lip-service to Islam throughout. The essence of Islam, however, permeates the whole Constitution, and the action component articles (the executive, legislative and judiciary articles) embody secularisation without divorcing them from the values expressed in Islam."[4]

Coming back to June 2002, the overwhelming sentiment witnessed in the Emergency Loya Jirgah was one of unity, rather than division, and this speaks more truly of Afghanistan today than anything else. *The Kabul Times* reported, "Asked which ethnic group he represented, Mohammad Rafiq Shahir, belonging to Western Herat, replied, 'Afghanistan. We are one nation and (are) putting the divisions behind us.'" The newspaper wrote, "Much of the blame for the country's past twenty-three years of conflict was laid (at the Loya Jirgah) on its volatile ethnic divides, but delegates were united in seeing themselves first and foremost as Afghans. 'There has really been no disagreement between ourselves. We have all been living together, eating together, talking together,' said Mohammad Karim, a Pushtun delegate from the Laghman province who shared a dormitory with (his) Uzbek and Tajik counterparts. His view was echoed by fellow Laghman representative Juma Gul, who said (that) the shared miseries endured by the Afghans over the years had created a common bond. 'This talk of disagreements and prejudice is wrong. We have been talking, joking, all week, Hazaras, Uzbeks, Tajiks,' he told AFP (the French news agency). 'Whatever problems we have had are over. We are all just Afghans.'"[5]

"The mood for the Loya Jirgah was fantastic," recounted leading Afghan woman activist Nasrine Gross of Negar – Support of Women of Afghanistan. "The anticipation was euphoric and contagious; for Afghans to have a chance to experience a peaceful and democratic event of this scale felt like a collective nightmare was finally coming to an end. We were happy that we had invited over fifty women delegates to our conference and, therefore, had very good contacts on the floor of the Jirgah."

The event with 2,000 people in one compound, she said, was like Afghanistan itself in miniature. The men and women's fashions alone, not to mention the variety of languages, dialects, accents, greetings, even religious orientations, bespoke of the pluralistic nature of the country. And how wonderful to recognise each one on his/her own merit as a true Afghan!

The achievements of the Loya Jirgah for women and for Afghanistan were considerable. The election of Hamid Karzai was very orderly. The secret ballot, the voting booths, the procedures to follow, gave each delegate a taste of democracy at work, of how orderly conduct could produce results and of how people with different points of view could also have arguments and common interests. This was a powerful lesson in a country that lengthy war had literally separated into many groups and chaotic governance.

Continuing her graphic description of the Grand Assembly, Gross said, "I could see that the stiff greetings of the first few days were giving way to broad smiles by the end of the Jirgah. The ice was thawing. People could feel that in spite of their differences, they also had the same aspirations for Afghanistan. They also were beginning to realise that they all had at least one irrefutable thing in common; they had all suffered and experienced together six years of complete separation. One side being totally ruled by the Taleban and suffering the worst of the militias' victimisation and Pakistani propaganda; the other side experiencing the ravages and deprivations of an imposed war and not knowing what was happening to their brothers/sisters on the other side. Everytime I saw a few of them talking with each other or eating at the same table or praying together, I knew I was looking at another, albeit small, step of healing, reconciliation and unity."

An important aspect of the Loya Jirgah, held only a little over six months after the fall of the Taleban, was the conspicuous role the women delegates played. Gross recalled, "Two hundred twenty women delegates from all over Afghanistan added a weight that could not be ignored. And they were vocal and visible. Massouda Jalal's precedence-setting candidacy for the presidency of the state of Afghanistan did not draw any criticism even from those who have in the past eschewed women's political role (the only criticism of her was from people who were pro-Karzai and did not want to see the vote split in any fraction). This fact alone made it very worthwhile for us."

"The presence of women in so many dress codes," she said, "from the extreme of veils of several layers to the very ethnic clothes to the professional attire and no veils, also showed Afghanistan's special place in the community of nations (many came with chadari from their districts but none wore it in the compound or in the meeting tents, although I would have preferred to see a few come in with it). It showed the pluralistic nature of this society and hence its tolerant stand in allowing different communities to pursue their individual preferences. Actually, this was true for men also, dressed in very traditional or ethnic or many kinds of religious outfits or modern, professional office suits and many different head coverings. Also, in the last few days of the Jirgah we could see that (the) same dress codes were getting more relaxed."[6]

Throughout the Emergency Loya Jirgah, one thing that stood out was the capability of the Afghans to readily acknowledge their traditional ethnic divides and, at the same time, to emphasise that years of internecine warfare had taught them the value of national unity with one identity for all. To return to *The Kabul Times*, "Halim Nuristani, who takes his name from the Nooristan ethnic group and eponymous province in the eastern Afghanistan, said that there were signs of tension at the beginning of the Loya Jirgah. 'At the start, there was a little bit of problem. Some people were acting together and only thinking that their group should get the main jobs. But now the atmosphere is like (that) of a brotherhood. We are all of one mind and one opinion on this.' Abdul Wahib, a Pushtun representing Afghan refugees in Pakistan, agreed that there had been early divisions and called for a national campaign to promote ethnic awareness. 'In the beginning, there were some ethnic divisions inside the tent (the venue of the Loya Jirgah) but these have gone now,' said Wahib. 'By every passing day, our national unity is getting stronger and there's more interaction between ethnic groups inside the tent.'"

Wahib also came up with a suggestion which is likely to gain ground. "For national unity," he said, "there should be a special programme in Afghan schools and in the media."[7]

Talking to the author a few days after the Transitional Government had taken over, its Finance Minister, economist and former World Bank and United Nations official Dr Ashraf Ghani Ahmadzai referred repeatedly to the participation of a rich Afghan businessman Rajab Ali Andishman in the Loya Jirgah as a prime example of Afghans of all hues getting together in the service of the country.[8] He mentioned that while the successful businessman domiciled in Japan had been extending assistance in various forms to the non-Taleban forces and gifted a Mercedes Benz for the use of Mr Hamid Karzai, his very participation in the Grand Council indicated that the efforts to rebuild the country were receiving the cooperation of all Afghans. "He is a very rich businessman in Japan and nobody had expected him to get involved with the national enterprise of reconstruction to such an extent, but his spontaneous participation in the Loya Jirgah proved that working closely with his countrymen who came from all walks of life was natural for him. While we leave it to the discretion of each Afghan domiciled abroad to participate in the reconstruction process, Mr Andishman is an example of how selflessly they can serve their country in its hour of need."

While the Transitional Government is confident that Afghans domiciled abroad will return to participate in the reconstruction of the country, Dr Ahmadzai made a significant remark. He said, "We want that kind of (Afghan) technocrats (living abroad) who believe that the people of this country are extremely sophisticated even if they are illiterate. Afghanistan is poor but the Afghans are rich."

One purpose of quoting extensively from Dupree's analysis of the 1964 Constitution and from the deliberations of the Emergency Loya Jirgah of mid-June 2002, is to record certain attributes of the Afghan people not generally taken note of, as has been seen repeatedly in both media and academic responses to the global war against terrorism, which was initiated with the United States-led alliance attacking the Taleban-al-Qaeda forces in Afghanistan.

Both the 1964 Constitution and the Emergency Grand Council show that the Afghans are intrinsically capable of adopting secularism and are proud of their nation. The popular perceptions about them, as discernible from the torrent of media and academic exercises since 11 September 2001 (the day the United States was attacked by terrorists belonging to al-Qaeda), however, continue to present them as inherently backward and feudal, orthodox and incapable of forging national unity. The international emphasis continues to be on the role of the warlords in eventually wrecking any attempt to build a politically united, modern society. The degree of scepticism about the Afghans building a democratic and modern society from the rubble of the war years, as evident in these judgmental writings and pronouncements, is unique, to say the least. As for the United Front, the worst possible judgments were made of its past actions and future intentions, and it is rare to see a scholar or journalist expecting a good deed or two from it in the event of its dominating the post-Taleban government.

For example, participating in a Roundtable on Afghanistan: Governance Scenarios and Canadian Policy Options, after Operation Enduring Freedom had been launched, this was what an Afghan scholar, Omar Zakhilwal of the Institute for Afghan Studies, said, "Given the time constraint, it is not possible for me to discuss a full picture of all the possible post-Taleban alternatives. However, I can focus on one very alarming and, therefore the worst yet, a very possible case scenario: that is the return of the Northern Alliance (United Front) to Kabul as a government."[9]

Further comments by the scholar revealed that he was actually pitching for King Zahir Shah as the head of a post-Taleban government. "Let me share with you the fact," he said, "that after 11 September (2001) many Afghans expected that before there was any military campaign, the United States and its allies would push for and help with forging a post-Taleban provisional regime. A regime that was composed of personalities who, at the minimum, were not associated with any serious war crimes against their own innocent Afghan civilians. It was also expected and still is that such a regime would be formed around the former king who enjoys an overwhelming popular support and respect among all tribal and ethnic groups in Afghanistan."

Continuing, he said, "Realising his important role, the king started to gather a broad coalition against the Taleban and started to position some of his influential people along the borders of Afghanistan. The news we were getting from the king's people in the field was encouraging. There were reports of successful contacts with the moderate Taleban commanders and, as a result, there were reports of dissension (within) the Taleban."

"However, the premature and hasty US attacks on Afghanistan not only hindered the king's efforts but also greatly boosted the ability of the (United Front) to attack Kabul and perhaps retake it. This made it less likely for the (United Front) to even become an ally to the efforts of the king," he said.

Explaining his opposition to a United Front-led government in the post-Taleban period, Dr Zakhilwal said, "Few outsiders know of the ground reality that although an overwhelming majority of the Afghans, living inside or outside of Afghanistan, regardless of their ethnic, linguistic and regional background, distaste the Taleban regime, an equally parallel majority would not want them to be replaced by the (United Front). Because in the eyes of the Afghan public, every leader of the different factions that make up the United Front (qualifies), at best, is a war criminal."

Well off the mark, as would be evident to anybody who happened to be in Kabul in the aftermath of the fall of the Taleban-al-Qaeda regime, but nevertheless, the Afghan scholar's analysis, made one month after the 11th September terrorist attack and the 9th September 2001 assassination of Commander Ahmad Shah Massoud, deserves attention as it exemplifies the sharp polarisation amongst the Afghan people. It is much easier to agree with Dr Zakhilwal when he said, "Thanks to neighbouring countries, particularly Pakistan and Iran for their deliberate creating and fuelling of ethnic tensions, ethnic divisions now run at the top among the factors that (are) keeping Afghanistan divided. All the warring factions in

Afghanistan are extremely ethnocentric and at numerous times throughout the civil war each faction committed serious war crimes against people of rival ethnic groups.

"For that reason the (United Front) does not and never did and perhaps never will enjoy the backing of the majority Pushtuns, whose support is absolutely fundamental for the survival of any government in Afghanistan. (Realising) that weakness, a few weeks ago, an envoy of the (United Front) signed a memorandum of understanding, perhaps for power-sharing, with the king, who is ethnically a Pushtun and, therefore, the (United Front)'s association could bring them some vital support from the Pushtuns. However, that same day the President and the Foreign Minister objected that their envoy did not consult them before he put down his signature on the document. Even if the (United Front) succeeds in reaching an agreement on an alternative post-Taleban arrangement with the king, it is not guaranteed that they will keep to it. In fact, the reverse is highly likely."

Once again, totally off the mark, for if anything, the post-Taleban period has been witnessing a remarkable adjustment among the various ethnic factions without which the implementation of the Bonn Agreement till date would have been impossible. However, the scholar was hitting the nail on the head when he said that the (United Front) was the last government Pakistan would want to see in Afghanistan "and Pakistan, therefore, will create another force (if they cannot reactivate the Taleban) within Afghanistan to confront it (a United Front government) successfully".

The same intensity of distrust was visible in the words of another Afghan, who also spoke at the roundtable, Jawed Ludin, who was working for British Overseas NGOs for Development. "By providing unconditional support to one warring faction (the United Front) in the Afghan conflict," he warned, "the United States and Britain are effectively reinforcing the dynamics of conflict and undermining the possibilities of a comprehensive solution. Using the (United Front) as a de facto ground force may seem the obvious option, but this is inappropriate and potentially dangerous. Warlords are the problem, not the solution in Afghanistan. It is hard to imagine that, given our exerience of their past, the (United Front) can be trusted to deliver the country to peace. There must be no doubt that these extremely violent and organisationally anarchic forces simply cannot produce the effective leadership the country needs."

Examples of such intense mistrust of the United Front, equating it oftener than not with the Taleban-al-Qaeda as far as devilishness goes and, in any case, describing it as nothing more than a disparate group of warlords as bad as the others, are galore, especially in the September-November 2001, period when the outcome of Operation Enduring Freedom was getting to be somewhat discernible but the future of the Afghan state remained obscure. What strikes a non-Afghan observer as unusual is the uniform tendency to disregard, almost contemptuously, all those statements that Commander Massoud and other spokesmen of the United Front had been making to the world at large throughout 2000 and until his death in 2001 outlining the United Front's position on a political settlement.

If one takes cognisance of those statements, the developments in the post-Taleban period should not surprise anyone. For example, the Rabbani Government's ambassador in New Delhi, Masood Khalili, said (the Taleban-al-Qaeda regime had fled Kabul and the United Front forces had taken over the capital five days earlier), "The United Nations special envoy for Afghanistan is expected in Kabul in the next two days and the (United Front) is very keen that they facilitate the setting up of an interim government. The (United Front) is very clear that they are not going to set up such an interim government. If tomorrow President Rabbani were to initiate such a process, the people would look upon him with suspicion and insist he was doing it to install himself as president. The initiative must come from the UN; we have reposed faith in them. Two processes are possible. The arrangement will either be brought about at the initiative of the former king of Afghanistan, Zahir Shah, or else the UN will have to set up a Loya Jirgah where people will decide who their next leader is going to be. We are not against either scheme. A final government will only be set up after there have been elections. The (United Front) will accept the decision either way."[10]

"Once this broad-based, multi-ethnic government is in place," he continued, "the UN (will have) to ensure that our neighbours, especially Pakistan, are not allowed to destabilise it as they have done so in the past. The US must keep a check on our neighbours. After all, it cannot be forgotten that traditionally, problems in Afghanistan have been created for us not from insiders but from outsiders."

Nearly seven months earlier, addressing a press conference in Paris, Commander Massoud held out his vision of Afghanistan in the post-Taleban period. "We believe," he said, "that the future government should be formed by means of general elections, via the people's ballot, through the vote of both women and men. The only form of government able to ensure social justice and equality between Afghanistan's various ethnic groups is democracy and the people's vote."[11]

"Our future government and the Taleban will be incomparably different," he continued with his vision. "We have always opposed and continue to oppose any kind of extremist or radical movements, even if they claim to be Islamic, and we do not believe they are good for Afghanistan, the region or the world. As I have repeated earlier, we believe in elections with the participation of both women and men.

"We fully respect human rights, we support it, we will protect it.

"We prescribe against the cultivation and trafficking of illegal narcotics; we believe they are haram (forbidden by Islam), and they are detrimental to all humankind and destructive to our own country.

"As during the jihad (holy war), we fully oppose terrorism and terrorist activities. No one had ever witnessed a terrorist attack by the mujahideen (freedom fighters), even when the Russians were in Afghanistan. Terrorism is wrong and we are against it."

Especially germane to the present task of rebuilding the country were the following words, "We not only support women's education, women working and women's participation in society, but we encourage it. Women can play an instrumental role in rebuilding the country after these many years of war."[12]

Ms Otilie English, the Public Affairs Representative of the Islamic State of Afghanistan (the formal identity of the Rabbani Government) later explained Commander Massoud's optimism about the eventual outcome of the civil war, despite the bleak outlook at the time, and what she said in response deserves repetition, "He's optimistic about the future because he is seeing that Afghans are tired of war. The Afghans now realise (that) they have been invaded again, and they hate the Taleban. And they hate the foreign 'guests'(the official description of al-Qaeda fighters under the Taleban regime). They have realised that these people are not Afghans – they're Chechens, Uighurs, Punjabis and Arabs of every stripe."[13]

Despite the Taleban-al-Qaeda regime's determination to bring about a military solution to the Afghan problem by defeating the United Front on the battlefield, for which Commander Massoud and his men were constantly required to be prepared and frequently passed through ups and downs, the legendary fighter kept on sending signals for peace talks. Twenty-six days before he was assassinated by two Moroccan terrorists masquerading as TV journalists at Khoja Bahauddin, Commander Massoud told AIM Television, "We have repeatedly said that two steps are crucial for restoration of peace in Afghanistan. One, that resistance is strengthened and expanded in Afghanistan and, secondly, international pressure is increased on Pakistan. If international pressure is increased on Pakistan, I believe that the Taleban will be compelled to sit at the negotiating table."

A year earlier, in his celebrated interview to A. Raffaele Ciriello, he had said, "Our message to the Taleban is clear; if they are truly relying, as they state, upon the unconditional support of the Afghans and above all Pushtun ethnics, the largest in number, why do they keep on rejecting free and democratic elections? Why do they continue fighting when they are aware that without the continued support of Pakistan, they could not last a week, notwithstanding the huge quantity of arms and means at their disposal, including (Osama) bin Laden's 3,500 men?"[14]

Addressing a press conference in Dushanbe on 9 April 2001, Commander Massoud said, "Despite all the existing problems, we have always been ready to sit down at the negotiating table with the Taleban. We may even accept the setting up of a provisional government jointly with the Taleban, but for a term no longer than half a year or a year."

Speaking at the first International Conference on Massoud Studies, held in Kabul, 7-8 September 2002, this author said, "Time and again, the Afghan leader used every opportunity that came his way to urge the world, till then supremely indifferent to the developments in Afghanistan as 11 September (2001) was mercifully yet to happen, to turn its attention to his unfortunate country and ensure that the Taleban, shorn of the baleful influence of the eastern neighbour, come to the negotiating table, a peace process was initiated and an all-inclusive political dialogue with a view to seek a political solution was started.[15]

"(Commander Massoud) himself spoke movingly about the plight of Afghanistan and the urgency to correct the situation in his Message to the People of the United States of 8 October 1998, 'I have spent the past twenty years, most of my youth and adult life, alongside my compatriots, at the service of the Afghan nation, fighting an uphill battle to preserve our freedom, independence, right to self-determination and dignity. Afghans fought for God and country, sometimes alone, at other times with the support of the international community. Against all odds, we, meaning the free world and Afghans, halted and checkmated Soviet expansionism a decade ago. But the embattled people of my country did not savour the fruits of victory. Instead, they were thrust in a whirlwind of foreign intrigue, deception, great gamesmanship and internal strife. Our country and our noble people were brutalised, the victims of misplaced greed, hegemonic designs and ignorance. We Afghans erred too. Our shortcomings were as a result of political innocence, inexperience, vulnerability, victimisation, bickering and inflated egos. But by no means does this justify what some of our so-called Cold War allies did to undermine this just victory and unleash their diabolical plans to destroy and subjugate Afghanistan.'"

The extent of the complexity of the situation in today's Afghanistan can well be gauged by taking stock of the present state of affairs. Under the auspices of the United Nations and according to the provisions of the Bonn Agreement, a broad-based transitional government is presently in office, tasked specifically to steer the country towards the drafting and adoption of a democratic constitution and holding of parliamentary elections after a fifteen-month period.

At the same time, the government is required to set up a full-scale bureaucracy, defence and police forces, initiate and carry forward various development projects and introduce modern economic activities including banking and a well-regulated curency. Above all, it is also expected to improve the security situation all over the country adequately so that the reconstruction of the country in all fields of human activity can progress without obstacles. It goes without saying that the international community is committed to assist the transitional government not only financially but also technically in all these duties and responsibilities.

As the world looks at today's Afghanistan, the complexity of the situation is enhanced further by the traditional and historical ethnic and tribal conflicts endemic to the Afghan nation. While, contrary to the doomsday predictions of both Afghan and non-Afghan scholars, these conflicts have not so far achieved anything close to a derailing of the process of rebuilding Afghanistan and each major step forward, such as the holding of the Emergency Loya Jirgah, election of the President of the country and the composition of the Transitional Government, has been gone through successfully, the scope and apprehension for such an eventuality is considered everpresent. Hence. the suggestion that the Pushtuns and the Tajiks sit down together and thrash out a political consensus before it is too late. Neither the people of Afghanistan nor the world at large wishes to see the country sliding back to anarchy.

The most visible indicator of the pitfalls that seek to bedevil the country is the close relationship between security and drug trafficking; it is thus with good reason that both the United Nations and the United States, as the country spearheading the reconstruction of the country, are equally concerned that opium exports have begun to rise again, neutralising the

Options Before Afghanistan

compensation scheme for farmers switching over to cash crops during 2002. If the trend continues, international efforts at normalising Afghanistan will have received its first major body blow.

During his several visits to Afghanistan in 2002, the author was struck by the evident display of the cash richness of the elite and professional classes, while the country at large remained abysmally poor (even in the eyes of a South Asian, used to the poorest part of the world). All consumer goods, whether white or food products or cosmetics, were exorbitantly priced, since the afghani commanded no respect in bazaars and every saleable item was quoted in terms of the US dollar. Yet, the elite and professional classes enjoyed all the benefits of good life. The question often arose: wherefrom did they earn the kind of money they were apparently spending? The answer was difficult to find because there were very few lawful avenues of earning and often, these were not adequately paying.

The answer that the author got from various knowledgeable sources, including foreign diplomats posted in Kabul, was that only a few Afghans would be completely innocent of one or another kind of link with opium poppy cultivation and opium production and smuggling. The surmise is that almost anybody with some length of cultivable land has opium poppy sown and cultivated and is paid handsomely by agents of opium factory owners, transport operators and smugglers. The system, built over the decades, is now so omnipresent that little effort is wasted in arranging cultivation and subsequent transportation to factory and eventual smuggling across the border, either into Pakistan or into Central Asia. The very fact that despite the interim administration's total ban on opium poppy cultivation exports of opium have actually increased during 2002 indicates that the infrastructure so carefully placed and nurtured by the Taleban-al-Qaeda regime continues to operate, and it can do so only because a vast majority of the population is connected one way or the other with the trade.

Today is not much different from what the situation was during the Taleban rule. Ahmed Rashid tells us about Wali Jan, "a toothless, elderly farmer", who says, "We cannot be more grateful to the Taleban. The Taleban have brought us security so we can grow our poppy in peace. I need the poppy crop to support my fourteen family members." Rashid adds, "The Taleban objective of re-establishing peace and security in the countryside has proved to be an immense boon to opium farming. On his small plot of land, Wali Jan produces 45 kilograms of raw opium every year and earns about US $1,300 – a small fortune for Afghan farmers. Wali Jan knows that refined heroin fetches fifty times that price in London or New York, but he is more than happy with what he gets. The results of this cash flow are evident everywhere, for there is more reconstruction going on in villages around Kandahar than anywhere else in Afghanistan."[16]

One should note that both the interim administration and the Transitional Government have opted to leave Kandahar and the southern Afghanistan undisturbed, not bothering to establish their writ in any manner whatsoever. The chief reason is the desire to avoid any showdown with the people associated with poppy cultivation and transportation, who include local warlords and their sizeable militia.

The United Nations Drug Control Programme has calculated that while Afghan farmers receive less than one per cent of the total profits generated by the opium trade, another 2.5 per cent remains in Afghanistan and Pakistan in the hands of dealers, while five per cent is spent in the countries through which heroin passes while en route to the West. The rest of the profits is made by the dealers and distributors in Europe and the United States. Even with this low rate of return, "it is conservatively estimated", writes Rashid, "that some one million Afghan farmers are making over US $100 million a year on account of growing poppies. The Taleban were thus raking in at least US $20 million in taxes and even more on the side."[17]

To be honest, the Taleban only inherited and improved upon the benefits of nurturing opium poppy cultivation and conversion into heroin, for before them it was the mujahideen warlords who profited enormously by participating in the trade. The drug money brought them unprecedented prosperity; the Taleban cleverly expanded both the area under poppy cultivation and the drugs trade and thus earned much more (a twenty per cent tax was imposed) to fund their war against the United Front and the jihad against the "infidel" countries like the United States, Israel, India and the Russian Federation.

For understandable reasons, the international community is not over-emphasising the supreme need of ridding Afghanistan of the scourge of drug trafficking immediately, for as we have seen above, the Afghan society is so intimately connected with the phenomenon over such a long period of time that even if the world comes forward and offers alternative sources of income, it would be not just difficult but outright impossible for the Afghans to shake it off within a year or two. As a matter of fact, the United States has come forward and a cash compensation scheme has been put in place; but the response of the population has been less than meagre.

So, what is the best way out? Speculating nearly three years before the Taleban-al-Qaeda regime fell, Rubin offered the following, "Indeed, whatever political group might take control of Afghanistan (obviously, the concept of a broad-based government taking over did not strike him at the time, though the idea had been in the air for sometime), the economic incentives for misgovernment are nearly irresistible. Only the drug and transit trade are really worth the effort of taxation, while the rest of the economy is hardly productive enough to make governing it worthwhile. It is difficult to recover the cost of more than a very sparse administration of such an economy and society. Such a political economy would leave the power bidders as unaccountable to most Afghan people as they were under previous regimes. Most of the population would be left to fend for themselves, in conditions of greater security, but without a development agenda, public services or reforms, notably in the status of women."[18]

Rubin's words bear an almost uncanny resemblance to the situation today. For illustration, we may consider just one aspect, the warlords. Earlier in this chapter, we have heard President Karzai venting his frustration over the continuing depredations of warlords while talking to a team of *Washington Post* journalists on 4 February 2002 (factional fight had broken out in Gardez, capital of Paktia province, in which at least sixty people had been killed).

The fact is that both General Abdul Rashid Dostum, running his virtual government in Mazar-i-Sharif in the north and General Ismael Khan, lording over Herat, have been wisely enough left undisturbed, though enough trouble has rocked Dostum's fiefdom during 2002, forcing international aid agencies to stop functioning for some time in the region. The inhabitants of southern and eastern Afghanistan, who continue to harbour remnants of the Taleban-al-Qaeda regime and its forces, are equally allowed to live as wildly as before, for the simple reason that the central government in Kabul continues to be weak without a worthwhile army and police force. This is just one example of how right Rubin was in his forecasting three years before the event.[19]

Pointing out that in such a scenario, the "expanding drug trade, money laundering and smuggling would undermine governance in several countries", Rubin came out with the suggestion: "A more challenging alternative is to consider peacemaking in Afghanistan as part of a larger problem, of transforming the political economy of a region. It has finally dawned on Europe and the United States that nothing less will work in the Balkans. There is no reason to think that Central and Southwest Asia will be a simpler problem."

As of today, fourteen months since the collapse of the Taleban-al-Qaeda regime and installation of a broad-based government with international support in Kabul, nothing of the kind of regional economic-political reconstruction is even being considered, not to speak of being planned and readied for implementation.

Far worse, even the relatively modest reconstruction of country and economy that should have been initiated is yet to take off. The entire Transitional Government is now openly criticising the international community for failing to live up to its promises of aid made in the midst of fanfare in Tokyo and Geneva (US $1.8 billion in nation-building and "tens of millions of dollars" for reconstructing security forces).

Talking to the author, Finance Minister Ashraf Ghani Ahmadzai said in Kabul on 29 June 2002, "...The truth is that we are terribly short of funds to run the government in all its paraphernalia and that is creating problems. The promised money has been extremely slow in coming, holding up work in all spheres. The flow of aid and investment that we expected has not happened. But I am not complaining. These are natural hiccups for a country devastated by years of warfare and just getting about to try to stand on its own feet."[20]

More than two months later, Foreign Minister Dr Abdullah echoed the Transitional Government's disappointment at the slow release of funds by the international community. He said, "Yes, it is true that we continue to be hampered in the job of restoring normalcy in the country due to the extreme lack of resources. The government lacks revenue; it is only in the process of preparing its budget estimates for the year. The banking system is not fully operational. The security forces are yet to be adequately recruited, trained, armed and deployed. No major development project has been started. Yes, even a casual observer will find out that there is scarcely any nation-building activity in Afghanistan. At the root lies the acute resource crunch. Not to speak of foreign investment, even the promised foreign aid is taking an inordinately long time to reach us."[21]

On 12 October 2002, Afghanistan's anguished cry for funds went up again; President Karzai told a meeting of foreign donors that the bulk of foreign aid money sent to Afghanistan in 2002 had gone to humanitarian organisations and the United Nations, not to his administration. Yet, it was this government which had been tasked to rebuild a completely devastated country. He called on the donors to channel financial assistance toward his government's own reconstruction projects as a means of reducing gradually the dependence on foreign aid. "I learned some time back that Afghanistan had received $890 million (in aid this year)," he said. "Of that amount, $800 million has gone to the United Nations and aid agencies" to support humanitarian programmes in Afghanistan.

Yet, the international community readily agrees that timely foreign aid would be crucial for the restoration and sustenance of peace and democracy in the country. Why then the debilitating delay, even at the risk of encouraging revival of terrorism and anarchy?

In response, two reasons are primarily cited; the red tapism inherent in international humanitarian and developmental aid as well as red tapism incidental to individual donor countries and the failure of the Transitional Government to put in place ministries that function satisfactorily.

Options Before Afghanistan 59

Donor countries explain that the unseemly delay in releasing aid and development funds to Afghanistan is due to both factors; while the international aid agency bureaucracy and national bureaucracies take their own time in budgeting, appproving and finally releasing the funds, it is the pronounced inadequacies of the Afghan administration, with the majority of ministries working with few professionals and just recovering from the terrible misgovernance of the Taleban-al-Qaeda period, that requires the donors to be extra vigilant about the very business of funding.

"This is unfortunate but reality," said Peter Tomsen, Ambassador-in-Residence, Centre for Afghanistan Studies at the University of Nebraska at Omaha and Special Envoy to the Afghan Resistance during 1989-92.[22] Tomsen should know because he has been involved with Central and Southwest Asia for over three decades. "While the US administration is bad enough, taking on an average one year to facilitate project funding, the Europeans seem to be worse practitioners of red tapism. Yet, the international community is well aware of the special status of funding the reconstruction of Afghanistan, that this is an extremely urgent case and does not brook any conventional approach. The problem has become so acute that the Bush administration has been forced to draft a Bill, which is in the process of being adopted by both Houses of Congress, which will separate funding for Afghanistan from other country-specific funding. Once the Bill becomes law, it should take the administration much less time to provide the urgently needed funds for the reconstruction of Afghanistan."

Tomsen was full of praise for the Indian government which appeared to have startled the international community earlier by providing three jet airliners to boost the functioning of Ariana airlines, Afghanistan's national carrier which was subjected to United Nations sanctions during the latter part of the Taleban-al-Qaeda rule, had its flights suspended and its assets frozen. The airline still functions from the bombed-out Kabul Hotel building in Kabul.

"Such an act of handing over as many as three jet airliners would have taken Washington not less than one year, which the Indian government did in a few months' time, cutting through red tape without mercy," said Tomsen. "This should be the approach of every international aid agency and donor country if succour has to reach Afghanistan before it is too late."

India is, in fact, the most appreciated country today in Afghanistan because it is reaching out exactly in those sectors where the welfare of the individual is the uppermost factor. Thus, Indian assistance in restarting primary and secondary education, hospitals and the entire health sector including supply of pharmaceuticals (Indian drugs being cheaper than those from developed countries) and the public transport system is both self-evident and genuinely appreciated.

During this author's September 2002 visit, a typical instance of the swift and timely Indian response to Afghanistan's intensely humanitarian needs manifested itself. While talking to the author about the resurrection and functioning of his university, President of the Kabul University Prof. Mohammad Akbar Popal remarked that he had a request to make to the Indian government. "Can you kindly tell your ambassador that if he gifts five buses to the university, we can restart our night university?"

Saying that this was a very special request, Prof. Popal then proceeded to explain the significance of resuming the night university classes. "You see, it was mostly women who work in government ministries who used to attend night university classes, in order to upgrade their education and improve their chances at places of work. The women, however, gradually stopped attending classes as the university was on the frontline during the mujahideen days when fights erupted everyday and the university was shelled. Thereafter, the women had to stop education altogether when the Taleban came to power."[23]

Continuing, he said, "Now that peace has been restored and the university has resumed functioning, we would very much like to restart the night university for the benefit of the women students. We are, however, not in a position to do so because the university campus is far away from the city and buses scarcely ply in the late hours in the area. It is for this reason that the women students have not yet returned to the night university. Otherwise, they keep appealing to us every now and then to restart the classes; but to do so, we first need a reliable bus service to the city and suburbs."

Resident editor of the Calcutta-based newspaper, *The Telegraph*, Bharat Bhushan, who was present at the interview, promptly conveyed the university president's request to Ambassador Vivek Katju who responded with equal promptitude, "Please request the president to write to me immediately about the five buses. Consider that the job is already done." It is only such responses that would bring genuine succour to the thoroughly devastated and traumatised country.

Thus, the options before Afghanistan are already enumerated, that either the country develops and entrenches itself steadily into the well-defined norms of parliamentary democracy and travels unflinchingly on the path to political, social and economic development and overall progress, quickly establishing the ethos of good governance and observance of human rights or it relapses into chaos, anarchy, intolerance and mayhem. Since Afghanistan has, in the last two decades and more, experienced the very catastrophe attendant upon the disintegration of the state and because the international community cannot conceivably be insensitive enough once again to allow the country to slip back into the Talebanesque hell, it is obviously the sane choice of a sustained return to civilisational existence and nation-building activities that will henceforth identify the country.

****

Endnotes

1. Interview of Foreign Minister of Afghanistan Dr Abdullah Abdullah on 25 June 2002, in Kabul.
2. Dupree, L., *Afghanistan*, pp.651-652.
3. ibid., pp.577-578.
4. ibid., pp.579-580.
5. *The Kabul Times*, 25 June 2002.
6. Gross, Nasrine, interview taken in Kabul on 5-6 September 2002.
7. *The Kabul Times*, 25 June 2002.
8. Interview taken in Kabul on 29 June 2002.
9. Roundtable on Afghanistan: "Governance Scenarios and Canadian Policy Options", held by the Department of Foreign Affairs and International Trade, Government of Canada, in Ottawa, Canada, on 12 October 2001.
10. Interview in *The Times of India*, New Delhi, 18 November 2001.
11. Press conference held in Paris on 4 April 2001, during Commander Ahmad Shah Massoud's European tour. The trip to Paris proved to be diplomatically disastrous as President Jacques Chirac refused to receive Commander Massoud. In fact, despite the utmost efforts of former minister Brice Lalande, a close friend of Massoud, neither the President nor Prime Minister Lionel Jospin agreed to meet the United Front Defence Minister, fearful that such an official recognition of the Afghan opposition at the highest level would irritate

relations with Pakistan, which was an important customer of the French defence industry. As a face-saver, Foreign Minister Hubert Vedrine agreed to host a luncheon for Commander Massoud. According to Lalande, who talked at length to the author on the subject, the French government's behaviour left a bitter taste not only in the United Front camp but also in France and Italy where the Afghan resistance leader enjoyed considerable popularity, his military exploits in particular being well-publicised in both countries.

12. ibid.
13. The interview of Ms Otilie English, the Public Affairs Representative of the Islamic State of Afghanistan, given to the *Omaid Weekly*, issue # 477.
14. "In the Lair of the Lion", interview with Commander Ahmad Shah Massoud, by A. Raffaele Ciriello, at Darqad, north Afghanistan.
15. Paper read at the first International Conference on Massoud Studies, entitled "Commemorating Commander Ahmad Shah Massoud". The conference was attended by leading experts on Afghanistan from abroad and by eminent Afghans, including President Hamid Karzai. The two-day conference was marked by the presence of a galaxy of Afghan mujahideen leaders, including the first mujahideen president Sibgatullah Mujaddedi as well as the president of the Islamic State of Afghanistan Prof. Burhanuddin Rabbani.
16. Rashid, Ahmed, *Taliban*... pp.117-124.
17. ibid., p.119.
18. Rubin, Barnett, "The Political Economy..."
19. The United Nations High Commissioner for Refugees on 2 July 2002.
20. The interview of Finance Minister Dr Ashraf Ghani Ahmadzai in his office in Kabul on 29 June 2002.
21. The interview of Foreign Minister Dr Abdullah in Kabul on 7 September 2002.
22. The interview took place in Kabul on 2 September 2002.
23. The interview took place at the Intercontinental Hotel, Kabul, on 7 September 2002.

2
Horror Called the Taleban

It was a morning the employees of the war-ravaged Kabul Museum will not be in a hurry to forget. The morning of 1 March 2001 had begun the way all mornings did (the official announcement of the Taleban that they had begun to destroy all statues at the Kabul Museum, however, came on 1 March 2001). But then, as the dull morning progressed, about a dozen Taleban fighters walked in, a bunch of very polite young men, and asked to see if everything was honky dory with the museum. The employees had their misgivings but did not know what to do. Then, as the young Taleban began to walk around, they took out hammers and went about demolishing statues with a deadly determination. The infamous Taleban culture police had reached one of Asia's most valued museums. By the time they left, priceless statues had been reduced to rubble and dust. Among them, the world famous headless statue of Emperor Kanishka, the greatest Buddhist king to rule the vast Kushan empire in the second century AD, now a mere collection of rubble lovingly collected and preserved by the museum employees (American historian Nancy Hatch Dupree, writing on 20 April 1998 and updated on 26 May 1998, listed the

Kanishka statue as still in the possession of the museum even though the civil war between various mujahideen factions since 1992 had damaged and destroyed the museum extensively).

Considered to be the depository of the most comprehensive record of Central Asian history, the Kabul Museum possessed artifacts dating back to pre-historic times; one of its largest displays was the magnificent Bagram Collection, discovered in 1939 by archaeologists excavating a Kushan fort; it contained as many as 1,800 pieces from India, Rome, Greece, Egypt and Central Asia. The Greek and Roman coins found near Kabul formed one of the largest collections of such artifacts anywhere in the world.

The origins of the Taleban, their nature of functioning and their objectives continue to fascinate the world even after they had passed into history. Were they indigenous to Afghanistan? How did their religious fanaticism, which was actually tantamount to barbarism, develop? Why did they quite consciously decide not to develop a nation-state even though they controlled nearly ninety per cent of the national territory and apparently enjoyed the confidence of the people in the initial days?

To answer the first question, were the Taleban, the so-called student storm-troopers from the madrassas (religious schools) in Pakistan and Afghanistan, an entirely indigenous or foreign-origin force? For good reasons, attempts were made at various periods of time and places to conceal or, at the very least, confuse anyone looking for it, about the identity of the militia with its members ranging in age anywhere from the early teens to mid-forties. Two facts about the movement, which appeared mysteriously in the civil war-riven Afghanistan in 1994, are certain, that the majority of them were schooled in madrassas set up in the refugee camps in north-west Pakistan and that some of those who led the Taleban in later years were among the mujahideen and fought against the Soviet occupation.

It is usually not fashionable to take notice of the Taleban's own claim of being indigenous to Afghanistan, but we will, nevertheless, record it here. History, according to the Taleban, was like this: Afghanistan's jihad against communism and foreign occupation began under the banner of Islam. It was on the basis of the teachings of Islam that a small, ill-equipped nation succeeded in defeating a superpower who seemed well-positioned to dominate the world. "As students of Islamic teachings, the Taleban played a paramount role in mobilising, planning and directing the holy jihad," the official Taleban literature says.[1]

"This role was not new to the Afghan history," the publication adds. "In the past, whenever a foreign power invaded Afghanistan and threatened freedom and independence of the Afghans, the Islamic students (called Talaba) left their schools or madrassas to fight at the head of the Afghan armies."

Based on this "historical" tradition, the official history of the Taleban claims, and on their "complete" devotion to the holy teachings of Islam, the Taleban were naturally opposed to the communists and their "decadent materialistic philosophy and atheistic view of the world". Before the communists were helped to power by the direct support of the Soviet Union in 1978, the Taleban used preaching and religious guidance as the major means of fighting against the atheistic ideology and corruption. After the communist coup d'etat, it was clear that "preaching and religious education had to be complemented by practical jihad if the people of Afghanistan were to be saved from vices that were being promoted by the communists and their supporters.

Thus, the Taleban changed their strategy and called on the nation to take up arms and render assistance against the atheist regime and its collaborators, the official history of the movement informs.

The struggle continued relentlessly, the official account says, and it was organisationally centred around a number of different political parties called Tanzeemha. The Islamic ulema and the Taleban were particularly attached to two of these political parties, Harakat-i-Inquilab-i-Islami Afghanistan (Afghanistan's Movement of Islamic Revolution) under the leadership of Maulvi Mohammed Nabi Mohammedi and Hizb-i-Islami (Islamic Party) under the leadership of Maulvi Mohammed Younis Khalis.

Summing up the jihad, in which neither the United States nor Pakistan and Saudi Arabia played any role (to go by the Taleban version), the publication describes the Soviet withdrawal and the immediate aftermath as follows: "With the Soviets gone in disgrace, and their puppets defeated, the Taleban perceived their task accomplished, and soon returned in large numbers to their madrassas, to take up their search for knowledge and spiritual advancement. The period described above that lasted from 1978 to 1992 can be called the First Phase of the Taleban mission in serving their faith, their people and their country."

But soon enough, the devout scholars were required to take up arms again. Describing the factional fighting that soon erupted among the various mujahideen groups, with foreign powers, Iran, Russia, Uzbekistan and India (no mention of Pakistan) rushing in to intervene and promote their protégés (Iran promoting Hizb-i-Wahdat, Russia and Uzbekistan supporting "communist" Abdul Rashid Dostum and India providing technical and financial assistance to Burhanuddin Rabbani and "his military strongman Ahmad Shah Massoud"), and with the unrest spreading to the countryside, the official history of the Taleban says that the people began to ask, "Why our religious scholars and students, who preach justice and peace, do not do something to save us from injustice and war?"

"In response to this important calling directed to them by the innocent and suffering people of Afghanistan, the Taleban stood once again to their feet, closed their books and came out of their madrassa classrooms to begin the second phase of their holy jihad against the wickedness and the corruption," the history says. The rise of the Taleban was accompanied by a fatwa (religious decree) issued by Islamic scholars, confirming the legitimacy of their uprising against corruption and vice. In this way, the new movement was called the Taleban Islamic Movement of Afghanistan.

"The Taleban Islamic Movement of Afghanistan is a genuine grass-roots movement that draws its power and support from the masses of the Afghan people," the history claims. After the Taleban succeeded in driving the "corrupt" forces of Rabbani and his military commander from Kabul in September 1996, they were able to establish a central administration in the capital, "run by people of good faith and intention". This was the first administration in almost twenty years that was truly interested in the well-being of the citizens and trying hard to make life easier for them.

Taking stock of their "accomplishments" in four years of rule, which also formed the basis of the Taleban government's case for granting of United Nations membership by unseating the Burhanuddin Rabbani government from the membership, the Taleban history claimed in 2000 that the achievements of the regime were as follows:

1. Restoration of full security of the citizens
2. Pursuance of honest and sincere negotiations
3. Support for the United Nations and Organisation of Islamic Conference peace efforts
4. Respect for United Nations rules and principles

5. Search for mutual respect and friendly relations towards all countries
6. Establishment of a credible and accountable Islamic regime
7. Protection of human rights and liberties
8. Restoration of women's safety, dignity and freedom
9. Observance of Islamic hejab or the veil
10. Women's education in the Islamic Emirate of Afghanistan
11. Establishment of a representative government on the basis of Islamic Sharia
12. The Islamic Emirate lends full support to the United Nations agencies and non-governmental organisations
13. Efforts to combat production and consumption of illicit drugs
14. The Islamic Emirate is against all forms of terrorism
15. The Islamic Emirate of Afghanistan intends to rebuild the war-torn country

The history of Afghanistan since the resistance against the Soviet invasion and occupation, as related by the Taleban, is not only acutely fanciful but also downright devilish. For, while the official website was trying to persuade the world about the fictional purity of the so-called students' movement, which was claimed to be entirely indigenous, the international community had long come to recognise the Taleban regime as the most brutal, sadistic and oppressive government anywhere in the post-Cold war period. Each of the so-called "accomplishments" was in fact the very opposite of what was actually happening in the country; and it was not even as if the world was ignorant about the reality.

Tracing the origins of the Taleban, Ralph H. Magnus and Eden Naby say, "The madrassas (in rural areas of Afghanistan left undisturbed during the jihad) attracted numbers of taleban and aspiring taleban according to the reputation and scholarly qualifications of their maulvis (teachers)... the number of small madrassas grew and hence that of taleban, who had always been a feature of traditional rural society. The informal network of these maulvis provided the basis for the Harakat-i-Inquilab-i-Islami Afghanistan of Maulana Mohammed Nabi Mohammedi, which had proven to be the most widespread of the mujahideen parties in the early years of the resistance... The fourteen years of the jihad produced a similar phenomenon among the Afghan refugees in Pakistan. A considerable number of Afghan refugee orphans entered into the network of madrassas of the Northwest Frontier Province, especially in tribal territories, where they were supported as a charity by Islamic organisations. The Jami'at-i-Ulema-i-Islam (Society of Islamic Scholars, JUI), a long-established (1945) political party led by Maulana Fazlur Rahman, went so far as to establish madrassas specifically for the orphans of the Afghan jihad. Its intellectual origins were in the Islamic University of Deoband (in India) and its version of Islam has always emphasised strict Hanafi Sunni orthodoxy and the dominant role of the ulema."[2]

The Jamaat-i-Islami had been favoured by the Zia-ul Haq regime (in Pakistan) during the jihad as its principal Islamic contact with the Afghan mujahideen and, particularly through the ISI, with (Gulbuddin) Hekmatyar. The JI followers were bitter rivals of the JUI; and the rivalry was such that, during her first prime ministership, Benazir Bhutto thought it wiser to leave the Afghan policy in the hands of the "heirs of Zia" in the military, which was followed during the prime ministership of Nawaz Sharif. But, when Bhutto came back in her second prime ministership, she changed the handling of the Afghan policy by handing it over to her father Zulfiqar Ali Bhutto's adviser for Afghan and frontier affairs retired army general Naseerullah Babar, who had become the Interior Minister in her Cabinet.

Pakistani brigadier Mohammad Yousaf, former head of the Afghan Affairs Bureau of the Inter-Services Intelligence (ISI) (who was directly responsible for the training and operations of the mujahideen for the period 1983-87), notes in his book *Bear Trap* (p.105) that in 1987 Gulbuddin Hekmatyar received twenty per cent of the Western military aid, Burhanuddin Rabbani nineteen per cent and Abdul Rasul Sayyaf eighteen per cent, while Maulvi Mohammed Nabi Mohammedi's Islamic Revolutionary Movement obtained a mere thirteen per cent. This was reflective of the utterly lopsided distribution of military aid amongst the various mujahideen groups because at the time the Taleban, under the banner of Nabi's party, accounted for as much fifty per cent of the total strength of mujahideen fighters. On the top of it, only one-third of the military aid meant for the party actually reached it; some equipment, instead of landing with the fighters, ended up in the black market having been siphoned off by Nabi's sons and his bureaucrats and some more would actually reach the very opposite camp, Afghan Maoist groups like the Sholayees in Nimrooz province. While Yousaf explains that the obvious disparity meted out towards the Nabi group was due to the latter's lack of willingness to participate in the jihad, the fact, according to Afghan sources, was that the Pakistani bureaucracy and Islamic fundamentalists did not wish the Taleban to receive larger support in the fight against the Soviets.

A pamphlet, entitled *Facts about Taliban*, which purports to present the Taleban's views on the developments since the Soviet invasion, says, "There is no doubt that General Zia-ul Haq (President of Pakistan) believed in the promotion of Islamic fundamentalism. He was a firm believer in the myth of an Islamic revolution carried out by the fundamentalist movements throughout the Islamic world. This is against the beliefs of the Taleban. The Taleban do not advocate the idea of a global Muslim revolution in collaboration with the Ikhwani forces who are seen to have deviated from the path of the Sharia and the teachings of the Koran and that of the Prophet Mohammad (PBUH)."

How did the concept of a global Islamic revolution become part of Afghanistan's recent history? According to the pamphlet, the stage for the foundation of such a revolution was set by Zia when he finally got rid of former Pakistani leader Zulfiqar Ali Bhutto after his 1977 coup. When the Russians invaded Afghanistan, Zia and the ISI were behind the transformation of Hekmatyar, Rabbani, Massoud, Sayyaf and others into political leaders. The mujahideen organisations, "created by Pakistan", were intrinsically modelled upon some other fundamentalist Islamic organisations like the already existing Jamaat Islami of Pakistan and the rest, all of which followed the political philosophies of the Ikhwan-ul-Muslimeen leaders such as Hassan-ul Bana, Sayed Qutb and Moudodi, the founding father of the Pakistani Jamaat Islami. By establishing such "fundamentalist networks", Zia wanted to unify the Pushtun brethren under the camouflage of Islamicism.

The pamphlet says that the Soviet invasion provided Zia with the opportunity to organise and transform into political leaders (those) elements who had in the guise of Islamicism previously proven to be anti-Afghan. "Hekmatyar, Massoud and Rabbani had failed in their previous Pakistan-instigated attempts in Laghman and Panjsher in 1975 because of a lack of public support. But with the Soviet invasion, they no longer had to worry about support from the nation: the Afghan refugees who were fleeing to Pakistan in thousands would now constitute the basis of their public support. This is how Pakistan came to monopolise the Afghan jihad, by making their own agents, who had previously desperately failed in their subversive activities, jihadi leaders."

Talking to the author in June 2002, in Kabul and Panjsher valley, members of the family of Commander Ahmad Shah Massoud and some of his long-time associates explained the 1975 adventure thus: Massoud and his associates were young men without adequate experience of the ways of governments and were thus lured into the misadventure to rise against the Daoud government by staging a revolt, without bothering to find out how such a rebellion could be sustained without strong indigenous popular support. As a result, the revolt was quelled swiftly, but it took many years for Massoud and his associates to realise the Pakistani gameplan in having involved them in the futile attempt to topple the Afghan government. According to the Massoud family, Islamabad thus wished to compromise the young Afghans to a perpetually adversarial relationship with the Afghan government in order to exploit them in the future. Rashid writes, "Hekmatyar and Massoud had both participated in an unsuccessful uprising against President Mohammad Daoud in 1975. These Islamic radicals had then fled to Pakistan where they were patronised by Islamabad as a means to pressurise future Afghan governments. Thus, when the Soviets invaded Afghanistan in 1979, Pakistan already had effective Islamic radicals under its control who could lead the jihad. President Zia-ul Haq insisted that the bulk of CIA military aid was transferred to these parties, until Massoud became independent and fiercely critical of Pakistani control."

Ahmed Rashid describes the Taleban leadership thus, "The Taleban leadership can boast of being the most disabled in the world today, and visitors do not know how to react, whether to laugh or to cry. Mullah Omar lost his right eye in 1989 when a rocket exploded close by. The Justice Minister Nuruddin Turabi and the former Foreign Minister Mohammed Ghaus are also one-eyed. The Mayor of Kabul, Abdul Majid, has one leg and two fingers missing. Other leaders, even military commanders, have similar disabilities."[3]

The Taleban's wounds, he says, were a constant reminder of twenty years of war, which had killed over 1.5 million people and devastated the country. The war wounds of the Taleban leaders also reflected the bloody and brutal style of war that took place in and around Kandahar in the 1980s. The Durrani Pushtuns who inhabited the south and Kandahar received far less aid through the Central Intelligence Agency (of the United States) and Western aid pipeline which armed, financed and provided logistics such as medical facilities to the mujahideen, as compared to the Ghilzai Pushtuns in the east of the country and around Kabul.

This was so, he explains, because the aid was distributed by Pakistan's Inter-Services Intelligence, who tended to treat Kandahar as a backwater and the Durranis with suspicion. As a consequence, the nearest medical facilities for a wounded Kandahari mujahideen was a bone-shaking two-day camel ride to Quetta across the border in Pakistan. "Even today (in 2000), first-aid amongst the Taleban is rare, doctors are all too few and surgeons on the front line non-existent. Virtually, the only medical practitioners in the country are the hospitals of the International Committee of the Red Cross (ICRC)," he adds.

Speaking about how the resistance against the Soviet invasion began, he writes that it was initially based around Kandahar on the tribal network of the Durranis. In Kandahar, the struggle against the Soviets "was a tribal jihad led by clan chiefs and ulema (senior religious scholars) rather than an ideological jihad led by Islamicists". In Peshawar, there were seven mujahideen parties which were recognised by Pakistan and which received a share of aid from the CIA pipeline. Significantly, none of the seven parties was led by Durrani Pushtuns. In Kandahar, all the seven parties had a following, but the most popular parties in the south were those based on tribal ties such as Harakat-i-Inquilab Islami (Movement of the

Islamic Revolution) led by Maulvi Mohammed Nabi Mohammedi and another Hizb-i-Islami (Party of Islam) led by Maulvi Mohammed Younis Khalis. Before the war, both leaders were well-known in the Pushtun belt and ran their own madrassas. Rashid's account tallies with that of the official Taleban history as far as the beginning of the resistance in the south was concerned.

The contradictions within the Pushtun mujahideen leadership were to weaken the Pushtuns as the war progressed, and the seeds of the future rise of religious fundamentalism were sown during the resistance with the Islamicists, who had even lacked a base in Afghan society, building themselves up into a "tremendous clout" with money and arms from the CIA pipeline and with support from Pakistan. "The traditionalists and the Islamicists fought each other mercilessly so that by 1994, the traditional leadership in Kandahar had virtually been eliminated, leaving the field free for the new wave of even more extreme Islamicists – Taleban."

For those mujahideen, who had fought the Najibullah regime and had then gone home or continued their studies at madrassas in Quetta and Kandahar, the situation in Kandahar, with warlords fighting each other incessantly, was particularly galling. Rashid quotes Governor of Kandahar Mullah Mohammed Hassan Rehmani reminiscing, "We all knew each other – Mullahs Omar, Ghaus, Mohammed Rabbani and myself – because we were all originally from Oruzgan province and had fought together. I moved back and forth from Quetta and attended madrassas there, but whenever we got together we would discuss the terrible plight of our people living under these bandits. We were people of the same opinions and we got on with each other very well, so it was easy to come to a decision to do something."

Other mujahideen groups in the south were also engaged at the same time in discussing the situation and trying to find a way out. Rashid quotes Minister of Public Health in the Taleban government Mullah Mohammed Abbas saying, "Many people were searching for a solution. I was from Kalat in Zabul province (85 miles north of Kandahar) and had joined a madrassa, but the situation was so bad that we were distracted from our studies and, with a group of friends, we spent all our time discussing what we should do and what needed to be done. The old mujahideen leadership had utterly failed to come up with a solution and things were getting worse. So we came to Kandahar to talk with Mullah Omar and joined him."

According to Rashid, the Taleban were born out of these meetings and discussions among people who were deeply concerned over the situation in the country. "All those who gathered around Omar were the children of the jihad but deeply disillusioned with the factionalism and criminal activities of the once idealised mujahideen leadership," he says. "Many of them had been born in Pakistani refugee camps, educated in Pakistani madrassas and had learned their fighting skills from mujahideen parties based in Pakistan. As such, the younger Taleban barely knew their own country or history, but from their madrassas they learnt about the ideal Islamic society created by the Prophet Mohammed 1,400 years ago and this is what they wanted to emulate."

Mullah Mohammed Omar (born around 1959 in Nodeh village near Kandahar city), the most secretive leader "in the world today", never photographed and never interviewed by Western diplomats (the first foreign diplomat he met was the United Nations special representative for Afghanistan Lakhdar Brahimi in 1998 in order to avoid a possible attack by Iran) and journalists, ran the Taleban government in a unique manner. Though the seat of the government was in Kabul, he always remained in Kandahar, visiting the capital for brief periods only twice. But the reins of the government remained firmly in his hands, though towards the end, divisive forces within the initially monolithic Taleban were growing powerful, leading to speculations that Mullah Omar and his inner circle could be toppled one day.

One of the few authentic portraits of the man, who in the years to come became one of the most feared and wanted men in the world, is available in the interview he gave to Pakistani journalist Rahimullah Yusufzai, which appeared in *The News on Sunday*.[4] At the time of the interview, Yusufzai writes, Mullah Omar was dressed in the Afghan salwar-kameez and jacket. Draped in chaddar, he wore a black turban, a Taleban trademark, making him look tall and imposing. He had a flowing beard, again a Taleban essential, and talked in measured tones. He displayed a peculiar sense of humour, which helped make the conversation pleasant, and the Taleban in the room often laughed. He reclined on a bed, instead of sitting cross-legged on the carpeted floor.

Yusufzai reports that while the interview progressed, Taleban military commanders and officials waited in the darkened room waiting to speak to him. One of his aides whispered into his ears from time to time and at least twice took a key from him to open a box stuffed with Afghan currency notes, which he passed on to someone in the room. It was this chest which was probably the famed treasury of the Taleban government which always remained by the side of the exalted Amir-ul Mumineen. Mullah Omar himself never wrote letters or notes; while he talked, his secretaries would be taking notes of his instructions, which would then be passed on to the commanders and officials concerned. Compliance of his instructions was always taken for granted.

Rashid describes the man as tall and well-built with a long, black beard and a black turban, with a dry sense of humour and a sarcastic wit. An extremely shy person when outsiders were present, especially foreigners, and a poor public speaker without any charismatic appeal, he was, nevertheless, always accessible to the Taleban. At the beginning of the Taleban movement, he used to pray every Friday at the main mosque in Kandahar and mingle with the people afterwards, but he grew increasingly reclusive and seldom ventured out of the administrative mansion where he lived. Even his visits to his native village grew infrequent, and when he went there, he was always accompanied by a convoy of imported vehicles with darkened windows. The secretiveness of his life apparently accompanied him everywhere.[5]

All available accounts of the Taleban movement agree that its beginning was marked by an incident in the spring of 1994 when his neighbours in Singesar village in Mewand district of Kandahar province (where Mullah Omar had functioned as the village mullah and ran a small madrassa before he joined the jihad) approached him for help to rescue two teenage girls, taken hostage by a Kandahar commander. He was told that the heads of the girls had been shaved and that they had been taken to a military camp where they had been repeatedly raped. According to one account, the girls were members of a family that was travelling on 20 September 1994, from Kandahar to Herat, had been overtaken on the way and looted, the male members molested and the girls abducted and taken to the camp.

Upon hearing of the plight of the girls, Mullah Omar collected about thirty Taleban with sixteen rifles between them, attacked the military base, freed the girls and hanged the commander from the barrel of a handy tank and, in the process, captured an unspecified quantity of arms and ammunition. Speaking to Suzanne Goldenberg of *The Guardian,* four years after the incident, Mullah Omar said, "We were fighting against Muslims who had gone wrong. How could we remain quiet when we could see crimes being committed against women and the poor?"⁶

After some time, the Taleban were again required to perform a similar act of rescue and retribution. Two commanders had fallen out with each other over the possession of a boy both wanted to sodomise, and in the process fighting had started in which civilians had been killed. As Mullah Omar and his talibs duly rescued the boy, the helpless people began to approach them with more and more appeals to help out in local disputes. In return, the Taleban wanted nothing except a commitment to follow Mullah Omar in establishing a just Islamic system in the country. Popular following began to grow, facilitated by the rampant lawlessness all around.

Apparently encouraged by the growing popular response, Mullah Omar sent emissaries to test how the mujahideen commanders were feeling about the situation. They met with Ismael Khan in Herat and, most importantly, emissary Mullah Mohammed Rabbani called on President Burhanuddin Rabbani in Kabul in September 1994. Since the Taleban, who were all Pushtuns, were vehemently opposed to Gulbuddin Hekmatyar who had continued his fight with the Kabul government, President Rabbani agreed to support them with funds if they actively resisted Hekmatyar.

It was also around this time that Pakistan was finally feeling tired of Hekmatyar's failure to make advances on Kabul and to garner following amongst the Pushtuns. The Pushtuns had, in fact, come to hate him for his religious fanaticism. It was clearly time for Islamabad to replace Hekmatyar with some other Pushtun group. As the events unfolded, it would be the Taleban, who were in any case already close to Pakistan, who would be ultimately chosen as the heir to Hekmatyar.

For Pakistan, the necessity to replace Hekmatyar also coincided with the urgency of finding an alternate route to

Central Asia via the northern Afghanistan. So long, the efforts were channeled to find such a route from Peshawar to Kabul across the Hindu Kush mountains to Mazar-i-Sharif and then upwards to Tirmez and Tashkent in Uzbekistan. As Afghanistan's bloody civil war continued, there was little prospect of this route ever becoming viable for Pakistan. It was, therefore, imperative that an alternate route was quickly found. This turned out to be a route from Quetta to Kandahar, then onwards to Herat and thereafter onwards to the Turkmenistan capital, Ashkabad. The advantage of following this route was self-evident: no murderous Afghan factions were fighting along this route, though dozens of rapacious local commanders were available to demand bribes to allow goods-laden trucks to pass. The new route was strongly advocated by the Pakistani transport and smuggling mafia, who had suffered enormously because of the internecine fighting in Afghanistan, the JUI and Pushtun military and political officials.

Rashid records that Pakistani surveyors and ISI officials arrived in Herat in September 1994, travelling from Chaman on the Pakistan side, to survey the viability of the route. The then Interior Minister of Pakistan, Pushtun-born Naseerullah Babar also visited Chaman at the time. Negotiations with the southern warlords and commanders began, as also with Ismael Khan in Herat to allow Pakistani transporters to ply through Kandahar, Herat and Ashkabad.[7]

In a display of deliberate snubbing of the Rabbani government and to score the point that the government's existence need not be taken notice of any more, Pakistani Minister Babar escorted a group of six ambassadors (from the United States, UK, Spain, Italy, China and South Korea) on 20 October 1994, to Kandahar and Herat without bothering to inform Kabul. The Pakistani team included officials from the departments of the Railways, Highways, Telephone and

Electricity. The Minister told the ambassadors that Pakistan wished to raise US $300 million from international lending agencies to rebuild the highway from Quetta to Herat. This was followed by a meeting on 28 October 1994, between Prime Minister Bhutto and Ismael Khan and General Dostum in Ashkabad when the Pakistani prime minister urged the two Afghan leaders to open a southern route so that Pakistani transporters could ply between Pakistan and Central Asia after paying road toll taxes and without the hassle of interference by mujahideen groups.

Both these significant events took place in the immediate backdrop of a major event heralding the advent of the Taleban in a telling manner. On 12 October 1994, approximately 200 Taleban collected from madrassas in Kandahar and Pakistan gathered at Spin Baldak, a small Afghan border post on the Afghanistan-Pakistan border opposite Chaman. Spin Baldak was frequented by the transport mafia for trucking and refuelling halts and was held by the Hekmatyar forces. At Spin Baldak, Afghan trucks would pick up goods from Pakistani trucks which were contraband in Afghanistan and fuel smuggled in from Pakistan for the various armies run by the Afghan warlords. The Taleban had now arrived at the post to wrest its control from Hekmatyar because the Pakistani transport mafia had donated several hundred thousand Pakistani rupees to Mullah Omar and had promised a monthly stipend if the Taleban could clear the roads of the impediments and guarantee the security for the goods traffic.

The battle that followed was brief but intense; after a while, Hekmatyar's men fled. Pakistan now stepped in, allowing the Taleban to capture a large arms dump outside Spin Baldak hitherto guarded by the Hekmatyar forces. The dump yielded for the Taleban nearly 18,000 kalashnikovs, dozens of artillery pieces, large quantities of ammunition and a large number of vehicles. The battle of Spin Baldak signified the arrival of the Taleban as a formidable force to reckon with with the full and open backing of Pakistan.

The battle for the opening of a safe route through Afghanistan for Pakistani transporters to travel to Central Asia was now nearing its climax. On 29 October 1994, under Minister Babar's supervision, a 30-truck Pakistani convoy carrying medicine left Quetta for Ashkabad with eighty former Pakistan army drivers, carrying Pakistan's consul-general in Herat, Colonel Imam, the most prominent field officer of the ISI, and Mullahs Borjan and Turabi of the Taleban. The convoy was held up by Afghan commanders twelve miles outside Kandahar city, who demanded money, part of the consignment and a guarantee that Pakistan stop supporting the Taleban.

As the negotiations began between the commanders and Col. Imam, the Pakistan government imposed an embargo on any news about the hijacked convoy and asked the Taleban to rescue it. Rashid quotes a Pakistani official explaining that the government had earlier considered various options to free the convoy, like despatching Pakistan army commandos, before deciding on the Taleban. The Taleban arrived at the location on 3 November 1994, and the commanders fled fearing that the Pakistan army had moved in. One of the commmanders, Mansur Achakzai, who had been controlling the Kandahar airport, was chased, caught and killed and his body left dangling from the barrel of a tank for public display.

Within hours, the Taleban descended upon Kandahar city and, after two days of sporadic fighting, captured it. The easy capture was facilitated in a large measure by the lack of resistance by the most prominent commander, Mullah Naquib who had 2,500 men under his command. It was later said that the ISI had already bribed the man. In any case, the Taleban gained an enormous armoury in Kandahar, dozens of tanks, armoured cars, military vehicles, weapons, six Mig-21 fighters and six transport helicopters at the Kandahar airport, all left behind by the Soviet army.

Rashid writes, "In just a couple of weeks, this unknown force (the Taleban) had captured the second largest city in Afghanistan with the loss of just a dozen men. In Islamabad, no foreign diplomat or analyst doubted that they had received considerable support from Pakistan. The fall of Kandahar was celebrated by the Pakistan government and the JUI. Babar took credit for the Taleban's success, telling journalists privately that the Taleban were 'our boys'. Yet, the Taleban demonstrated their independence from Pakistan, indicating that they were nobody's puppet. On 16 November1994, Mullah Ghaus said that Pakistan should not bypass the Taleban in sending convoys in the future and should not cut deals with individual warlords. He also said (that) the Taleban would not allow goods bound for Afghanistan to be carried by Pakistani trucks – a key demand of the transport mafia."[8]

The road from Pakistan to Central Asia was finally opening up for the transport mafia. The Taleban had removed the chains from the roads, set up a one-toll system for trucks entering Afghanistan at Spin Baldak and guarded the highway. The first Pakistani convoy consisting of fifty trucks carrying raw cotton fromTurkmenistan arrived in Quetta in December 1994, after paying the toll of 200,000 Pakistani rupees (equivalent to US $5,000) to the Taleban. At the same time, thousands of young Afghans, studying at madrassas in Baluchistan and the North West Frontier Province of Pakistan, rushed into Kandahar to join the Taleban. "They were soon followed by Pakistani volunteers from JUI madrassas, who were inspired by the new Islamic movement inAfghanistan," writes Rashid. "By December 1994, some 12,000 Afghan and Pakistani students had joined the Taleban in Kandahar."[9]

In an interesting departure from the familiar history of the Taleban as recorded by Rashid and others, Yossef Bodansky, director of House Task Force on Terrorism and Unconventional Warfare of the US Congress, says, "...the Taleban resulted from the calculated organisation and activation of Islamist Pushtun forces sponsored jointly by Teheran and Islamabad. The populist myth is correct in that the hard core of the Taleban were Pushtun religious students and young Islamist clergy. Many of them were veterans of the war in Afghanistan, and all were graduates of training camps and higher schools in Iran and Pakistan. Nationalist and Islamist, they were eager to rebel against the corrupt ISI-installed warlords and crime bosses. Until they began receiving support from the ISI, however, they were unable to do anything. Former Pakistani Interior Minister Naseerullah Babar acknowledged in fall 1998 that the Taleban were organised under his guidance in 1994. "(The) Taleban were also given military training when I was interior minister in 1994," he said. "Once empowered, (the Taleban) initially established themselves in the Kandahar area, where the destruction of the long-established tribal royalist leadership left a void to be filled. The Taleban's first success – the seizure of Kandahar in November 1994, was considered the beginning of their campaign."[10]

Both Teheran and Islamabad now accepted the reality of the collapse of the Afghan state, writes Bodansky. "In late fall 1994, both governments concluded that it was imperative for their respective intelligence services to consolidate a certain degree of control over the regional ethno-political dynamics to preserve the power position of their governments. Southern Afghanistan would be the first stage. After the Taleban's initial success in stabilising Kandahar in mid-November (1994) and relying on the unquestionable popular support they enjoyed, Islamabad was ready to capitalise on the Taleban to expand

Pakistan's hold over the Pushtun-populated parts of Afghanistan. The surge into Afghanistan, including the creation and empowerment of the Taleban, has been a sacred mission supported by all governments in Islamabad – including Bhutto's – and implemented by the ISI."

Bodansky reports that by mid-December (1994) between 3,000 and 4,000 religious students had moved from madrassas in western Pakistan across the border to join the Taleban, as recorded earlier by Rashid. "By early January 1995, the movement had become a flood," he says. "Most Taleban came from Sunni madrassas in Pakistani Baluchistan, particularly from the Afghan refugee camps established in the mid-1980s by the ISI to alter the demographic character of Baluchistan. Baluchistan is a fiercely independent province of Pakistan whose unique population, the Baluchi tribes, have repeatedly rebelled against the central government. By February 1995, the Taleban forces were some 25,000 strong, predominantly Pushtuns but including over a thousand Tajiks and Uzbeks. These troops were recruited by Pakistan to add military skills and expertise to the Taleban 'army'."

Noting that by mid-1995 the Taleban had virtually secured control for Pakistan of the sole non-Iranian route between the Indian Ocean and Central Asia, he says, "Afghanistan was then ready to support a serious expansion and improvement of the support system for terrorists – the establishment of the Imarat, run by (the Saudi promoter of international terrorism) Osama bin Laden. This role defined bin Laden as a prominent leader in the world of conservative-traditionalist Islam."

As the world perceived that Pakistan was in fact gaining control over southern Afghanistan through the medium of the Taleban and that the Rabbani government was in no position to resist, pressure was mounted on Islamabad for an explanation. Prime Minister Benazir Bhutto issued the first formal denial on 17 February 1995, while visiting Manila. "We have no favourites in Afghanistan and we do not interfere in Afghanistan," she said. "I cannot fight Mr. Rabbani's war for him. If Afghans want to cross the border, I do not stop them. I can stop them from re-entering but most of them have families here (in Pakistan)."[11]

While by early 1995 the Taleban were at the gates of Kabul, it would be September 1996, before they would complete their victory over the Rabbani government. Meanwhile, the true nature of the Taleban was suddenly in awesome display, stunning first the Afghans and then, the external world as the word spread slowly of the developments in the devastated country. The strictest imaginable interpretation of the Sharia was in force in the areas under the control of the Taleban; education for girls and employment for women were banned, TV sets were smashed wherever they were noticed, putting the fear of God in anyone possessing a TV set, almost all sports were prohibited, and all males were ordered to grow flowing beards. Overnight, the darkness of medieval barbarity had suddenly descended upon the twelve provinces controlled by the Taleban. It would, however, be many more months before the Taleban would be able to wrest the control of Herat, the all-important station on the way to Central Asia, in the quest to resume the drug, arms and smuggled goods traffic between Pakistan and Central Asia.

Following the capture of Kandahar, the Taleban had run over at a frightening pace in just three months as many as twelve of Afghanistan's thirty-one provinces and stood at the outskirts of Kabul in the north and of Herat in the west. Thousands of Afghan and Pakistani students of madrassas continued to stream across the border and join the ranks of the student army. But, while the euphoria remained and the whole country was looking astonished at the swift victories that came their way, the student army seemed to have suddenly met with the first resistance by professional military leadership and apparently lacked an answer.

The resistance by Commander Ahmad Shah Massoud in Kabul and by General Ismael Khan in Herat exposed the reasons for the Taleban's victories; in many instances, the local commanders just gave up fighting as they were unnerved by the popular upsurge in favour of the Taleban; in others, they were bribed; and it was in some cases that Taleban actually had to fight their way into a town. The kind of chicanery that the Taleban employed in winning battles was best illustrated in the case of Helmand province. This province was of particular importance for the Taleban because of its lucrative poppy fields. While the forces of Ghaffar Akhunzadeh controlling the province offered fierce opposition, the Taleban bribed smaller drug warlords to rise in revolt against Akhunzadeh and managed to capture the province in January 1995. It was also the time when Pakistan had succeeded in forging an alliance between Gulbuddin Hekmatyar, who had continued to receive the largest quantum of Pakistani aid, and General Dostum and the Hazaras of central Afghanistan who were controlling a part of Kabul.

Hekmatyar was growing unhappy over the Taleban's rapid progress towards Kabul and his worst fears were confirmed when the latter captured Wardak, 35 miles south of the capital, on 2 February 1995, bringing Hekmatyar's bases around Kabul under threat.

On 14 February 1995, the student militia captured Charasyab, where Hekmatyar's headquarters were located, forcing his forces to flee towards Jalalabad. Massoud withdrew his forces into Kabul and prepared to confront the Taleban.

Fearing another impending onslaught on the already severely battered capital, the United Nations sought to move in and facilitate a cease-fire and peace talks. The UN special representative for Afghanistan Mehmoud Mestiri attempted to seize the moment by appealing for a cease-fire but the two deadly enemies, the forces of Massoud and Taleban, were then ready to fight.

Massoud, however, uneasy over the role that the Hazaras holding the southern suburbs of Kabul could play in the event of a battle with the Taleban, sought to buy time by holding negotiations with the enemy and conferred twice with Taleban commanders at Charasyab. The talks, however, failed as the Taleban remained inflexible in their demand that President Rabbani step down and that Massoud surrender. Massoud rejected both demands.

The Taleban then met with the UN special representative Mestiri and offered to join peace talks provided their units formed a "neutral force" to guard Kabul, only "good Muslims" were made members of an interim administration to run the country, which was made genuinely representative of the entire country. Both the UN and the Rabbani government turned down the Taleban conditions as the latter insisted that they should dominate the interim government.

Massoud, the great tactician that he was, first planned to neutralise the inimical Hazaras by attacking the southern suburbs. As the Hazara civilians fled the city and the suburbs were reduced to rubble, the Hazaras, who were Shias, sought a deal with the Taleban, who were Sunnis of the most rigid kind ever seen. But, in the thick of the battle, something unexpected happened that turned the tide in favour of Massoud. The Hazara leader Abdul Ali Mazarai, who was in Taleban custody, was killed, leading the Hazaras to allege that he had been done to death by the Taleban by being pushed out of a helicopter as he tried to seize a gun. The Hazaras said that the Taleban were taking him as a prisoner to Kandahar. This marked the rift between the two sides and the Hazaras would never again forgive the Taleban for their leader's death. Massoud's task was made lighter by this particular development. He seized the moment and mounted a massive attack on the Taleban on 11 March 1995. Hundreds of Taleban fighters were killed in the battle, forcing the militia to leave Kabul. This was the first major battle lost by the Taleban.

It was around February-March 1995 that the Taleban renewed their bid to get at Herat. They captured Nimrooz and Farah, both provinces controlled till then by Ismael Khan and advanced on Shindand, where the former Soviet airbase was situated, and which lay south of Herat city. As Ismael Khan's position became threatened, Massoud swung into action and sent his planes to bombard the Taleban front lines and airlifted his men to reinforce the defence of Shindand and Herat. As the Taleban casualty mounted, they retreated by the end of March 1995, suffering a staggering loss of 3,000 fighters and losing all the territories they had gained during the march to Herat. The student army had thus lost on both the north and west fronts and their control over territory was reduced to eight, instead of the twelve provinces they were controlling in the wake of the capture of Kandahar. The Rabbani government, on the other hand, expanded its control to six provinces around Kabul and the north and Ismael Khan regained his control of three provinces. For the moment, therefore, the transport mafia's dream of opening up the Quetta-Kandahar-Herat-Ashkabad route was thwarted.

The Taleban, however, did not give up their plan to capture Herat and soon, they had their opportunity. Unfortunately for Ismael Khan, his popularity and prestige had dwindled to such an extent that around the time the Taleban were aiming at Herat, official corruption and high-handedness towards civilians had become rampant in the city and, as Rashid records, customs officials were charging every passing truck the exorbitant sum of 10,000 Pakistani rupees or US $300, "a sure way to make an enemy of the transport mafia". Rashid quotes Mullah Wakil Ahmad telling him, "Ismael is weak, his soldiers will not fight because they have not been paid and he is widely discredited amongst his people because of the corruption in his administration. He stands alone and has to be propped up by Massoud."[12]

On the top of it, Ismael Khan erred militarily by deciding to attack the Taleban on the apparently mistaken notion that following their consecutive defeats, the Taleban had become demoralised. Initially, his offensive proved to be successful, as his large mobile force first captured Dilaram on 23 August 1995, and then parts of Helmand and thus presented a threat to the defence of Kandahar.

But the successes also meant that Ismael Khan's army was overstretched in a hostile territory. Doubly unfortunately for him, the Taleban army had been revitalised with generous Pakistani and Saudi Arabian supplies of arms, ammunition and vehicles, and the force had a new command structure built up with the assistance of ISI advisers. The ISI had also brokered a deal between the Taleban and General Dostum, following which the latter's technicians repaired the Mig fighters that had fallen into the student army's hands when they captured the Kandahar airport a year ago and thus the Taleban came to possess their first air power. To add to Ismael Khan's woes, Dostum sent his planes to bombard Herat.

In less than a week after Ismael Khan had advanced towards Kandahar, the Taleban forces pushed him back all the way to Shindand and on 3 September 1995, the base fell as Ismael Khan abandoned it without putting up a fight. On 5 September 1995, Ismael Khan abandoned Herat as well and crossed over to Iran with a part of his force. The Taleban thus came to control the entire western Afghanistan.

On 6 September 1995, a pro-government mob raided the Pakistani embassy and wounded the ambassador while government soldiers stood by as onlookers and President Rabbani publicly accused Islamabad of trying to dislodge him through the Taleban.

Under the Taleban rule, Herat soon became a wasteland, with the local population, highly sophisticated and cultured, totally kept out of the administration. Women in Herat suffered much more than elsewhere because they had traditionally lived a more liberal and productive life. While hundreds of the local people were arrested, all schools were closed down and the Sharia came to be implemented in a more ruthless manner than experienced in Kandahar.

Cooley writes, "People of Herat speak Persian. They are well-educated, liberal and traders in outlook. Many women were well-educated and followed fairly liberal employment practices and dress codes. The Herat people regarded the invaders as Pushtun peasants. They were stunned and shocked when a young man, said to have shot two members of the Taleban, was hanged from a crane – a practice the Taleban later adopted in other parts of Afghanistan – in the presence of the assembled public, while loudspeakers blared Koranic slogans."[13]

It would be another year before the Taleban would be able to capture Kabul; this interregnum was marked by some of the most brutal fightings and destruction of the capital as the student army kept on hammering the city with rockets. In a macabre replay of Gulbuddin Hekmatyar's rocketing of Kabul for two years during 1993-95, the Taleban achieved the dubious distinction of firing as many as 866 rockets in just one month, April 1996, killing 180 civilians, injuring another 550 and adding fresh signatures of destruction to the already badly mauled city. The rocket attacks were accompanied by repeated attacks against Massoud's troops in the south and west of the city.

Once again, the sheer brilliance of Massoud's military leadership came to the fore. Despite the overwhelming superiority of the Taleban's fire power and manpower, the "Lion of Panjsher" valley managed to fend the attackers off time and again, breaking up their formations. But his limited manpower prevented him from stretching out and driving the Taleban away and thus creating a safe buffer zone to protect Kabul.

Time was also running out for him. The Taleban, determined as ever before to defeat their most formidable enemy, were reinforced with liberal doses of logistical supplies by Pakistan and Saudi Arabia in a final bid to defeat Massoud. However, in a surprise tactical move, the Taleban moved upon the eastern city of Jalalabad on 25 August 1996. While they moved from the south, Islamabad played its role of the good Samaritan by opening up the frontier and allowing hundreds of madrassa students to swell the ranks of the attackers. The head of the Jalalabad Shura, Haji Abdul Qadeer (later assassinated on 5 July 2002, when he was the Vice-President of the Islamic Transitional Government of Afghanistan) was said to have been bribed to the tune of US $10 million, fled to Pakistan on 10 September 1996, and the very next day the city fell as the acting governor Mehmoud was killed and a brief firefight followed.

In their typical swift mobility, the Taleban then captured Nangarhar, Laghman and Kunar provinces in a matter of few days and arrived on 24 September 1996, at Sarobi, 45 miles away from the capital and the gateway to the seat of government. Sarobi itself offered little resistance as government troops were pushed back to Kabul in the face of the fast moving Taleban forces. The student army kept on marching right into Kabul, and others joined in from the south, and with the Bagram airport falling into the hands of the attackers, the capital lay open to the invading army.

Two evenings later, on 26 September 1996, the Taleban fighters descended on Kabul, with Massoud troops retreating a few hours before. Speaking about the retreat four years later, Massoud justified the withdrawal thus, "...I am still convinced (that) it was a clever decision. The arrival of the Taleban in Kabul's outskirts was totally unexpected; a last-minute defence would have meant to tear apart the city and to exact an unbearable toll of victims among civilians."[14] What he did not mention was that the capital had been surrounded on all the four sides and that defence was militarily impossible without, as he noted rightly, exacting a terrible human cost, which he could not afford, for he still hoped that he would be back one day when the Taleban would be gone.

What followed immediately after the fall of Kabul has been recounted many times over, for the sheer barbarity that was practised by the victorious army cannot be easily matched. At around 1 a.m. on 27 September 1996, a five-men team, reported to have been led by Governor of Herat and commander of the forces deployed to capture Kabul, Mullah Abdul Razaq, entered the United Nations compound, walked straight into the room where former President Najibullah (1986-92) had been staying since his deposition, beat Najibullah and his brother Shahpur Ahmadzai senseless, threw them into a pick-up van and drove to the Presidential Palace. The former President was castrated in the palace, then he was tied to a jeep and dragged around the palace for several rounds and finally shot dead. His brother was also tortured and throttled to death. Then the two bodies were hung on a concrete traffic control post outside the palace for public display. When residents of Kabul came out in the morning, they found unlit cigarettes stuck into the fingers of the two men and afghani currency notes bulging out of their pockets, the Taleban's unique way of telling the world that the two men were corrupt and debauches. The manner of the execution of Najibullah and his brother also told the world that the Taleban had thrust upon it a deliberate, calculated act of cruelty and defiance.

One question that has always bothered the international community is the comparative ease with which Najibullah was captured while in UN protective custody. There was little doubt at the time that the United Nations had failed miserably in honouring its own protective custody rules. But the gruesome death was also a combination of factors, one important point being the role that the Pakistan government played.

With his family finding safe shelter in New Delhi, the former President, who was completely unemployed, had little choice to pass time and was inordinately fond of Hindi movies, was being supplied with Hindi movie videos every day by the Indian embassy. Thus, the latter was in touch with him every day. Sources in the embassy told this author during one of his visits to Kabul that Najibullah had decided to stay put in the UN compound principally because he believed that being a Pushtun himself, the Taleban would never stoop so low as to harm him.

But, according to the sources, something happened a few hours before Kabul fell on 26 September 1996 that actually sealed his fate. He received a communication from Islamabad assuring him of protection after the Taleban would take the city over. He had nothing to fear, the ISI-sponsored message conveyed the assurance to him, and he believed in its truthfulness. His violent death was thus engineered by this act of treachery. And in any case, as his murder showed clearly, the Taleban had planned his execution in minute details well before they burst upon the capital.[15]

Rashid notes that on 24 September 1996, when Sarobi fell, Najibullah approached the United Nations office in Islamabad asking UN mediator Norbet Holl to arrange the evacuation of his brother, personal secretary and bodyguard and himself. There was, however, no UN official in Kabul to take the charge of Najibullah and the request for evacuation thus fell on deaf ears. Massoud, attempting a last minute rescue act on the afternoon of 26 September 1996, sent one of his senior generals to ask Najibullah to get out of Kabul with the retreating government forces, promising him safe passage to the north, but Najibullah refused, probably because even at that stage he preferred to rely more on the Pushtun Taleban than on the Tajik Massoud.

While the Taleban's capture of Kabul and the retreat of the Burhanuddin Rabbani government to the north marked the beginning of the rabid fundamentalist group's regime in Afghanistan, Bodansky examines a very vital aspect of this development in the context of the international terrorism that had already spread around the world and in which Pakistan and the civil war-ridden Afghanistan had been playing a significant role. He shows that the fall of Kabul served to strengthen the international terrorist network and the international terrorism schedule that Osama bin Laden and his group were planning at the time. "The emergence of bin Laden's terrorist empire in Afghanistan was made possible by two key developments," he notes. "His relocation to Afghanistan and the establishment of the Taleban's rule over that country."[16]

According to Bodansky, the Islamic terrorist infrastructure in Afghanistan had been consolidated with the assistance of Pakistani intelligence, the ISI. In spring 1995, the Armed Islamic Movement had started transferring some of its key training camps for Sunnis to Afghanistan. The most important of these were the training camps for martyrdom operations used for recruits from numerous Arab, Islamic and even European countries. The key training camps for sophisticated and spectacular terrorist activities – including martyrdom operations – using sophisticated explosives such as C-4 and

SEMTEX were in Paktia and Chahar-Asiab in eastern Afghanistan and run by Gulbuddin Hekmatyar's Hizb-i-Islami.

The importance of these assets, Bodansky says, was clearly shown by Pakistan's efforts to save them as Afghanistan slid into a ruthless fratricidal civil war. By fall 1995, it had become increasingly difficult for Islamabad to conceal and deny the extent of the ISI's sponsorship of international and regional terrorism. A senior Arab official and a supporter of Pakistani premier Benazir Bhutto tried to reconcile her declared pro-Western inclination with the growing support provided by the ISI to the "Afghans" and other Islamist terrorists. Despite Bhutto's desire "to please the Americans" by joining the struggle against Islamist terrorism, the Arab official explained, "she was thwarted by domestic difficulties and by a political-military-economic trend opposed to surrendering the Arab 'Afghans'. This trend encompassed military intelligence, civilian political parties and the drug merchants' lobby. All of these groups were – and still are – anxious to protect these Arab fundamentalists, including those wanted for crimes in their own countries."

The strongest supporters of the Arab "Afghans" and of Islamabad's continued sponsorship of their operations was the Pakistani defence establishment. Islamabad, the senior Arab official explained, "uses groups of 'Afghans' in the war that is being waged against India in Kashmir. They are also used in the factionalist war in Afghanistan. Because of all this, the official Pakistani campaigns to expel Arab 'Afghans' lost their effectiveness." The Arab "Afghans" had always been able to remain in Pakistan, although they had to stay away from the centre of Islamabad.

In principle, Bodansky says, militant Islamists, including known terrorists, had little to worry about in Pakistan-Afghanistan: "Despite the fact that the Americans demanded that Benazir Bhutto take action to purge the security agencies, and she did, she was unable to carry out a serious counter-terrorism campaign and, at least, get rid of the 'Afghans' who were known to be extremists and who were wanted for crimes in their countries," he quotes the Arab official saying.

Predictably, during the Taleban offensive on Kabul, the Pakistani ISI took over these specialised training camps. The ISI moved many of the Arab "Afghans" – from Egypt, Algeria and Sudan – to special training centres it was running in Lahore, Pakistan. There the terrorists' skills and expertise were further upgraded after a few months of intensive training. The Arab "Afghans" were then regrouped and sent back to Afghanistan with the help of Qazi Hussain Ahmad, the leader of the Pakistani Islamic Group. Consequently, in spring 1996, a solid, well-organised base emerged for the "Afghans" and "Balkans" in Afghanistan. This infrastructure was ready for the arrival of Osama bin Laden and his assets.

It was then that Osama bin Laden arrived in Afghanistan, establishing his headquarters in an encampment in Nangarhar province with Maulvi Mohammed Younis Khalis, the head of Hizb-i-Islami during the jihad who had received bin Laden's assistance earlier. The Arabs had already set up three semi-autonomous Imarat (singular: Imarah, country, region or district headed by an emir in Kunar, Wakhan and Paktia provinces). The Arab "Afghans" and "Balkans" had training centres, hiding places, logistics coordination units and command and communication centres for their forces in Egypt, Saudi Arabia, Algeria, India, Tajikistan, Azerbaijan and some other Arab countries.

One gets a chilling glimpse of the extent of terrorist infrastructure that the Arabs had established from the following description by Bodansky, "Extremely important in the terrorist effort were the fortified villages used by the Arabs. These power centres included power generators, satellite telephone and television equipment, workshops for printing secret bulletins, and huge quantities of modern weapons, ranging from weapons supplied to the Afghan mujahideen during the 1980s to recently acquired, more modern systems delivered via Pakistan. Moreover, the Imarat in Afghanistan served as long-term rear-area bases for Islamist terrorists; they deployed from them to augment and run high-quality operations in the Middle East, India (not just Kashmir), and increasingly Western Europe."

"This vast, comprehensive terrorist infrastructure could not have been sustained without extensive support from the ISI," he says. "The patronage of Qazi Hussain Ahmad ensured active support for the Islamist terrorists from his followers throughout the Pakistani defence establishment. Ahmad Wali Massoud, the pre-Taleban Afghan government spokesman in Kabul, complained that these 'Arab Afghans are ensconced in fortified villages previously loyal to Hizb-i-Islami. They continue to maintain Pakistan's approval and support.' The 'Afghans' and 'Balkans' enjoy freedom of travel through Pakistan, and all their international movements as well as the flow of goods, services and international communications are conducted via Pakistan."

The point to note is that while the Arab "Afghans" had already set up the Imarat in Afghanistan, the capture of Kabul and the beginning of the Taleban government coinciding with the arrival of Osama bin Laden in the eventful latter half of 1996 reinforced the regime of international terrorism. Thus, it is important to consider the Taleban period in Afghanistan in the wider context of the growing pace of international terrorism engineered by Islamicist forces. And, above all, the intimate and crucial role that Pakistan played in the entire drama also marks that country out as a unique instance of a nation-state aligning itself with and actually encouraging the votaries of international terrorism as a tool of its foreign policy.

****

Endnotes

1. A Taleban publication, *A Reminding Glimpse of the Islamic Jihad*, 1978-92, posted on http://www.taleban.com
2. Magnum, Ralph H. and Naby, Eden, *Afghanistan: Mullah, Marx and Mujaheed*, Harper Collins Publications India, 1998, pp.179-191.
3. Rashid, Ahmed, *Taliban*... pp.17-30.
4. The interview appeared in the 10 March 1997 issue of the newspaper.
5. Rashid, Ahmed, *Taliban*... pp.24-30.
6. The account was published in *The Guardian* of 13 October 1998.
7. Rashid, Ahmed, *Taliban*... p.27.
8. ibid., p.29.
9. ibid.
10. Bodansky, Yossef, *Bin Laden: The Man Who Declared War on America*, Prima Publishing, California, pp.97-99.
11. Rashid, Ahmed, *Taliban*... p.29.
12. ibid., p.39.
13. Cooley, John K., *Unholy Wars*... p.145.
14. The interview of Commander Massoud by A. Raffaele Ciriello.
15. The author's conversations with senior Indian diplomats in September 2002, on condition of anonimity.
16. Bodansky, Yossef, *Bin laden*... pp.186-189.

3
The Dark Age Descends

The way to the Panjsher Valley from Kabul takes one past a vast wasteland, with thousands of houses mowed down, farmlands and orchards weeded out, and inactivated landmines lurking almost everywhere beneath the uneasy, dusty and bedraggled surface. This is the Shamali Plains, once one of the most beautiful parts of the country, a sea of greenery capable of soothing the most tired of eyes, and now, so chillingly devastated that the sight literally numbs the mind.

Rashid thus describes the transformation of the Shamali Plains. In mid-July (1997), Massoud broke the military stalemate north of Kabul by recapturing Charikar and the Bagram airbase, killing hundreds of Taleban fighters. By September (1997), Massoud's forces were once again positioned a mere twenty miles north of Kabul. Both sides traded artillery and rocket bombardments, forcing nearly 180,000 civilians to flee the "lush" Shamali Valley which was then the front line.

As the Taleban retreated from the valley, they poisoned water wells and blew up small irrigation channels and dams in a bid to ensure that the local Tajik population would not return in a hurry (and thus recreate a friendly buffer for Massoud). The war was now not just uprooting and killing civilians but destroying their very means of livelihood and turning Kabul's agricultural belt into a wasteland.

If the Shamali Plains stand as a macabre monument to the butchery of the Taleban, a more celebrated monument lies further north-west, the Bamiyan caves. On 26 February 2001, Mullah Mohammed Omar issued an edict declaring that statues, including the Bamiyan Buddhas, were insulting to Islam. "Because God is one and these statues are there to be worshipped, and that is wrong, they should be destroyed so that they are not worshipped now or in the future." The edict was published by the Taleban-run Bakhtar News Agency.

Before they were demolished, the two giant Buddhas had stood in their caves in the beautiful Bamiyan Valley for around 1,500 years. Jet van Krieken of SPACH (Society for the Preservation of Afghanistan's Cultural Heritage), the Netherlands, who was earlier involved in the preservation and restoration of the extant and smuggled out Afghan artifacts, describes the Buddhas in the perspective of the Gandhara art, "In this Buddhist richness of inspiration, two masterpieces were produced which stand out head and shoulders above the others, the Buddhas of Bamiyan. These two giant Buddhas (53 m and 38 m tall respectively) stand in the beautiful Bamiyan Valley, situated 230 km north-west of Kabul at an altitude of 2,500 m. The caravans on the Silk Route invariably made a stop in this valley. It was one of the major Buddhist centres from the second century up to the time that Islam entered the valley in the ninth century."[1]

The two statues were hewn out of the rock (estimates of dates vary, but most probably, around the fourth and fifth centuries AD). They were covered with a mud and straw mixture to model the expression of the face, the hands and the folds of the robes. This was then plastered and, finally, the statues were painted: the smaller Buddha was painted blue and the larger one red, and their faces and hands were painted gold. "They must have been quite impressive for monks travelling through the harsh surrounding landscape, who finally reached the beautiful valley with the peaceful Buddhas making the gesture of reassurance," Krieken remarks.

The statues, however, apparently attracted vandals throughout the centuries, obviously iconoclasts. The damages inflicted on the statues were clearly dictated by a desire to deface them in order to rob them of their identity. The iconoclasts left their mark on the frescoes painted around the Buddhas and in the cells meant for monks; all the faces in the frescoes were carefully obliterated.

Krieken reports that one of the factions in the civil war had used the feet of the larger Buddha as an ammunition dump in the mid-1990's but it was in 1997 that a Taleban commander, who was trying to take the Bamiyan Valley from the Northern Alliance (United Front), warned that he would blow the statues up the moment he would capture the valley. His threat raised immediate protests around the world, and the Taleban were forced to declare that far from destroying the Buddhas, it would be their endeavour to protect the Afghan cultural heritage. Following the intervention of the SPACH, a general Office for the Preservation of Historical Sites in Hazarajat (which included the valley) was set up.

However, as the valley came to be in the possession of the Taleban in the autumn of 1998, the Buddhas were in constant danger and were actually being damaged. Krieken says that it was around this time that the head and part of the shoulders of the smaller Buddha (representing Buddha Sakyamuni, according to W. L. Rathje, Senior Editor, *Discover Archaeology*; B. Rowland describes the statue as "really a gigantic magnificence of a Gandhara image", *The Evolution of the Buddha Image*, The Asia Society, 1963) were blown off, partly by a rocket, partly by explosives. Even worse, the Taleban commander who had earlier threatened to damage the statues succeeded in drilling holes in the head of the larger Buddha (representing Vairocana the "Light Shining throughout the Universe Buddha", according to Rathje; "an enlargement of an Indian Buddha statue of the Gupta period", Rowland) with the intention of inserting dynamite into the holes. The statue would probably have been dynamited there and then, but the Taleban governor of the province intervened at the SPACH's urgings. Tyres were then burnt just above the mouth of the larger Buddha "so his entire face is now blackened", Krieken writes in 2000. The commander was since arrested, and Krieken commented (in 2000), "It seems, nevertheless, a miracle that these incredible Buddhas have more or less survived in a country in which they have become strangers who were not able to flee."

Destroying the Buddhas, however, proved to be a truly gigantic task for the Taleban. After the first batch of media correspondents were taken to the Bamiyan Valley to see their handiwork, the Taleban revealed that it had taken them all of twenty days, beginning on 1 March 2001, to finish the statues off. "It took us twenty days to destroy the statues," Reuters quoted a Taleban official saying on 26 March 2001, at the site. "It was a hard job to finish them. We had to use explosive materials." While the larger Buddha was completely obliterated, only part of an elbow of the smaller Buddha was visible; the Reuters correspondent wondered if the partial elbow would be spared as the only reminder to future visitors of the Buddhas that had dominated the valley for so many centuries. The Taleban also took care to completely erase the remnants of the frescoes in the monks' cells.

Why did the Taleban destroy the two giant Buddhas in the face of worldwide protests, in which the entire Muslim world, including the Taleban's mentor Pakistan, joined? Rathje tries an answer.[2]

First, he says, it is important to remember that the "Bamiyan massacre" had little to do with religion. The Buddha was never a god. "During his lifetime of eighty years, Buddha Sakyamuni only allowed his image to be recorded as a reflection in rippling water." Buddha images did not appear for at least 400 years after his death and even then these were created only to remind Buddhists of their own innate "Buddha nature".

Then, the Buddhas were destroyed because Buddhism was traditionally an easy target for fundamentalist Muslims. (Richard Foltz writes in *Religions on the Silk Road*, "Although Islamic law offered protection to 'peoples of the Book', namely, Christians, Jews, and by some interpretations, Zoroastrians, the early Muslims were generally hostile towards Buddhists. They referred to Buddhists as 'idol-worshippers', which had unfortunate associations with the portrayal of the Prophet's Meccan enemies in the Koran.") So, even though the Buddha stood against idolatry, the Taleban had a tradition to uphold on the Silk Road.

Secondly, Bamiyan was a base for the Massoud forces, and destroying the Buddhas could be an effective way of humiliating the locals, who were after all culpable of sheltering the enemy. Thirdly, the Taleban government was incensed at the time with the international community which had not responded to their appeals for larger humanitarian aid in the wake of the protracted civil war, earthquakes and a severe drought but which was eager to spend millions of dollars to save the "un-Islamic" stone statues.

At the time, a hugely indignant world thought that the statues could perhaps be replicated at a later stage. After the collapse of the Taleban and the advent of the Interim Government in December 2001, international efforts were undertaken to review the position. At an international seminar held in Kabul in early 2002, under the auspices of the Unesco, archaeologists, museologists and historians came to the conclusion that the construction of replicas of the giant Buddhas would not be feasible. The idea of filling up the void in the cliff by placing replicas was, therefore, given up and instead, it was wisely decided to set up an international centre of Bamiyan studies in Kabul in order not only to keep alive the world's memory of the giant Buddhas but also to enrich research in allied subjects. The Unesco member-countries are expected to provide the requisite funds for the proposed centre. In early October 2002, however, a fresh initiative was launched to explore the scope for replicating the statues. Not many details about the project have since emerged in the public domain; the point to note, however, is the intense desire in the intellectual world to undo the horrible damage caused to the world heritage by the Taleban.

While the demolition of the statues began on 1 March 2001 and the world came to know of the devilish act by 2 March 2001, the Islamic State of Afghanistan (the official name of the government run by the United Front) came up on 3 March 2001, with the accusation that it was the Pakistan government which was behind the diabolical act.

The opposition government alleged that the Taleban's efforts to demolish the two statues was "a Pakistani engineered plot". "The Islamic State of Afghanistan vigorously condemns the issuance of this despicable decree by the Pakistani-Taleban and warns the international community of the irremediable aftermath of the decreed frenzy of the statues' destruction in Afghanistan by the Pakistani-Taleban," it said. "The Islamic State of Afghanistan earnestly calls upon the United Nations and the entire international community to pay serious heed to the urgency of taking preventive measures in dealing with the impending Taleban leader's destruction order on the statues sooner than later, through bold and effective pressure on both Pakistan and its Taleban mercenaries." The government's ambassador in New Delhi Masood Khalili told the author, "The move to destroy the Buddhas is a major step towards the growing international isolation of Afghanistan, which is actually the chief aim of Pakistan's Afghan policy. The more isolated the country becomes, the tighter Pakistan's grip will be on it. By implementing the Pakistani advice to ignore the plea of the international community to spare the statues, the Taleban are now more securely in Islamabad's hands."[3]

The Indian reaction was typical of the horror and disgust felt all over the world. The Indian Parliament condemned on 2 March 2001, the "barbaric and anti-civilised" destruction of the Buddhas and a Rajya Sabha (upper house) resolution sought United Nations intervention to ask the Taleban to desist from this "senseless, destructive act". "We hope," the resolution said, "the world community and especially the United Nations will take note of this and prevail upon the Taleban regime in Afghanistan to desist from this senseless, destructive act." The Indian government offered to bring the surviving Buddhist relics free of cost for preservation, an offer made by several other countries as well, particularly Greece and Italy.

The devastated Shamali Plains and the void in the Bamiyan cliff today remain as grim reminders of the Taleban regime. Fortunately, many of their misdeeds have now been replaced by the return of normal life in the country. It is, nevertheless, profitable to recount some of them in order to sense the extent of medieval barbarity that was practised during those fateful years.

The very first measures in the name of establishing a pure Islamic state that the Taleban took in the areas they captured were aimed at severely curtailing and, in most cases, abolishing completely individual freedom to live a normal life in pursuance of education, gainful employment and rearing of families. The Taleban intruded right into the very centre of the family life by dictating how male and female adults and male and female children would live. Thus, male adults were forced to grow flowing beards at the pain of fine but to a specific length crossing or falling short of which used to invite severe punishment; women of course were immediately banned from any activity outside their homes; girl students were debarred from attending school; women unaccompanied by male relatives were forbidden to leave home, whatever the urgency could be; and even though the measure paralysed the two vital sectors of health care and primary education, women doctors and nurses and teachers were banned from joining duty. And every Afghan, whether male or female, adult or child, was banned from indulging in any kind of entertainment, listening to and performing music, portrait painting, photography of human beings and playing games. Even children's toys, including dolls and kites, were banned. Pet parakeets and, of course, alcohol and cigarettes, were absolute taboo; by inserting unlit cigarettes into the fingers of the dead Najibullah and his brother, the Taleban had tried to depict their immorality. Towards the end of their rule, mainly at Pakistan's endeavour, a cricket team of Afghanistan was gathered and sent to Pakistan to play the game.

In what was possibly the last interview Commander Ahmad Shah Massoud gave before his assassination on 9 September 2001, AIM Television asked him on 13 August 2001, "Is the Taleban's approach to human rights and women's education rights coming from within or is this also being dictated by

Pakistan?" What Massoud said in response goes a long way in explaining the retrograde steps that were initiated during the Taleban rule.

Massoud said, "I briefly want to mention one thing in this regard, with the help of which you can analyse and interpret the actions of the Taleban. In order to swallow and usurp Afghanistan, it is one of the dangerous policies of Pakistan to reduce Afghanistan from the level of a state to tribalism. In this way, the Pakistanis have begun destroying (the) foundations of the state so that no government worth its name exists in Afghanistan in the future. It has been many years since the Taleban are governing a large part of Afghanistan but Pakistan has never wanted to see that the Taleban (have) a regular and organised army. There is no doubt that the Taleban, when their real face had not yet been recognised, had gained popularity among the people and the nation. But, during this period, Pakistan never wanted to bring thousands of Afghani and Pushtun educated scholars who were living in Peshawar and elsewhere in Afghanistan and make them part of the Taleban administration so that it could improve and the administrative condition become better. Instead, they created worse conditions for them. They used Hizb-i-Islam of Hekmatyar to threaten and murder Afghani scholars. Morever, under the threat of (the) Taleban, those scholars were forced to flee Pakistan and seek asylum elsewhere. The Afghans themselves initiated steps and established a university in Peshawar, so that the Afghan refugees could study there but the Pakistanis closed down that university and constructed a mosque in that place. They let the Taleban establish more madrassas but did not allow an institution to continue which could serve the future of Afghanistan. Certain observers are of the view that Pakistan does not have enough control over (the) Taleban to restrain them from taking steps on human and women's rights. *It is Pakistan, which has been providing weapons, fighters and other financial help; how is it not possible for it to restrain the Taleban from destroying the Buddhas?*"

"The problem is different," said Massoud. "Actually, Pakistan wants to show that Afghans are uncultured and uncivilised and they had nothing in the past and have always led a tribal life and have become accustomed to tribal habits and will always remain so and thus, it is their (Pakistan's) strategy to destroy the identity of Afghans. This is the most dangerous part of their strategy and policy with regard to Afghanistan. *They want to bring down Afghanistan from the level of a state to tribalism.*"

Admittedly, the plight of women under the Taleban rule exceeded all limits of decency and civilisation. Jan Goodwin writes, "Thirty thousand men and boys poured into the dilapidated Olympic sports stadium in Kabul, capital of Afghanistan. Street hawkers peddled nuts, biscuits and tea to the waiting crowd. The scheduled entertainment? They were there to see a young woman, Sohaila, receive 100 lashes, and to watch two thieves have their rights arms amputated. Sohaila had been arrested walking with a man who was not a relative, a sufficient crime for her to be found guilty of adultery. Since she was single, it was punishable by flogging; had she been married, she would have been publicly stoned to death."[4]

As Sohaila, completely covered in the shroud-like burqa veil, writes Goodwin, was forced to kneel and then flogged, Taleban "cheerleaders" had the stadium ringing with the chants of onlookers. Among those present there were just three women: the young Afghan, and two female relatives who had accompanied her. The crowd fell silent only when the luckless thieves were driven into the arena and pushed to the ground. Physicians using surgical scalpels promptly carried out the amputations. Holding the severed hands aloft by the index fingers, a grinning Taleban fighter warned the huge crowd, "These are the chopped-off hands of thieves, the punishment for any of you caught stealing." Then, to restore the party atmosphere, the thieves were driven in a jeep once around the stadium, a flourish that brought the crowd to their feet, as was intended.

Earlier that same week, three men accused of "buggery" had been sentenced to death by being partially buried in the ground and then having a wall pushed over on them by a bulldozer, a bizarre and labour-intensive form of execution dreamt up by the supreme leader of the Taleban, the thirty-six-year-old Mullah Mohammed Omar, says Goodwin. After another man, a saboteur, was hanged, his corpse was driven around the city, swinging from a crane. "Clearly, there is nothing covert about the regime's punitive measures. In fact, the Taleban insure (that the measures) are as widely publicised as possible."

In March 1997, the regime's radio station, the only one allowed in the areas under the Taleban's control, broadcast that a young women caught trying to flee the country with a man who was not her relative, had been stoned to death. On another occasion, it was announced by the radio that a total of 225 women had been rounded up and sentenced to a lashing for violating the dress code. One woman had the top of her thumb amputated for the crime of wearing nail polish. Goodwin also mentions the castration and hanging of former President Najibullah and his brother and their corpses hung for public display for three days. "Photographs of the corpses appeared in news magazines and newspapers around the world."

The things that women were not allowed to do, as Goodwin recounts: no education, no jobs, no nail polish or jewellery or eyebrow plucking or cutting hair short or colourful clothes or sheer stockings or white socks and shoes, no high-heel shoes of course and no loud walking or talking or laughing in public. It is little wonder that after the Taleban fell, the media the world over went on publishing photographs of women walking around in Kabul streets, some without the burqa. It was indeed news.

Goodwin mentions the experience of a young woman, Torpeka, who had ventured out of her home in order to rush her child, who was dangerously ill, to the doctor. Even though she was dressed according to the diktat of the Taleban, a teenage Taleban guard aimed his Kalashnikov at her and repeatedly fired directly at her, hitting her. She was badly injured but still kept going so that the child would be examined quickly. When the crowd in the street saw what was happening, it intervened, and that was how the young desperate mother was saved and her child could be treated. When her family complained to the authorities about the guard, it was told that the fault was Torpeka's, for in the first instance, she had no business going out of her home.

"Women's Health and Human Rights in Afghanistan", a report prepared by JAMA (Journal of the American Medical Association), examines the position of women under the Taleban. The violations of women's rights were justified by the Taleban in the name of religion and culture. However, the Taleban's decrees represented a striking departure from past religious and cultural practices in Afghanistan. Before the Taleban took control of Kabul, schools were coeducational with women accounting for seventy per cent of the teaching force. Women represented about fifty per cent of the civil service corps, and forty per cent of the city's physicians were women. Afghan women who were once free to choose their dress, move about in public independently, and pursue their careers, were under the Taleban rule subject to harsh punishment, usually in the form of summary public beatings, if they violated Taleban decrees, which were enforced by the regime's "religious police", members of the Department for the Propagation of Virtue and the Suppression of Vice. Afghan staff members of international organisations had reportedly faced threats, harassment, beating and arrest while conducting their professional duties.[5]

The situation for women deteriorated further when in September 1997, the decree of segregating hospitals for males and females was finally implemented. What this meant on the ground was unacceptably cruel; the Ministry of Public Health ordered all hospitals in Kabul to suspend medical services to the 500,000 women living in the city with only a single badly equipped clinic made available to them. Two months later, in November 1997, after an intervention by the International Committee of the Red Cross, most hospitals were officially restored to women but, as the report notes, "despite this policy reversal, women have less access to hospital care than they did before the Taleban had banned women from hospitals". Prior to the imposition of the ban in September 1997, approximately twenty-five per cent of the medical and surgical hospital beds dedicated to adults were available for women but, as of May 1998, only twenty per cent of hospital medical and surgical beds dedicated to adults were available for women while seventy per cent were allocated to men. The ban on women working in hospitals as doctors, nurses, pharmacists and technicians was also reversed later as the public healthcare system was on the verge of collapse leaving the government with no choice but to eat the humble pie and women were allowed to return to their jobs.

The JAMA carried out a sample survey of Afghan women living in both Afghanistan and Pakistan as refugees. The findings regarding human rights abuses these women

The Dark Age Descends

experienced were as follows: the respondents reported harassment, physical abuse and restricted activity as a consequence of the Taleban occupation of Kabul. Sixty-nine per cent of them reported that they or a family member had been detained in Kabul by the Taleban religious police or security forces. Overall, twenty-two per cent reported a total of forty-three separate incidents in which they were detained and abused. Of these incidents, seventy-two per cent followed the charge of non-adherence to the Taleban dress code for women. Specific offences included not wearing a burqa; not completely covering the face, hands, wrists or feet; and wearing stylish clothes, white socks or shoes or shoes that made noise while walking. Twelve per cent of the respondents were detained for being unaccompanied by male chaperons in public. Among other detainees, two disabled women, both of whom lost a leg from rocket blast injuries, were detained and beaten for entering a public building through an entrance designated for males. Thirty-five of the forty-three detentions lasted less than one hour; however, thirty-six detentions led to public beatings and one to torture.

The survey established that since the beginning of the Taleban occupation of Kabul, the health and physical conditions of the majority of the respondents declined significantly. The respondents also reported an inadequate control over their reproduction. "After having experienced years of armed conflict and injuries to themselves or their families, they are now forbidden from working and receiving formal education, restricted in their activities in public, and targets of attack by the Taleban militia. These oppressive violations of women's human rights are likely to have a detrimental influence on health, particularly in the types of stress-related symptoms related here," the survey said.

The survey concluded that the current health and human rights status of women described in this study suggested that the combined effects of war-related traumas and human rights abuses by Taleban officials had had a profound effect on Afghan women's health. The majority of Afghan women interviewed reported deteriorating physical and mental health during the last two years of the Taleban regime. The extent of mental health problems, in particular, indicated an urgent need to address both the cause and the long-term consequences of such suffering.

A reassuring finding of the survey was the strong support that the women accorded to human rights. The survey concluded that while the Taleban regime did not recognise international treaties, agreed to by their predecessor governments, citing their irrelevance to Afghan culture and Islamic law, the "strong support for women's human rights held by participants in this study suggests that the Taleban's rejection of international norms of human rights is incommensurate with the interests and needs of Afghan women."

The five years of Taleban rule, 26 September 1996-13 November 2001, were marked by frequently changing fortunes in the battlefield; the Taleban and their only adversary, the Northern Alliance (later, the United Front) fought tooth and nail to prevail over each other, their fight to the finish conditioned at periodic intervals by the annual snowfall and, at other times, by natural calamities visiting the hapless country. The battles were also punctuated by instances of massacres as provinces, cities and villages and highways were occupied, vacated and reoccupied by the two sworn enemies.

While the post-jihad period was pockmarked with scores of massacres, one of the goriest took place in Mazar-i-Sharif in the aftermath of a Taleban misadventure to wrest the most important northern city from General Abdul Rashid Dostum. Ever since the September 1996 fall of Kabul, the Taleban were widely expected to move northward and try their luck in Mazar-i-Sharif. It was vital for the Taleban to gain control over the north, because while the population was concentrated in the south and east, the natural resources were predominantly located in the northern provinces, natural gas (estimated to be 100 billion cu. m.) being the foremost. There is also some oil, estimated to be around 11.63 million tons. Besides, there are iron ore, copper and bauxite yet to be exploited and coal and salt, apart from lapis lazuli in the Panjsher Valley. Mazar-i-Sharif had on its own become a major port of call in the multimillion dollar smuggling racket involving Pakistan, Afghanistan and the Central Asian republics. The smuggling boom also brought in handsome revenue for General Dostum, the undisputed warlord of the region, in the form of transit taxes and duties levied on transporters.

As the period of uncertainty and frequent battles continued, thousands of residents of Kabul fled north to Mazar-i-Sharif which, under the forceful rule of Dostum, looked an oasis of peace in the troubled country. In fact, the city was never touched by the traumatic years of the jihad and the mujahideen in-fighting. Besides, it was traditionally a major place of pilgrimage, housing as it did the Tomb of Ali, cousin and son-in-law of the Prophet Mohammad and the Fourth Caliph of Islam, greatly revered by the Shias.

The days of tranquility were, however, coming to an end. Dostum and his second-in-command General Malik Pahlawan fell out over the murder of the latter's brother General Rasul Pahlawan in June 1996. The surviving brother felt threatened that his life too could be in danger and secretly contacted the Taleban. On 19 May 1997, Pahlawan betrayed Dostum, along with three other Uzbek generals. This development also coincided with widespread unrest among Dostum's troops who had not been paid wages for five months. Sensing their moment of victory, the Taleban moved fast from Herat and Kabul, and as the unique joint Pushtun-Uzbek advance moved north, with the northern provinces capitulating without much fuss, Dostum fled to Uzbekistan and then onwards to Turkey.

The Taleban-Malik collaboration, however, broke down immediately after the Taleban forces took Mazar-i-Sharif over, disarmed the fierce Uzbek and Hazara fighters, closed down all educational institutions including Balkh University, the only functioning university in Afghanistan at the time, declared Sharia law in force and took various other measures to convert the traditionally liberal and open city into yet another bastion of intolerable orthodoxy and medievalism. As the alliance was about to break up, with Malik feeling slighted with the Taleban offer of the insignificant deputy foreign ministership in Kabul, Pakistani diplomats and ISI officers arrived at the city to attempt a patch-up job, for it was vital for Pakistan that the rift between the Tajiks, Uzbeks and Hazaras in the north was sustained in order to weaken the military strength of Commander Massoud and simultaneously strengthen the Taleban. It was also the juncture when Islamabad extended its recognition to the Taleban government as the legitimate Afghan government on 25 May 1997, and successfully persuaded Saudi Arabia (a close collaborator in financing the Taleban, which extended its recognition on 26 May 1997) and the United Arab Emirates (on 27 May 1997) in following suit. Rashid quotes the Pakistani Foreign Minister Gohar Ayub declaring the Afghan crisis had been resolved with the Taleban forming a broad-based government. "We feel that the new government fulfils all criteria for de jure recognition. It (the government) is now in effective control of most of the territory of Afghanistan and is representative of all ethnic groups in that country." Within hours of the congratulatory Pakistani statement, however, the Taleban were forced out of Mazar-i-Sharif.

The afternoon of 28 May 1997 saw the beginning of one of the goriest massacres in the blood-soaked history of modern Afghanistan. An uprising, catching the uninitiated Taleban off guard, spread rapidly as a group of Hazaras first resisted being disarmed, followed by the Hazaras rising in revolt, and then the entire population erupted against the invading Pushtuns. For fifteen hours, the mayhem continued, with Taleban fighters fighting desperately to escape from the city which had suddenly turned into a giant death-trap for them. At the end of the massacre, 600 Taleban soldiers lay dead in the streets and over 1,000 were trapped and captured at the airport. As many as ten high-ranking Taleban political and military leaders were either killed or captured, including Foreign Minister Mullah Mohammed Ghaus, Mullah Abdul Razaq (who had led the Taleban force) and Central Bank Governor Mullah Ehsanullah and the Pakistani ambassador who was soon released. Pakistanis, mostly students, wherever they were found, were instantly put to death. As Malik's men looted the city, the offices of United Nations agencies became victims, forcing aid workers to flee and the agencies to close down their humanitarian activities.

General Malik's forces advanced out of the city and recaptured all the four northern provinces (Takhar, Faryab, Jowzjan and Sar-i-Pul) the Taleban had taken over on their way to Mazar-i-Sharif a mere five days back. Fighting raged for retaking the remaining three northern provinces of Balkh, Samangan and Kunduz. The massacre of Taleban fighters and Pakistani students continued; and hundreds of bodies were thrown into mass graves. As the Taleban were kept busy escaping from the north after the terrible misadventure at Mazar-i-Sharif, Commander Massoud utilised the opportunity, advanced south and retook the strategic Jabal-ul-Seraj, which lay at the entrance of the Salang tunnel. By blowing the tunnel entrance up, he succeeded in trapping the fleeing Taleban fighters in the north as travelling south from the Salang Pass became impossible. The misfortune that had visited the Taleban in the north was repeated in the north-east as Massoud recaptured several towns close to Kabul; and the massacre of Taleban fighters continued in the region as well. Hazaras rose under the leadership of Karim Khalili and drove the Taleban out of the Bamiyan Valley in the north-west of Kabul. It was a grim scenario all around not only for the Taleban, who had suffered as many as 3,000 dead and injured and nearly 3,600 fighters taken prisoner at various places by Generals Malik and Sayyid Jaffar Naderi (leading the Ismaili militia) and Commander Massoud, but also for the Pakistani government for the battles had led to the killing of over 250 Pakistanis with another 550 in opposition custody.

There were two major follow-ups of the events in Afghanistan: first, the Central Asian republics and the Russian Federation were truly concerned over possible Taleban attacks north of the border with Afghanistan and, consequenly, upgraded and tightened their security apparatus and arrangements. Secondly, Massoud made a major gain by obtaining access to the Kuliab airport, southern Tajikistan, opening up an invaluable military supply line from Russia and Iran. The opposition alliance established the "United Islamic and National Front for the Salvation of Afghanistan" on 13 June 1997, reappointing Burhanuddin Rabbani as the President and appointing Massoud as the Defence Minister. Just when opposition unity had begun to appear entrenched, fresh differences broke it up as the three military commanders, Massoud, Malik and Khalili failed to resolve their mutual differences. Their differences became irreconcilable as misgivings about Malik's fidelity persisted and were proved correct when Taleban remnants, numbering about 2,500, managed to retake Kunduz, quickly turning the city into a Taleban stronghold by daily shipments of men and materials from Kabul by air.

The Taleban, who never gave up the idea of retaking the north, drew considerable inspiration from the continuing differences within the opposition alliance and bided time for the eventual collapse of the collaboration among the Uzbeks, Hazaras and Tajiks. Meanwhile, Massoud had advanced dangerously close to the capital, digging in with his troops a mere twenty miles away to the north (September 1997); both Charikar and the Bagram airbase had fallen back into his hands. The Taleban had been forced to withdraw from the Shamali Plains, and while retreating, they performed their infamous scorched earth policy, leaving behind a huge wasteland of poisoned wells, ruined irrigation channels and dams and uprooted orchards and farmlands and torched and demolished Tajik homes.

President Burhanuddin Rabbani of the Islamic State of Afghanistan, writing to the United Nations Secretary-General in the aftermath of the massacres in the Shamali Plains, said in a letter dated 19 August 1999, "The Pakistani and Taleban troops continue to barbarously pursue their campaign of systematic ethnic cleansing and genocide by means of scorched-earth policy. In addition to troop mobilisation, heavy artillery bombardment and ground artillery barrage, they have targeted civilian neighbourhoods. The widespread use of hundreds of incendiary and cluster bombs, the levelling and burning down of entire villages, the mass killing of hundreds of innocent civilians, mostly women and children and the forced displacement of over 40,000 women, elderly and children to the barren hot deserts of Jalalabad, where a dozen women and children have died daily from excessive heat and lack of water and food, in addition to the already 300,000 internally displaced refugees, all present the latest predicament and catastrophe in Afghanistan. Also, the latest crackdown by the Taleban in Kabul, with the arrest of thousands of people at Khair Khana on the northern outskirts of the city, where over 10,000 were forcibly deported and sought refuge after the 28 July Pakistani-Taleban attack on their villages in the Shamali Plains, is another dimension of the ongoing genocide."

Lamenting the complete lack of action by the international community in the face of the mounting genocide, Rabbani remarked with bitterness, "If it were to be claimed that the international community, non-governmental organisations and aid agencies had adopted an attitude of indifference, it would not be an exaggeration. Justice and equal rights of mankind – two sacred principles – having always been attributed to the guiding criteria by aid agencies and the international community, against the backdrop of the latest tragedy, have led to a predominant impression among our people that such notions are nothing more than empty rhetoric, bearing no weight whatsoever. It is exactly here that the Afghan nation, instead of forwarding their appeal to world leaders, take the liberty to express their grief to the conscience of the peoples of the world, and rather ask them for assistance."

The most important development in the north around this time was the return of General Dostum, who had embarked upon the twin objectives of driving the Taleban out of Mazar-i-Sharif and finishing off General Malik's forces. Chaos also returned to the city with the United Nations agency offices, once again a helpless prey in the hands of marauding Uzbeks. While the Taleban retreated into Kunduz, Hazaras troops in effect took over Mazar-i-Sharif, forcing Dostum to shift his headquarters to Shiberghan. The opposition alliance weakened further as the Uzbeks and the Hazaras confronted each other.

Dostum was instrumental around this time in unearthing one of the worst massacres perpetrated during the civil war, the cold-blooded killing of more than 2,000 Taleban fighters in the Dash-te-Laili desert in Jowzjan province by General Malik's men. On his urging, the United Nations investigated the massacre and found that the prisoners were tortured and starved before being put to death and buried in twenty mass graves. The United Nations Special Rapporteur Paik Chong-Hyun, who investigated the massacre, reported thus: "The manner of their death was horrendous. Prisoners were taken from detention, told they were going to be exchanged and then trucked to wells often used by shepherds, which held about 10 to 15 metres of water. They were thrown into the wells either alive or if they resisted, shot first and then tossed in. Shots were fired and hand grenades were exploded into the well before the top was bulldozed over."

The massacres and counter-massacres to settle scores, in the wake of battle victories and defeats, had led Afghanistan by the last quarter of 1997 into a multipolarised society, with each major ethnic community deadly set against the other. While the Pushtun Taleban had killed Hazaras, Uzbeks and Tajiks en masse, the latter had with equal brutality retaliated by killing thousands of Pushtuns. In one sense, while the country was ethnically separated, there was also a geographical separation, as the Pushtuns were concentrated in the south and the three minority communities in the north and west. The polarisation along ethnic and geographical lines would continue until the fall of the Taleban on 13 November 2001, in the wake of Operation Enduring Freedom, and the consequent return of normalcy to the country. It was in this context that woman activist Nasrine Gross was enthused by the sight of Loya Jirgah delegates of various ethnic communities mixing together freely, in an obvious step being taken towards national integration after nearly five years of separation.

Evocative of those days of swinging fortune marked by no-holds-barred encounters, as the Taleban remained hell-bent on capturing the remaining northern and western provinces and Commander Massoud stood like a rock to frustrate their design, was the following despatch. "As severe winter holds Afghanistan in its grip, bringing all military offensives to a halt," the report said, "fresh huge supplies of military hardware have reached the Taleban for a major attack to be mounted after the snow melts. The offensive is expected to hit Takhar province in an effort to widen the area under the Taleban's control."[6]

With the United Nations virtually crying off as six years of search for a peace formula appeared to have proved fruitless, the prospects of a country, living in a state of war for the last eighteen years, seem to be as gloomy as the winter days.

In Kunduz province, neighbour to Takhar, the fundamentalist forces remained entrenched in Kunduz city with northern forces digging in all around with no intention to attack. The stalemate was expected to continue with both sides opting for defensive-offensive positions during the winter. "Our goal is to contain the Taleban in Kunduz city which we cannot afford to attack as it is dominated by the Pushtuns," said Afghan ambassador Masood Khalili.[7]

The Taleban threat to Mazar-i-Sharif appeared to have subsided and Faryab province was now being considered safe (from the viewpoint of the Northern Alliance). Badghis province remained evenly divided between the northern and Taleban forces. Plentiful of rain and snow had rendered the area unfit for combat.

"Meanwhile," the report continued, "the Taleban's enemies continue to be poised in the immediate north of Kabul with no intention to advance during the winter months. While the winter has rendered military offensive unproductive and forced all concerned to pursue diplomacy for a change, there is little likelihood of striking a way out for peace negotiations."

There was, nevertheless, some expectation from the Organisation of Islamic Conference (OIC) summit now in progress in Teheran. The summit was expected to adopt a resolution on Afghanistan today.

Even the parallel initiatives taken up by Iran and Pakistan in the recent days in this regard suffered from mutual contradictions. While Pakistan, embarrassed by growing evidence of its involvement with the Taleban, was clearly in a hurry to work out a framework for peace talks among some of the neighbouring countries and Afghan factions, Iran was apparently taking a relatively circumspect view. "Teheran is keen to utilise its three years of presidentship of the OIC to work out a peace plan and wishes to go about it in a deliberately phased manner," the report concluded.

Less than two months later, a major earthquake had hit the areas under the control of Commander Massoud's forces, and the following despatch showed how relief for the earthquake victims became a prey to the Taleban's military exigencies. "The Burhanuddin Rabbani government renewed its appeal to the international community to rush aid to the remote north-eastern province of Takhar close to the border with Tajikistan. Meanwhile, according to opposition government sources, the Taleban, who bombed the provincial capital Taloqan, 40 km south of Rustaq (hit by the earthquake), yesterday afternoon, were trying to obstruct the supply route. The Taleban must be stopped from achieving this as this would jeopardise any aid mission to the quake-hit areas, they said."[8]

The report noted that the Rabbani government had initiated several emergency measures to rush aid to the affected areas. While civilians in the neighbourhood had been asked to rush immediately to the quake-hit areas, the "limited armed forces" of the government had been instructed to begin the rescue mission, including the extrication of dead bodies and clearing of rubble. A "National Mourning Day" was observed, the report said, and the government called on the international community to rush aid to the affected province.

The last remaining months of 1997 also witnessed Afghanistan's relations with the international community reaching their nadir. The astonishing intransigence displayed by the Taleban in refusing to facilitate any peace bid by the United Nations frustrated UN Secretary-General Kofi Annan to such an extent that in one of the bluntest reports he had ever submitted to the Security Council, he remarked, after noting the damage being done by external powers in extending military assistance to the warring parties, "The Afghan leaders refuse to rise above their factional interests and start working together for national reconciliation. Too many groups in Afghanistan, warlords, terrorists, drug dealers and others, appear to have too much to gain from war and too little to lose from peace."

While the next two years, 1998-99, were marked by the protracted tussle between the Taleban and the Hazaras under the leadership of Karim Khalili's Hizb-i-Wahdat over the possession of Bamiyan province, with fortunes swinging every now and then and resulting in massive human suffering, the period also proved to be strategic for an extension of the Pakistan-Afghanistan under the Taleban-Osama bin Laden's international terrorism nexus to the Indian State of Jammu and Kashmir.

It was on 26 May 1999 that the Kargil war broke out between India and Pakistan, after a belated discovery by India that Pakistani infiltrators had encroached upon Indian territory and set up posts on mountain peaks on the Indian side of the Line of Control, thus clearly crossing the LoC and violating the provisions of the Simla Agreement 1972, between the two countries. An intensive two-month war followed, with India hovering often on the option of striking inside the Pakistani territory in order to halt infiltrations, a possibility that alarmed the world community and led to intervention by the United States government. Though the Indian government claimed that Indian defence forces had been able to push the Pakistanis out of Indian territory, the fact was that Pakistan was forced to withdraw its troops after United States President Bill Clinton summoned Prime Minister Nawaz Sharif to Washington on 4 July 1999 and literally gave him a dressing down. Sharif had little option but to give an undertaking that Pakistani soldiers would be withdrawn from the Indian side of the LoC; and on 26 July 1999, the Indian army announced that the last of the infiltrators had left.

The Kargil war also exposed for the first time in a decisive manner that international terrorists trained in camps run by Osama bin Laden in Afghanistan had been actively participating in the proxy war being waged by Pakistan in Jammu and Kashmir and that they were part of the infiltrators in the Kargil sector.

The author reported at the time, "The Inter-Services Intelligence (ISI) of Pakistan, the Taleban and the Osama bin Laden network had decided at a joint meeting to launch a fresh offensive against (United Front) forces in Afghanistan along with the armed intrusions into Jammu and Kashmir, the opposition Burhanuddin Rabbani government said today."[9]

Continuing, the report said that the Osama bin Laden group of terrorists had been provided a new base at the Hadda farm in eastern Afghanistan. The Taleban had been conducting training sessions for these terrorists inside the Taleban-controlled territories. At the suggestion of the ISI, the Taleban were providing safe haven for terrorists from Uzbekistan and Azerbaijan, the Rabbani government fighting the Taleban said.

The Rabbani government said that the Pakistani intrusions into the Kargil sector of Jammu and Kashmir were part of a hidden agenda of the ISI. It added, "What unravels in the Indian Kashmir today has been the scene of events in Afghanistan for the past seven years, all of Pakistani military activities under the pretext of the Taleban." It pointed out that just as Pakistan still maintained that in the Afghan conflict it did neither intervene nor had any favourites, so too it claimed that in Kashmir it only provided moral and diplomatic support to the "Kashmiri fighters".

"Obviously," the statement said, "the international community has viewed such propaganda with maximum scepticism." United States officials present at the 4 July 1999 meeting between President Bill Clinton and Prime Minister Nawaz Sharif, expressed their doubts as to whether the Pakistani prime minister would be able to guarantee a Pakistani military pull-back. The American officials also said it was obvious that the Pakistani military had taken the initiative in Kargil and "that still remains the case". "This is an admission by the US authorities of the fact that (the opposition government in Afghanistan) has continuously stated to (them) that such military adventures, including the Pakistani war in Afghanistan by the Taleban, are hegemonistic initiatives by the ISI."

The Rabbani government statement, quoted in the report, said that the following Pakistani forces and groups were at present fighting the (United Front) in Afghanistan:
(a) para-military groups such as the Sipah-e-Sahaba, the Sipah-e-Tayeba and the Harakat-ul-Ansar, mostly from Punjab (Pakistan);
(b) frontier militia forces from Pakistan's North-West Frontier Province;
(c) military units from the "Churat" and "Sahiwal" divisions and officers and soldiers from the Pakistani

military, mostly Punjabis. At present, a majority of these groups had been stationed in the garrisons of Rees-Khor (Kabul), Chehle-Tan (Paghman) and Kunduz.

As for the Taleban, the Rabbani government said that altogether five different groups of people came under the omnibus name. These were: the Pakistani ISI maintaining the command and control of military initiatives, Pakistani armed Taleban under the ISI command, the Afghan Taleban, extremist groups from Egypt, Bangladesh, Algeria, Uzbekistan, and several other countries, and the Osama bin Laden terrorist network controlling all the Arab nationals' activities, the report concluded.

Bodansky notes that since September 1998, the anticipated escalation in the Pakistan-sponsored Islamist terrorism in Kashmir had been associated with Osama bin Laden. For example, Ghulam, a Harakat-ul-Ansar (now called Harakat-ul-Mujahideen) commander in Srinagar, Kashmir, who had been trained in the Badr camp in Khost (eastern Afghanistan), stressed his loyalty to bin Laden. "Our 'father' bin Laden has sent brothers from Afghanistan to wage jihad," he explained. "The ISI has recently adapted existing organisational frameworks to reinforce the 'new character' of the war in Kashmir," Bodansky says. "Very important is the emergence of the Taleban-i-Kashmir organisation – ostensibly an Afghanistan-based Kashmiri Islamist terrorist organisation whose existence warrants the growing numbers of Afghan, Pakistani and Arab 'Afghan' terrorists in the ranks of the Kashmiri national liberation forces. These foreigners are largely Islamists fighting for a sacred cause, not the mercenaries the ISI recruited in the mid-1990s. There is already evidence of popular support for bin Laden in the ranks of the Islamist terrorists fighting in Kashmir. For example, on 1 November (1998), Indian security authorities engaged a well-armed Harakat-ul-Mujahideen detachment trying to cross over from Pakistan in the Poonch area. In the pockets of four Pakistani terrorists killed, the Indians found for the first time photographs of bin Laden along with the usual pocket Korans and a book on guerrilla warfare."[10]

Just as in the Kargil war Pakistan army regulars wore the salwar-kameez (the ethnic dress of loose trousers and long shirt), a despatch by the author spoke of similar camouflage worn by Pakistani soldiers fighting in Taleban ranks in Afghanistan. "The (United Front) in Afghanistan last night recovered the bodies of four Pakistan army regulars on the Old Road, north-east of Kabul, after fierce fighting with the Taleban," the report said. "According to (United Front) sources, Col. Ahmed Salim and three others of the Pakistan army were killed in the fierce battle on the 28 July night. Fifty attackers were taken prisoner, mainly Arab mercenaries and Pakistan army troops."[11]

The report said that two tanks of the attackers were destroyed, two others captured. Several Toyota pick-ups used for transporting the Taleban forces and their irregular armies were captured. The four bodies were recovered after heavy fighting broke out last night between the two sides on the Old Road and New Road areas, north of Kabul. Severe fighting was said to be continuing at Tagab, north-east of Kabul. The Arabs and Pakistan regulars attacked the (United Front) forces eight times on the Old Road and four times on the New Road last night. "The offensive seems to have gone so far rather badly for the attackers. On July 27, the first day, they suffered heavy losses. Yesterday, they broke the defence lines at Tagab, advanced for five hours but were pushed back. The massive Taleban offensive was launched from three directions north of Kabul – the Old Road from Phul Sofiaz, and the New Road between Kabul and the Bagram airbase. The third front was at Tagab, north-east of Kabul. The area is manned mostly by ISI and the Pakistan army. The Taleban and (their) allies were also concentrated at Dara-e-Suf in Samangan province, Shulgar in Balkh province and Kunduz."

Pointing out that the attack was launched with artillery and forces backed by the ISI, Pakistan army and Arab extremists sent by Osama bin Laden, the report said, "Sources said (that) for the last one-and-a-half month, the ISI, bin Laden's group, the Taleban and the Pakistani extremists had been mobilising forces to 'finish' the war in Afghanistan. The offensive was, however, postponed due to the India-Pakistan conflict in Kargil. Interestingly, the preparations for the 'final' offensive continued even as the United Nations-sponsored Six-plus-Two contact group met in Tashkent earlier this month. The group discussed ways of averting an escalation of war and seek a political settlement. Sources said (that) Pakistan was hardly committed to the Tashkent conference as the ISI was simultaneously mobilising the offensive by pumping in huge amounts of funds and weapons. Thousands of extremists were being transported to participate in the offensive."

On 25 October 1999, addressing a joint session of the Indian Parliament after a general election and assumption of office by a new government, President K. R. Narayanan said, "The situation in Afghanistan demands a careful assessment and a fresh approach. We shall work together with like-minded countries for an early return to stability in Afghanistan." Reporting the address, the author said in his despatch to *The Hindustan Times*, "(The President) added that an essential requirement for that (return of stability) to happen would be 'the cessation of outside interference in the internal affairs of Afghanistan'. The trickiest task would be delinking Pakistan from the Taleban. In fact, no initiative had so far even attempted it. The United Nations special envoy Lakhdar Brahimi had made a tactical retreat precisely because 'outside interference' had thwarted the move to defuse the situation. It is not yet clear how India proposes to launch its initiative. However, once the cease-fire holds and an interim administration takes charge, the initiative could move to the second stage – the holding of a political dialogue involving all Afghan sections."

The report was, however, naturally sceptical of any breakthrough in the near future and noted, "Judging by recent history, the initiative might well falter at this stage, for the numerous Afghan factions are not renowned for their interest in achieving a consensus. During his earlier tenure in office, Prime Minister Atal Behari Vajpayee had ordered a re-appraisal of India's Afghanistan policy. The outcome of the analysis was never made public but the feeling had gained ground that it was time India started playing a role in the affairs of a country that affected regional security. Throughout these years and especially since the Taleban swept into Kabul, India chose to stay aloof. There are many in this country who rue to this day India's abandonment of President Mohammad Najibullah. The new Vajpayee government is now apparently planning to adopt a proactive stance. Behind the seeming inactivity, however, New Delhi has been confabulating with 'like-minded' countries. Its exclusion from the Six-plus-Two initiative at Pakistan's behest led to heartburn but New Delhi was pragmatic enough to acknowledge the ground realities. The ground realities today are significantly different, and this has helped India plan its initiative. The upsurge in international terrorism is probably the most important contributor to the realisation among the international community that India should come forward to help demystify the Afghan situation."

Four days earlier, on 21 October 1999, the author wrote in a despatch to *The Hindustan Times*, "As United Nations resolutions on international terrorism pile up, there is growing concern in India and other front line victims over the international community's failure to combat the scourge seriously. While the resolutions are mostly inspired by countries experiencing the ravages of terrorism, the lengthening gap between their adoption and implementation exposes the cross-purposes at which UN member-states are working. These cross-purposes are apparently products of national interests superseding those of the international community. What India and others are, however, more concerned with is the indication that coinciding with the dithering by the world community, terrorist groups and their state sponsors are growing even more brazen."

Continuing, the report said, "The most telling example of this is the Taleban's response to UN Secretary-General (Kofi) Annan to the effect that they cannot just hand over Osama bin Laden to the Americans for his alleged role in organising terrorist attacks on the US embassies in Kenya and Tanzania last year. 'Afghanistan won its freedom (from the Soviet Union) thanks to fighters like Osama bin Laden,' the militia ruling (over) ninety per cent of Afghanistan have said. 'That's why a hand-over of bin Laden to America would amount to a betrayal of Islamic principles. And that's why we can't do it at any cost.'"

While the United States, Russia and India had identified Osama bin Laden as one of the principal organisers of terrorist groups, the report said that the Central Asian republics had now followed suit. "Kyrgyzstan has confirmed that terrorists attacking state institutions are sponsored by bin Laden. It has also stated that Uzbek fundamentalists active in Dagestan, a Russian province, and in its territory are both links in the same chain of terrorists being trained, funded and armed by bin Laden and people working closely with him. When one considers the defiant protection that the Taleban are providing to bin Laden and the close links between Pakistan and the fundamentalist militia, the Indian position that the world community must rise to the necessity of condemning the state sponsorship of terrorism is easily appreciated," the report said.

The year 2000 proved to be little different from the previous year in so far as the overall situation in Afghanistan was concerned. The Taleban remained entrenched in the east, west and parts of the north, while the United Front continued to hold on to the north, with pockets under its control in large tracts of land in the north, west and east. The two adversaries continued to attack and re-attack, with resultant sufferings for the civilian population. Driven by the never-ending war and occasional visits by natural calamities like earthquakes and drought, a massive part of the population remained as refugees in Pakistan, Iran and various other countries, while those who had little choice but to stick to their homes within the country, lived a kind of hopeless life few nations had experienced in world history. Women and children continued to be the worst victims of the situation. The international community had grown completely weary of the prolonged civil war; and while sporadic attempts were made by the United Nations and the Six-plus-Two contact group to convene a broad-based conference of the various factions, little positive was achieved. A process to convene a Loya Jirgah, focussed around the former king Zahir Shah, self-exiled in Rome, gathered momentum, encouraging other initiatives, such as, the Bonn process and the Cyprus process, which began to cooperate with the Rome-based initiative.

The devastated economy continued to rally around opium poppy cultivation, and Afghanistan was, for the second consecutive year, the largest opium producer in the world. The drought in 2000 proved to be the worst one in the previous thirty years, and whatever little agriculture was there, suffered enormously. At least, half of the population was badly affected by the drought, of them 3-4 million people were particularly severely affected. The entire country suffered from the ill-effects of the drought, forcing more people to migrate, livestock perished, the crop loss was at places as high as fifty per cent of the total annual production. All these happened on the top of an already badly languishing agriculture due to the civil war and large-scale displacement of the farming community. Agriculture was also restricted due to landmines planted all over the country. There was scarcely any industry, and trade centred on opium, fruits, minerals and gems; an important contributor to trade was, of course, the huge quantities of smuggled goods from Pakistan. Smuggling in all manners remained probably the most important source of income for a vast population. The fiscal situation was made worse by rival currencies, both highly inflated and floated by the two main warring sides. The World Bank, which had suspended operations since 1992 when the country ceased to contribute its share, estimated that in 2000 the per capita income was about $280 a year. There was limited reconstruction activity in the Taleban-controlled Herat, Kandahar and Ghazni.

Human rights continued to be violated by the Taleban; summary justice was the way of life, rather than exception, in areas controlled by them, and political and other extrajudicial killings, including targeted killings, summary executions and deaths in custody, continued to occur with a sickening regularity. Disappearances were also reported from time to time. Much of the serious abuse of human rights was traced to the Taleban's imposition and implementation of the strictest form of the Sharia law ever experienced anywhere in the modern world. The Ministry for the Promotion of Virtue and

Suppression of Vice was entrusted with carrying out such chillingly medieval punishments as stoning to death, flogging, public executions for adultery, murder and homosexual activity, and amputations of limbs for theft. Beatings of men and women and even children on the spot, usually the street, the moment an actual or imagined violation of the Sharia code of conduct had been detected, were among the usual activities of the government. None of the freedoms that citizens enjoyed in other countries existed in Afghanistan under the Taleban, among them the freedoms of speech and religion were the most restricted.

Little wonder, then, that in the twenty-first year of continuous warfare, there were more than 2.8 million refugees abroad and another 258,600 were internally displaced. Refugees kept returning from time to time in the hope that conditions may have improved relatively; under an agreement for voluntary repatriation brokered by the United Nations high Commissioner for Refugees, a total of 133,600 refugees returned from Iran, and another 50,000 joined the return trek independent of the agreement. International aid agencies and non-governmental organisations kept doggedly to work, despite the extreme harassment meted out by all the warring factions, as they knew only too well that they were the only source of assistance for the condemned people of Afghanistan.

In the midst of this atmosphere of unmitigated horror, there were signs that Afghans were unable to take their extreme deprivations any more, and even more significantly, the Taleban had begun to loosen their regime of torture just a wee bit. The most significant development was the very gradual and very quiet spread of educational facilities for girls, always within private homes where students and women teachers converged. At a workshop in Washington DC, hosted by the World Bank on the state of education in Afghanistan, this development was described as "lights within the tunnel, while there is as yet no light at the end of the tunnel". Country Reports on Human Rights Practices – 2000 Afghanistan, prepared by the US Department of State, said, "During the year, a degree of 'enforcement fatigue' seems to have led to an informal easing of various restrictions. Reports suggest that activities such as non-formal education for girls and women working in self-employed sectors increasingly are tolerated if engaged in quietly. Many households in urban areas own television sets. Significantly, the Taleban forces did not engage in scorched-earth policy of previous campaigns when they burned homes, killed livestock, uprooted orchards and destroyed irrigation systems."

The State Department reported that the Taleban forces committed a large number of political and other extrajudicial killings, both within the country and in the refugee community in Pakistan during the year. In June 2000, Amnesty International reported that over the previous two years, more than a dozen prominent citizens advocating an end to the war and establishment of a government representing all ethnic groups had been arrested and killed by the Taleban. Much of the political and extrajudicial killings in Afghanistan during 2000 occurred during the renewed conflict between the Taleban and the United Front in the summer, which was characterised by sporadic indiscriminate shelling and bombing.

A few examples: On 14 February 2000, indiscriminate bombing by the Taleban in the Panjsher Valley killed eight civilians. In mid-June, the Taleban began offensives in the Shamali and Kunduz areas, using aircraft to support ground troops. On 1 July, they launched large-scale attacks near the towns of Bagram and Charikar, approximately thirty miles north of Kabul. Civilians continued to be the primary victims of the fighting. On 1-2 July, they carried out air raids on the towns of Charikar and Jabal-ul Saraf, reportedly claiming civilian lives. In mid-July, there were reports, denied later by the Taleban, of summary executions of prisoners by their forces in the conflict areas. On 23 July, Taleban aircraft bombed several towns and villages in northern Afghanistan, reportedly killing three and wounding seven civilians. On 30 July, they used heavy artillery and aircraft to bomb Nahreen town before capturing it.

Capturing Taloqan proved to be particularly devastating for civilians. The State Department said that between 9 August and 5 September, when the city finally fell, intense fighting raged all through. Taleban aircraft frequently bombed the city. While no statistics were available on civilian casualties, nearly 75,000 residents fled the city and adjoining areas to escape the incessant fighting. In a typical incident, a village in the vicinity was bombed, burnt and some of the villagers killed; the throat of a man was cut in front of his relatives.

On its part, United Front forces continued to fire rockets into Kabul, killing scores of civilians in the process. There were killings of a different kind as well; rival commanders and their sympathisers were sometimes attacked and killed due to various factors, including personal and family feuds and battles over the drug and smuggled goods trade.

A particular incident reported at the time spoke of the extent of the abnormality of the situation in Afghanistan. On 5 August 2000, seven de-miners (those engaged in deactivating the landmines, a crucial humanitarian job) working for the United Nations-funded Organisation for Mine Clearance and Rehabilitation, were ambushed, killed and burned in Badghis province; the report said that one of the de-miners may have been alive while being burnt. It was never known who were the perpetrators; all that was known was that the de-miners were waylaid by a "large, well-organised and well-armed" group of men.

The year 2000 also began to see the first signs of weaknesses creeping into what was till then perceived widely to be a monolithic organisation, cemented by a pathological mission to spread a totally misinterpreted version of Islam throughout the world. In one of the earliest readings of the almost imperceptible changes occurring within the Taleban, ambassador Peter Tomsen wrote, "The Taleban's failed offensive in the fall of 1999 exposed the movement's declining military punch. A mostly non-Pushtun coalition in northern Afghanistan turned back the Taleban's attacks and has since pushed the front lines toward Kabul, capturing Taleban-controlled areas in northern, eastern and western Afghanistan. The popular enthusiasm that greeted earlier Taleban offensives has faded; Pushtun youth are no longer volunteering to join the Taleban, and Pushtun fighters are leaving the Taleban's ranks, gravitating back to their southern rural areas."

"Signs of the Taleban's disintegration abound. Afghans are growing suspicious of how heavily the ISI controls the Taleban; ISI officers and Pakistani religious-party firebrands have become ubiquitous in Taleban-controlled cities, including Kabul. Taleban adversaries are profiting from these suspicions. Moreover, corruption, inspired by the lucrative opium business, has now started to infect Taleban leaders; this has raised questions among their followers about their professed spirituality in order to gain personal wealth and power."[12]

On 12 July 2000, US Congressman Gary Ackerman, New York Democrat and Chairman of the Congressional India Caucus, declared that if South Asia faced the possibility of a nuclear conflagration, the real culprits were the powers that propagated and proliferated terrorism. Addressing a House International Relations Committee hearing, Ackerman pointed out that India, a long-time victim of cross-border terrorism, could lose its patience and abandon its policy of restraint and resort to a hot pursuit response, triggering a major conflict. "In South Asia today," he said, "the two crucibles of global terrorism are Pakistan and its vassal state, Afghanistan. It is from these two nations that fanatic forces of fundamentalist faith are spreading wanton mayhem and murder not only against India, a bastion of democracy, but also against Western democracies, values and interests. These forces of chaos, who make no distinction between civilian and military targets, cannot thrive and function in both Pakistan and Afghanistan without the cooperation and tacit blessings of the authoritarian regimes that have usurped power in Islamabad and Kabul."[13]

At around the same time, a bomb blast at the Pakistan embassy in Kabul led to the very first expression of Pakistani doubts about the consequences of close collaboration with the Taleban. The Pakistani media began to question the advisability of sticking to the Taleban. In a scathing editorial, *The Frontier Post* questioned the wisdom of the Pakistan government continuing its relations with the Taleban government and urged it to wake up to the ground realities. Terming the bomb blast an opportunity, the newspaper said, "The nation expects the Chief Executive, Gen. Pervez Musharraf to heed the blast as a warning that cannot be louder and clearer. It says, 'You must order a drastic re-appraisal of our commitment with whosoever is in the saddle in Kabul.'" Demanding that the Taleban government must accept responsibility for the blast, it said that if the government could not even protect the solitary embassy in its capital, it was no government. "We withdraw lock, stock and barrel. We should also make it absolutely clear to them that if any similar blast occurs anywhere in Pakistan in the near future, our first suspicion would be (the) Kabul hand in it. The government would be perfectly justified to serve (a) stern notice to Kabul's surrogates and agents inside Pakistan. Enough is enough."

The people of Pakistan were convinced right from day one that the decision of Zia-ul Haq to plunge Pakistan into the Afghan war had nothing to do with the people of Pakistan and was perverse. "The dictator is dead and gone. Not his surrogates who have been pushing Pakistan deeper and deeper into this bottomless dungeon because they lack moral courage to face the profoundly wronged people of Pakistan. Will anyone please explain why we, of all nations and states in the world, are the only one to have a full strength embassy in Kabul? Even the Saudi has quietly slipped out. So has the United Arab Emirates. There is no trace of the United States in Kabul whose war we are fighting."

The State Department Fact Sheet on Afghanistan, setting right the record of the United States policy on the country in the wake of the United Nations sanctions (which, the United States government took particular pain to emphasise, were directed against the Taleban rule and not Afghanistan per se), significantly picked on the Pakistani media to strengthen its case that there were people outside the realm of the United States who had also begun to see the demerits of the Taleban rule.

"Editorial opinion in Pakistani newspapers generally opposes (the) United Nations Security Council sanctions against the Taleban," the Fact Sheet, dated 17 January 2001, noted. "Some analysts, however, are uneasy with the Taleban's policies and understand the purpose of the sanctions. Several of these writers have called on the Taleban to comply with the United Nations Security Council Resolutions – for the good of Afghanistan and for the greater good of the entire region."

The Fact Sheet quoted *The Frontier Post*, dated 27 December 2000, to the effect, "Virtually the whole world (Pakistan being the sole exception) has kept the Taleban regime in Afghanistan at an arm's length. Do the Taleban really feel convinced that the whole world together is unwise and they alone are the peerless paragons of wisdom? The Taleban who rule Afghanistan should do some stiff heart-searching. They should try to figure out why they are in the kind of predicament that is now their lot... The leaders in Kabul had better start thinking of their country and government as part of the rest of the world."

The Friday Times wrote in its 22-28 December 2000 issue, "The Taleban have subscribed to laws, supposedly Islamic, that have brought both the militia and Islam into disrepute. Their treatment of women and children remains abominable. They have failed to govern the people or divert resources into rebuilding the country... They are involved in smuggling and have given sanctuary to criminals from Pakistan. Most significantly, while Pakistan has continued to go out on a limb to support them, the Taleban have shown a complete disregard for Pakistan's concerns, exposing Islamabad to international condemnation."

The Nation wrote on 17 December 2000, "What the Afghans need is not more Sharia but food, medicine, shelter and a normal life. Most Afghans were practising Muslims before you (the Taleban) came to power. If you would only follow a less rigid interpretation of Sharia and allow people to practise their faith as they have done for centuries, Afghanistan will again become a happy and peaceful country. If you really want an Islamic revival and renaissance, you will have to become tolerant and progressive. You will have to convince the Afghans that your first priority is their well-being and reconstruction and rehabilitation of your destroyed country. You will have to give hope and opportunity to the Afghans who reposed their trust in you in the belief that you would restore peace and stability, end lawlessness, put the country on the path to economic recovery, create conditions for the safe return of refugees, and make the daily life of an ordinary Afghan less harsh, fearful and sad than it was before you came to power."

Neither the Taleban nor the Pakistani government was, however, inclined to take note of the growing restiveness within Pakistan and the complete alienation from the international community that Kabul's policies had brought about. An addendum to the 1 February 2001 report submitted to the fifty-seventh session of the Commission on Human Rights by Special Rapporteur Kamal Hossain, dated 27 March 2001, read in part, "I received a letter dated 1 February 2001 from the Permanent Mission of the Islamic State of Afghanistan to the United Nations Office in Geneva in which it was reported that Taleban forces, in the course of military offensives in the provinces of Takhar and Kunduz, had engaged in mass killings of innocent civilians around 23 January 2001. It was alleged that the victims were found buried in two mass graves and a list of the names of victims in the villages of Bagh Zakheera, Rustaq and Mamayee was enclosed. By a letter dated 19 February 2001, addressed to the Human Rights Commission, the Taleban authorities reported that following an attack on the town of Bamiyan by the opposition forces, crimes and genocide had been committed upon entry into the town by those forces." Both sides later denied the mutual allegations.

The Special Rapporteur, thereafter, commented, "The reports of summary executions and massacres are a source of mounting concern as in recent years the continued conflict and the taking and retaking of particular areas by the warring parties have resulted in massacres involving reprisal killings and summary executions. A recurrent pattern is manifest from the (not exhaustive) list of such occurrences reported over the last four-year period, as follows: Mazar-i-Sharif/Dasht-i-

Laili (Shebergan) in May 1997; Mazar-i-Sharif Airport (Qezelabad) in September 1997; Qaysar in December 1997; Mazar-i-Sharif in August 1998; Kayan Valley in August 1998; Bamiyan in May 1999; Shamali Plains in August 1999; Khwaja Ghar in Takhar province in September 1999; Ghosphandi in Sar-i-Pul province in January 2000; Yakawlang in Bamiyan province in January 2001; Khwaja Ghar in Takhar province in January 2001; and Bamiyan in February 2001."

The Special Rapporteur noted that widespread concern had been expressed at the massacres and summary executions reportedly carried out by one or other of the warring parties at different sites. On 19 January 2001, the United Nations Secretary-General issued a statement expressing concern about "numerous credible reports" that civilians were deliberately targeted and killed in Yakawlang. The Secretary-General called on the Taleban to take "immediate steps to control their forces", adding that the reports required "prompt investigation" and that those responsible should "be brought to justice".

He also noted the statement issued by the United Nations High Commissioner for Human Rights on 16 February 2001, including the reported summary execution of over 100 civilians by Taleban forces in Yakawlang district of Bamiyan province in January 2001, in the following terms, "In view of the pattern of repeated massive violations of human rights and humanitarian law, I call upon the international community to establish an independent international inquiry into the massacres and other grave human rights violations by parties to the conflict in Afghanistan."

It was now increasingly recognised, the Special Rapporteur wrote, that the impunity enjoyed by those who had been responsible for ordering and carrying out the massacres and summary executions and the absence of accountability for such gross violations of human rights and grave breaches of humanitarian law, had contributed to the repeated occurrence of such violations. There was thus a growing opinion that in order to deter and prevent the occurrence of such atrocities, an effective international initiative was called for not only to document, denounce and then cut the sinews of war (arms supplies, external financial support, linkages with drug warlords) but also to expose and hold to account those responsible.

He said that the latest reports of summary executions and massacres provided a challenge and an opportunity to the international community to take the needed initiative. "Reports supported by reliable eyewitnesses document some of the summary executions and massacres carried out in January 2001 in Yakawlang. These reports indicate that in the taking and retaking of Yakawlang, breaches of humanitarian law were committed by both parties as they violated the neutrality of medical facilities in the district and disregarded the rights of civilians to be treated as non-combatants. Yakawlang was captured by the United Front forces (Hizb-i-Wahdat and Harakat-i-Islami) on 28 December 2000, but was recaptured by the Taleban in early January 2001."

He went on to describe what happened next: Taleban forces reached the district centre of Nayak on the morning of 8 January 2001. Following the retaking, there were reports of mass arrests followed by summary executions carried out between 8 and 12 January 2001. A number of aid agency personnel and a United Nations staff member were among those killed. The Human Rights Watch report, published on 19 February 2001, had identified (the) civilian victims, including a number of aid workers and staff of international humanitarian agencies, hospitals and local relief and assistance organisations.

"Crisis of Impunity", the Human Rights Watch (HRW) report, quotes a witness describing the Taleban advance into

Yakawlang. "On the evening of 7 January 2001, a friend told me that a helicopter had been heard flying into Feroz Bahar. Initially, people thought that it was supplying the United Front troops, but it turned out that it had been flying in Taleban troops. That night there were sounds of heavy fighting. In the morning again, we heard intense firing, and there was clearly a battle going on in Nayak (the district centre). Later that morning, Nayak fell and the fighting was over... From 2 p.m. on 8 January, we watched United Front troops retreating, walking past us and with their mounted column, heading west towards lower Yakawlang. There were so many of them that it took the rest of the day for them to pass us – they were trooping past us until late evening. They were heading for Deh Surkh and Daga."

On reaching Nayak, the Taleban organised eleven search parties; each party was allocated one sector of central Yakawlang where it moved from house to house, rounding up male occupants. The search party allocated to Dar-i-Ali commandeered twelve horses and so was able to travel extensively through the valley, only part of which was accessible by road.

The report then quotes another witness describing the capture of the district and the search operations in Dar-i Ali. He first learned of the Taleban advance when Hizb-i-Wahdat troops stationed near his office informed him that a helicopter had landed at Feroz Bahar and that they believed a Taleban attack was imminent. Between midnight and three in the morning, there was heavy fighting all around the area. When there was a lull in the fighting at 3 a.m., the witness fled to Dar-i-Ali. The fighting stopped altogether at around 8 in the morning. At approximately three in the afternoon, he sought shelter in a friend's house but was told by the family that the Taleban had started searching and it was, therefore, not safe to be there. As he came out of the house, the witness ran into a group of Taleban troops who ordered him to join a crowd of men already gathered and heading towards a local aid agency. Three bodies were lying in front of the aid agency; the Taleban soldiers explained that these men had tried to escape. The HRW report then quotes the witness saying, "A group of about one hundred men was gathered at the (aid) centre. After some time, the Taleban ordered us to move, and we were herded down towards Nayak (the district centre). At first, the pace was slow, but after some time we were met by a group of mounted Taleban and the soldiers started to whip the detainees and ordered us to move more quickly. When we got to Nayak, another group of Taleban was waiting there at the entrance to the bazar, armed with sticks. They beat us and told the Taleban in charge of the group to "take them to the Mullah". According to other witnesses, the detainees were herded to the office of a relief agency located at Nayak, where most were later executed.

The atmosphere of utmost panic that gripped the area was conveyed in the following testimony: A witness said, "The same day (10 January 2001), news came that the Taleban were searching houses as far as Girdbayd, some five kilometres from Nayak. People coming from there said that the Taleban had killed some of the people there. We all discussed among ourselves whether this could be true or not. After a couple of days (11 or 12 January 2001), eight or ten of the village elders decided that they must go to Nayak to discuss the security of the area with the Taleban. They set off on foot towards Nayak."

Later on, the witness learned from the elders what happened on the mission. As they were making their way to Nayak, they came upon a local Tajik commander, Jan Agha, sitting on a Taleban pick-up truck near the village of Qala Issa Khan, about 500 metres west of the district centre, and obviously pointing something out to them. But the elders could not fathom what he was pointing at and continued on their journey. As they entered Nayak, nobody stopped them so they went straight into the Taleban command post. They wanted to see Commander Mullah Abdul Sattar who, however, refused to see them; then they managed to see Commander Haji Faqoori and finally, Sattar agreed to meet them and told them that he had just received orders from Mullah Mohammed Omar in Kandahar declaring a general amnesty. He then instructed the elders to go and meet Hizb-i-Wahdat Commander Karim Khalili to tell him that the fighting must be stopped or there would be more killing.

It was on their return trip that Jan Agha clarified what he was trying to tell them earlier: a pile of bodies lying at the edge of Qala Issa Khan. A massacre had already taken place. As Khalili refused to give up fighting, however, many villagers began to leave for safer areas.

This particular group of elders appeared to have been luckier than several others. The HRW report mentions at least two instances when teams of village elders who were intrepid enough to seek to intercede with the Taleban seeking safety and security for their communities paid with their lives. On 9 January 2001, the entire group of elders of Kata Khana village was killed; only two were spared. When the elders of Bed Mushkin village called on the Taleban to discuss security, all except one were gunned down.

The HRW report says that the main execution site in Yakawlang, however, appeared to have been outside the relief agency in Nayak, the district centre, where the detainees from Dar-i-Ali were killed. Witnesses also reported seeing piles of bodies in four other locations in and around Nayak: outside the district hospital, in the ravine behind the mosque in the old bazaar area, outside the prayer hall of Mindayak village, and at Qala Arbab Hassan. "Of these, the largest pile of bodies was at Qala Arbab Hassan," says the report. Other killings were reported from neighbourhoods in areas surrounding the district centre, including outside the leprosy and tuberculosis clinics. A witness, who visited Yakawlang district four weeks after the incident, inspected one of the mass graves at Bed Mushkin village, in which twenty-six bodies had been found. One of the bodies was that of a seventeen-year-old boy, Mir Ali, much of his skin had been removed either prior to or after his death. In a separate case, seven men were shot dead at the Zarin crossroad near the leprosy clinic in Yakawlang.

The HRW report says eyewitnesses reported that personnel of the Centre for Cooperation on Afghanistan, a local aid agency, identified as Sayyid Sarwar and Sayyid Talib, were among the civilians rounded up at Dar-i-Ali and executed outside the relief agency office. Other staff members of relief agencies were identified among those killed. These included a driver named Daoud who was working for an international humanitarian agency; a man named Qasim who worked as an assistant in the leprosy clinic; and Sayyid Ibrahim and a man named Tahsili, both of whom worked in the district hospital and were staff members of a local assistance organisation. Witnesses reported seeing a Land Cruiser and a Russian-made jeep in the possession of the Taleban, both of which belonged to the Yakawlang offices of humanitarian aid organisations.

Commenting on the genocide in Yakawlang, Amnesty International said on 25 January 2001, "Taleban officials issued an order to its forces to kill all men between the ages of 13 and 70 living in the Yakawlang area. These deeply disturbing reports once again underline the need for action by the international community to ensure protection of the civilian population in Afghanistan. Numerous reports have emerged regarding the Taleban's latest acts of atrocities committed against the predominantly Hazaras population in central Afghanistan. Non-governmental organisations calculate that approximately 600 Afghans were killed and dozens more injured by Taleban forces, including humanitarian aid workers and even patients in medical facilities. According to the Afghan Islamic Press, opposition forces in Afghanistan have discovered three mass graves, containing at least seventy bodies, including those of many women and children, found 28 miles north of Taloqan.

Towards the end of October 2000, a development occurred leading to a fresh escalation in tension in the region. On 25 October, Russian Defence Minister Marshal Igor Sergeyev and his counterpart in the Islamic State of Afghanistan Commander Ahmad Shah Massoud met in Dushanbe, the capital of Tajikistan, the first ever meeting between the top Russian defence official and a leader of the United Front. At the meeting, which took place in the backdrop of a conference of the Commonwealth of Independent States and attracted wide attention for its significance, Russia pledged military support to anti-Taleban forces including possible air strikes. While no official version of the meeting was made available, the Russian media reported that the two sides had discussed Russian military aid to the embattled opposition forces which had been pushed north to the border with Tajikistan by the advancing Taleban forces. Massoud had launched a counter-offensive on Taleban positions in Takhar province but he obviously urgently required air and artillery support to recapture Taloqan, which had proved to be a strong base for the Taleban in northern Afghanistan.

Interestingly, Marshal Sergeyev also conferred with the Iranian Foreign Minister Kamal Kharazi. "We discussed regional security, including the situation in Afghanistan," the Russian Minister later told the media. "Central Asia is slowly becoming the capital of international terrorism with Islamic extremists trying to redraw the map of the region. If the Taleban move any closer to the Tajik border, then there will definitely be armed confrontation. Significantly, the Russian United Front defence ministers' meeting was preceded by two consultations the Russian government had held in the immediate past, one in New Delhi during the India-Russia summit and the other in Washington DC between the Russian Foreign Ministry and the US department of State. The indication was that the Russian offer of military help to Massoud was made only after these two consultations.

When the BBC asked "Amir-ul-Mumineen" Mullah Omar about the meeting in Dushanbe, this was what he said: "The Russians had oppressed the Afghan people, killed millions of Muslims in Afghanistan and destroyed the country. They are the root cause of all misfortunes suffered by the Afghan people. The meeting of Ahmad Shah Massoud with the Russian defence minister in an atmosphere of mutual security cooperation is akin to destruction for Massoud, because he used to consider himself to be from the mujahideen, but now he has proven, by throwing himself into the embrace of the Russians, that he is their puppet and deputy in Afghanistan."

A more substantive response came from the Taleban spokesman in Kabul, Abdul Hai Mutamain, who threatened, "The consequences (of Russian military help) would be very dangerous if it continues to do so. We can create lots of problems for the Russians and inflict heavy losses on them."

On 11 November 2000, ten mortar mines fired by the Taleban exploded near villages in Tajikistan, prompting a Russian warning that retaliatory strikes could be expected if the Taleban continued to shell the northern neighbour. The Tajikistan-Afghanistan border was being guarded by Russian forces. The Russian border guards said that Taleban artillery were frequently hitting Tajik territory across the border, apparently hoping to invoke retaliation. The guards were quoted by the Russian media saying that in order to avoid further damages to Tajikistan, "a decision may be taken to hit Taleban artillery which is deployed close to the border with Tajikistan".

While the year 2000 was drawing to a close, Dr Olivier Roy of the Centre National des Recherches' Scientifiques (CNRS), France, summed up the situation in the war-devastated country, "I see a strategic realignment in Central Asia now among the new republics. Tajikistan has supported Commander Massoud against the Taleban and is itself supported by the Russians and Iranians. On the other hand, Uzbekistan, a country that was until recently very opposed to the Taleban, has mended fences with them and is beginning some rapprochement with the Taleban. Turkmenistan has already made an agreement with the Taleban. We have on one side, Tajikistan, Russia and Iran, and on the other hand, Uzbekistan and Turkmenistan."[14]

Asked if the change in Uzbekistan's policy was driven by commercial interests, Roy said, "No, for Turkmenistan it's a commercial and trade issue, not for Uzbekistan. I think the problem for the Uzbeks is to assess what is the main threat. Tashkent is hesitating between two priorities. Either they consider that the main threat is Tajikistan – because of certain kind of pan-Tajikistan for example – or they consider the Islamists as the main threat. By getting closer to the Taleban, Tashkent hopes to win on both sides. Tashkent hopes to weaken the Tajik coalition and, also, hopes that the Taleban will decrease or even stop their support for the Uzbek Islamic Movement, which is presently based in Afghanistan."

Roy also analysed how the Islamist movement started in Afghanistan in the 1980s mainly to fight the communist regime and the Soviet occupation transformed itself from the mid-1990s to an international jihadi movement directed against Western interests. He said, "In the 1980s, the bulk of the mujahideen movements in Afghanistan was Islamist. By that, I mean that they wanted to establish an Islamic government in Afghanistan, and they were supported by Pakistan and the Pakistani religious movements. What we saw at the end of the 80s was sort of a gap between the Islamist movement in Afghanistan, whose members were mainly Afghan nationalists and more and more secular like Massoud, and an Islamist movement that retained strong supra-national and international connections. These connections were established in the mid-1980s when hundreds and thousands of foreign Islamic militants came to Afghanistan to fight against the Soviets. The bulk of these volunteers were supporting Gulbuddin Hekmatyar and groups that are now known as the Taleban. So, it was a kind of hijacking of a part of the Afghan resistance by international networks, who were not so much interested in the freedom of Afghanistan and the establishment of a stable government, but who were engaged in overall jihad, not only in Afghanistan, but also in Kashmir, Central Asia and other places. So, I would say that there was a growing gap between the Islamo-nationalist movements, that wanted to, first, free their own countries like Afghanistan and Tajikistan... and the international movement headed now by Osama bin Laden, who does not care about establishing a stable government, but wants to wage a universal jihad against the Russians, the Americans and even the Iranians."

****

Endnotes

1. Krieken, Jet van, "The Buddhas of Bamiyan: Challenged Witnesses of Afghanistan's Forgotten Past", International Institute for Asian Studies, Newsletter 2000, University of Leiden, Holland.
2. Rathje, W. L., "Special Report: Archaeological Terrorism: What's Behind the Assassination of Two Colossal Buddhas?", http://www.discoveringarchaeology.com, 19 April 2001.
3. An interview of Islamic State of Afghanistan ambassador in New Delhi, Masood Khalili, in April 2001.
4. Goodwin, Jan, "Buried Alive: Afghan Women under the Taliban", 27 February 1998.
5. Journal of the American Medical Association, 5 August 1998.
6. Mukarji, Apratim, *The Hindustan Times*, New Delhi, 10 December 1997.
7. In an interview to the author in New Delhi.
8. ibid., 7 February 1998.
9. Mukarji, Apratim, "ISI, Taliban and Osama bin Laden hatched plans for... simultaneous offensive in J & K, Afghanistan", *The Hindustan Times*, New Delhi, 9 July 1999.
10. Bodansky, Yossef, *Bin Laden...* pp.320-321.
11. Mukarji, Apratim, *The Hindustan Times*, 31 July 1999.
12. Tomsen, Peter, "A Chance for Peace in Afghanistan: The Taliban's Days are Numbered," Foreign Affairs, Jan.-Feb. 2000.
14. Roy, Dr Olivier, in an interview to Azadi Afghan Radio, 4 November 2000.

4
Terrorism at the Centre-Stage

On 30 September 2002, a confidential report was read out to the members of the United Nations Security Council which must have sent chills down the spine of many in the audience. An experts' panel, appointed by the Security Council, called the Monitoring Group to track the implementation of measures against terrorist groups, said in the report that a year after Operation Enduring Freedom and Operation Anaconda and the continuing operations in Afghanistan and Pakistan to hunt down the remnants of al-Qaeda and the Taleban, "Al-Qaeda is fit and well and poised to strike again at its leisure".

The report said that despite the plethora of international action, the al-Qaeda terrorist network had been able to retain its financial support and remained a deadly threat. "Members of al-Qaeda and their associates are deployed in many countries across the world and, given the opportunity, they will have no compunction in killing as many people as they can from those nations that do not conform to their religious and ideological beliefs and which they perceive as their enemies."

The report also said that despite having lost its physical base and sanctuary in Afghanistan, al-Qaeda continued to have operational links with militant Islamic groups in Europe, North America, North Africa, the Middle East and Asia, and remained able to recruit new members and plan and launch future terrorist attacks. "The terrorist organisation's diffuse leadership, loose structure and absence of centralised command and control make it hard to detect and eradicate," it added.

The Monitoring Group said that one problem ineffectively stemming the activities of al-Qaeda was a lack of coordinated action among the United Nations member-countries. This was due to the fact that only a few of those individuals detained, sought and identified by states were included on the United Nations' consolidated list of those under sanctions. Instead, the member-countries were using their own lists "unevenly", a practice which was seriously diminishing the effectiveness of responses to deal with terrorist groups and individuals. The member-nations would naturally have to make a "much greater use" of the United Nations' consolidated list.

The Monitoring Group also found out that even though the concerted action by the member-countries had succeeded in freezing al-Qaeda assets to the tune of $112 million, the network had continued to have access to "considerable financial and other economic resources". The group recommended increased intelligence and information sharing among the member-countries in order to achieve better results in detecting and arresting the course of funds transfers to al-Qaeda. It also urged greater efforts by the member-countries to track and close down businesses supporting al-Qaeda and to better regulate alternative banking systems.

The report further said that members of al-Qaeda and the Taleban "continue to move undetected across international boundaries" and urged that the member-countries adopt stricter border control regimes. As arms continued to be smuggled across to terrorist groups, the report recommended that the member-states should undertake certain measures to disrupt the illegal sales and supplies of arms and ammunition to al-Qaeda and its associates.

A little earlier in September, an article by the chief of the Pakistan-based terrorist group Lashkar-e-Toiba, Hafiz Muhammad Saeed had attracted wide attention, as he had asserted that both Osama bin Laden and Mullah Omar were safe despite the unrelenting satellite surveillance by the United States. While the Americans and the Pakistanis had been conducting search and extermination operations in eastern and southern Afghanistan and in the western border areas of Pakistan, the mujahideen had been able to regroup. "The patience and endurance shown by the Taleban and the Arab mujahideen and the tyrannies of the United States and its allies from Tora Bora to Guantanamo (Bay) has proved (that) the Muslims are the victims and the United States is a tyrant," Saeed wrote.[1]

While noting with some satisfaction that "even Pakistan, the most reliable ally of Washington in the Muslim world, has refused to support America in its aggression against Iraq, clearly saying that it will be an attack on an Islamic country," the terrorist chief said that "Muslim leaders should have taken a stand against the American operations against Afghanistan (under the Taleban)."

"We also request," he added, "the secular class of Pakistan and politicians to amend their ways. Their enmity and hatred against jihad and mujahideen has enabled the United States and Jews to make inroads into the country."

In a note of warning, Saeed wrote, "If the disbelievers have come in (to) the battlefield after naming jihad as terrorism, then the thinking of Muslims has also changed. Their hatred against the disbelief is changing fast into anger. Fidayeen missions in Kashmir and Palestine, where Muslim women are offering sacrifice of their lives along with young boys, is a mark of a new light."

In the backdrop of slowly rising incidences of terrorism in Afghanistan, exemplified by the 6 July assassination of Vice-President Haji Abdul Qadeer, the 5 September assassination attempt on President Hamid Karzai and the car-bomb explosion in Kabul killing over a score of civilians, Saeed said, "Jihad news are pouring in from Afghanistan. Mujahideen have recomposed themselves and have initiated their favourite job. They are also dominating in Kashmir, adding to the helplessness of occupying Indian forces."

On 27 September 2002, the former Taleban ambassador to the United Arab Emirates and presently the chief of Tehreek Jamiat Muslimeen (Movement of Young Muslims) Naseer Ahmed Rohni told a select group of journalists in Peshawar that Osama bin Laden and Mullah Omar were not only living in Afghanistan but were also in contact with each other.

Rohni made several other claims: one, that he had met Mullah Omar in Afghanistan a fortnight before, to receive "instructions". "Mullah Omar is in high spirits and is commanding mujahideen in Afghanistan," he added.

His second claim: over 5,000 Taleban fighters were engaged in fighting the United States-led coalition forces in Afghanistan. Thirdly, he claimed that his men who were fighting in Afghanistan had shot down a B-52 bomber in Bandsarda area of Paktia province and had ransacked and destroyed the office of a Christian missionary non-governmental organisation in Ghazni province. His fourth claim: while the Pakistan government had announced that it had handed over 400 Taleban leaders and supporters to the United States, Rohni said that the correct number was over 1,000.

There was some kind of confirmation of the speculation over the survival of bin Laden and Mullah Omar when *The*

Observer Weekly reported on 6 October 2002 that interceptions by United States spy satellites of a telephonic conversation between bin Laden and Mullah Omar that had occurred a month ago had revealed that both were living and meeting each other.

As revealed by the Americans, Mullah Omar and an aide were heard discussing the United States-led hunt for them. The two men were using a mobile Thuraya satellite phone and discussing tactics for several minutes. Mullah Omar was then heard turning to a third person who was obviously in proximity to him. After exchanging a few words with the third person, Mullah Omar was heard saying, "The Sheikh sends his *salaam* (greetings)." In Islamic terrorist circles in Afghanistan and Pakistan, bin Laden is referred to as the Sheikh. On the eve of general elections in Pakistan held on 10 October 2002, a letter purported to have been written by bin Laden was circulated in the frontier areas of Pakistan, exhorting the people to end the rule of President Pervez Musharraf. While the Pakistan government took little notice of the letter, there were good reasons to believe that it was a hoax.

As efforts to destabilise the post-Taleban Afghanistan are clearly visible, in which the shadowy presence of al-Qaeda and the Taleban is being felt, it is easier to appreciate that the true tragedy of Afghanistan that took place towards the end of the twentieth century and at the beginning of the twenty-first century was the "hijacking" (as Dr Olivier Roy calls it so aptly[2]) of the Islamist nationalist movement in Afghanistan by the international movement against established governments and nation-states spearheaded by a conglomerate of terrorist groups, the most visible face of which was the Saudi moth of international terrorism Osama bin L
Afghanistan was concerned, the hija
because the Taleban proved to

There are certain aspects of Osama bin Laden's life which are intimately interwoven with the recent Afghan history; and, therefore, the recalling of one necessarily brings in the other, too. For instance, bin Laden was one of the first Arabs to join the jihad in Afghanistan. While he proved to be an important contributor to the strengthening of the jihad in the years to come (he organised the Arabs' participation in the jihad, which meant that thousands of Arab militants joined and fought in the jihad against the Soviet occupation in Afghanistan by his courtesy), he himself came to regard his joining the jihad as a turning point in his life. "The Soviet Union invaded Afghanistan, and the mujahideen put out an international plea for help. I was inspired by the plight of Muslims in a medieval society besieged by a twentieth-century superpower… In our religion, there is a special place in the hereafter for those who participate in jihad. One day in Afghanistan was like one thousand days of praying in an ordinary mosque."[3]

Osama bin Laden's involvement with the Afghan jihad proved to be a boon for the cause. He not only paid passage fares up to Pakistan and Afghanistan for all Arab volunteers in the beginning but also set up training camps in Pakistan to prepare Arab mujahideen to fight in Afghanistan. In early 1980, he established Ma'sadat Al-Ansar, the main base at the time for the Arabs fighting the Soviet army. It was around this time that he also came in contact with Sheikh Abdallah Yussuf Azzam, a Jordanian, a PhD in Islamic jurisprudence from al-Azhar University, Cairo. Thus, the first ever contact between bin Laden, Azzam and the Egyptian Islamists came to be established, for Azzam had developed close contacts with the latter during his tenure at al-Azhar. Azzam and bin Laden, ording to some accounts, were already acquainted when was teaching at King Abdul Aziz University, Jeddah, en was a student. This particular point in the life of bin Laden and, indeed, in the history of international Islamist movement, gained in importance because this was when Azzam developed his doctrine of the centrality of the jihad to the eventual liberation of the Muslim world from the harmful effects of Westernisation. Bodansky quotes Azzam telling his students, "Jihad and the rifle alone; no negotiations, no conferences, and no dialogues."[4]

If the gradually lengthening role of Osama bin Laden and of Arab mujahideen in the Afghan jihad brought in Saudi Arabian influence on the resistance fighters, and through them on Afghanistan itself in the years to come, Islam itself in Afghanistan also began to change and acquire alien characteristics through the same process, albeit almost imperceptibly in the beginning. The end result of this process was only manifest years later, in the form of the Taleban who established the hardest form of Islam seen anywhere in the world.

The most striking aspect of Islam, as practised in Afghanistan through the centuries, was its liberalism; despite the Sunni Hanafi branch of Islam to which the majority Pushtuns belonged, the Islamic Afghanistan was traditionally characterised by a very potent presence of Sufism, which is mystical Islam and a highly tolerant, understanding, embracing rather than rejecting, kind of religious approach to life and god. Rashid quotes Arab traveller Ibn Batuta describing Sufism as: "The fundamental aim of the Sufi life was to pierce the veils of human sense which shut man off from the Divine and so to obtain communion and absorption into God."[5]

Three factors that provided leadership to the Afghan jihad ensured that this Afghan religious tradition of liberalism and tolerance was replaced decisively by Wahabbism, which was part of the Sunni Hanifi creed but exclusively Saudi Arabian in origin and character. The funding of the jihad, which was dispersed through the ISI and provided by the CIA of the United States and Saudi Arabia, also came to determine the eclipse of the genuinely Afghan resistance movement spearheaded by Jabba-i Najat Milli Afghanistan led by Sibgatullah Mujaddedi (who later emerged as the first mujahideen president of Afghanistan in 1992) and Mahaz-e-Milli, led by Pir Sayed Ahmad Gailani. Instead, the CIA-ISI nexus boosted Gulbuddin Hekmatyar, Ahmad Shah Massoud, Burhanuddin Rabbani and Abdul Rasul Sayyaf, the latter setting up a Wahabbi party called Ittehad-e-Islami. But Sufism was so strongly entrenched in the Afghan mind that Wahabbism, despite being promoted by the fund-providing CIA-ISI nexus, could not take roots amongst the Afghan mujahideen.

Yet, radical Islam came to Afghan mujahideen through the radical parties set up by the earliest protégés of Pakistan, Gulbuddin Hekmatyar, an engineering graduate of Kabul University, and Massoud, a student of the French Lycée in Kabul, both of whom received their political lessons from Jamaat-i-Islami, the most radical Islamic party in the neighbouring country (the JI itself drew its inspiration from Ikhwan-ul-Muslimeen or the Muslim Brotherhood). What did happen in Afghanistan only in the mid-1990s, the emergence of the rabidly fundamentalist Taleban, thus had its beginning in the convergence of young Afghan western-educated mujahideen and radical Islam of Pakistan under the benign patronage of the CIA-ISI nexus. A short time later, with the arrival of Osama bin Laden and the swift widening of Arab presence in the jihad, radical Islam did get a boost. And all this while, the traditional Afghan religious approach of liberalism and tolerance continued to be sidelined.

The remarkable story of the twist in the political inclinations of the Afghans during the jihad would not be complete without referring to the initial Taleban response. It was no coincidence that the majority of Afghan mujahideen, led by the poor and modest village-based mullahs, preferred to align themselves with the two traditional tribal-based parties, Harakat-Inquilab-i-Islami led by Maulvi Mohammed Nabi Mohammedi, and Hizb-i-Islami led by Maulvi Younis Khalis, rather than with the radical parties set up under the Pakistani patronage. It needs to be emphasised that Pakistan displayed considerable hesitation and even latent hostility towards the Taleban when the latter had launched their amazing rise to prominence. Islamabad tried its best to stick to Hekmatyar and that was why the latter's party continued to receive the largest chunk of the ISI patronage even after the Taleban had begun to gain territory. The ISI decided to chuck Hekmatyar only when his inability to deliver goods was established beyond doubt. He is, however, very much back in the ISI's reckoning, and according to reliable sources, he is active once again in eastern Afghanistan in a bid to destabilise the Transitional Islamic Government of Afghanistan with the blessings of the ISI.

Yet another transformation took place, this time within the young western-educated young mujahideen. Gulbuddin Hekmatyar grew in strength as his party, Hizb-i-Islami, continued to attract the largest share of the western booty through the open patronage of the ISI and, consequently, more and more Afghan adherents. Even Hekmatyar and Hizb-i-Islami would, however, be eclipsed by the fanaticism that was to be displayed by the Taleban in later years. But the seeds of what happened in Afghanistan between 1996 and 2001 were definitely planted and nourished in Pakistan in the early 1980s. Ahmad Shah Massoud, on the other hand, drew himself and his followers away from the influence of Wahabbism in a fast course of disorientation as he realised that the role of Pakistan in promoting the jihad was compromised by its desire to create and install its puppets in Kabul and thus retain Afghanistan as a perpetual vassal state to serve its geo-political interests and goals.

Rashid notes that the Talebanesque interpretation of Islam, jihad and social transformation was an anomaly in Afghanistan because the rise of the movement echoed none of the leading Islamicist trends that had emerged through the anti-Soviet war. "The Taleban were neither radical Islamicists inspired by the Ikhwan, nor mystical Sufis, nor traditionalists," he says. "They fitted nowhere in the Islamic spectrum of ideas and movements that had emerged in Afghanistan between 1979 and 1994." Where did the Taleban spring from, then? He provides the answer, "It could be said that the degeneration and collapse of legitimacy of all (the) three trends (radical Islamicism, Sufism and traditionalism) into a naked, rapacious power struggle created the ideological vacuum which the Taleban were to fill. The Taleban represented nobody but themselves and they recognised no Islam except their own. But they did have an ideological base – an extreme form of Deobandism, which was being preached by Pakistani Islamic parties in Afghan refugee camps in Pakistan."[6]

Bodansky, however, provides a geo-political analysis of the origin and emergence of the Taleban. According to him, the Jalalabad battle of March 1989 marked the beginning of the decline of Arab Islamicism as a principal contributing factor to the jihad and paved ultimately the way for the rise of the Taleban. The ISI literally pushed the mujahideen into the battle, which was heavily stacked against them. Jalalabad was very well fortified and the mujahideen stood little chance of taking it from the Soviets. The resultant massive carnage, therefore, was least surprising; but, to go by Bodansky's account, the ISI's purpose of decimating the resistance was fulfilled. "The road was open for Islamabad to organise and field its own 'mujahideen' force, now known as the Taleban," he says.[7]

An ancient Durga, saved by the Kabul Museum staff from the Taleban in April 2001.

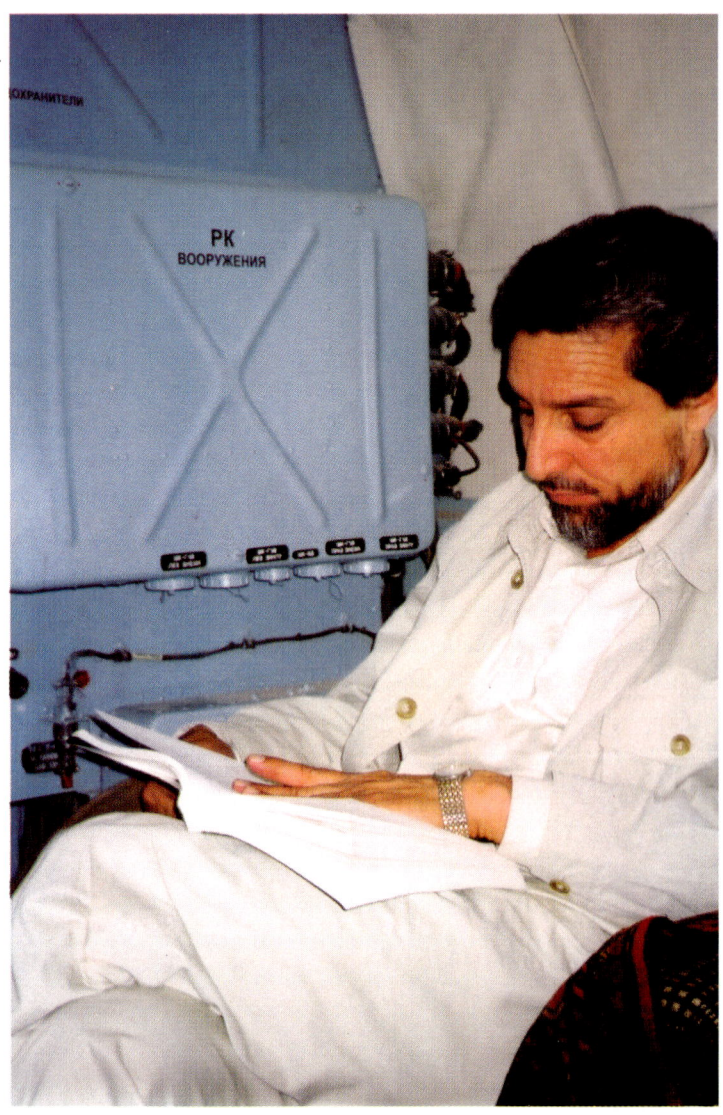

The last photograph of Commander Ahmad Shah Massoud, taken twenty-four hours before his assassination.
(*Photo:* Ambassador Masood Khalili)

Panjsher valley, the natural fortress, begins here. The Soviet army laid siege to the valley seven times and was forced to retreat each time.

Remnant of destroyed Soviet tank in Panjsher valley.

1981. Commander Massoud addressing the people in Panjsher valley during the early days of the mujahideen fight against the Soviets.

April 2001. Commander Massoud addressing the Afghan diaspora in Paris. Also seen is Masood Khalili, presently Ambassador of Afghanistan in India. (*Photo:* Reza)

He notes that Osama bin Laden and many Arab mujahideen participated in the battle and saw for themselves the effects of the ill-advised offensive, and on their return to Pakistan, discussed the "betrayal" perpetrated on the dedicated mujahideen by the ISI. Sheikh Azzam was said to have been furious; and as discussions ensued, Azzam, Osama bin Laden and others reached the conclusion that the foolhardy but deliberately planned offensive was actually part of the American conspiracy, implemented through the Pakistanis, to discredit and thus weaken the very concept of Islamic jihad. Azzam immediately got on to the job of reviving the original spirit of the Afghan jihad and thus, apparently, became the main obstacle to the ISI's gameplan. Shortly thereafter, Azzam and two of his sons were killed in a powerful car-bomb explosion in Peshawar. While the hand behind the killing was never revealed, suspicion hovered around the ISI, for it gained enormously from the prompt removal of Azzam from the scene.

The Nida'ul Islam magazine, which propagates the concept of the Ummah (the re-establishment of the Caliphate, a transnational Muslim region, and, thereby, uniting the Muslim world in one political system) offered an interpretation of the rise of the Taleban and their role in Afghanistan in the light of the tenets of the international Islamicist movement. "The emergence of the Taleban movement and its control over more than eighty per cent of the Afghan lands has undoubtedly upset the equilibrium, on the regional and international levels. Thus, conspiracies were installed to influence it, in order to preserve the interests of various sides. These dangers that face the movement materialise as follows: firstly, the trials of assimilation; secondly, the Shiaite-Communist Confederation."[8]

The first factor is regarded as the more serious danger on the movement due to the following reasons:

- The integration of many leaders from different parties to the movement. The concern being the lack of solid organisational correlation with the chief leaders, which may be utilised by the enemies of Allah like the United States and its puppets;
- The Saudi attempts to attract some of the leaders by way of exploiting the glistening lands of the two Holy Mosques in accepting them as visitors for Umrah and Hajj and by showering them with money and gifts;
- The United Nations' activities in using its programmes to control or influence some of the regions, especially its food and health programmes;
- The activities of the American-Arab intelligence who spread their officials in different Afghan cities, especially the capitals. It is no surprise if they were involved in the bombing of the police headquarters in Jalalabad; and
- The activities of the Pakistani government in order to control them, noting that Afghanistan represents an important ground for the general politics of Pakistan, even with the different successor governments, its enmity with India, Iran and others remain the same.

Speaking about the Taleban-Arab mujahideen relations, the fundamentalist magazine said, "With the movement of Sheikh Osama bin Laden to Afghanistan upon the compliance of the Sudanese government with the American-Saudi pressure to expel him, bin Laden resided in the company of one of the leaders of Hizb-i-Islami, Maulvi Mohammed Younis Khalis, in the Nangarhar region. He was then surrounded by the Arab mujahideen who dispersed, after the end of the jihad against the communist invaders, in Pakistan and areas of Afghanistan because they were pursued by Arab intelligence officials, even though many of them were occupied with seeking knowledge, business or securing sustenance for themselves and their families."

The Arab pressure, the magazine continued, especially that of the Saudi, for handing over bin Laden, increased. Younis Khalis refused this instruction and said to Sulaiman Al-Ali, the Saudi family ambassador to Afghanistan: "O Sulaiman! We are the Afghans. If the livestock in the lands of the two Holy Mosques, the cattle, sheep and camels, sought our protection, we will surely protect it in the best manner and we would not hand it over to no one. So, in what way do we deal with a man who we saw from nothing but support, jihad and bestowment? And these are the graves of his brethren and their martyrs are in every region of Afghanistan? This will not be!"

When the Taleban entered Jalalabad, the magazine said, and their rule became stabilised, the movement's deputations passed by the Sheikh, saluting him in honour and dignity. One of the commanders said to Sheikh Osama – this account was from an eyewitness: "O Sheikh! Our lands are not the lands of the Afghans, but it is the lands of Allah; and our jihad was not the jihad of the Afghans, but it was the jihad of the Muslims. Your martyrs that are in every region of Afghanistan, their graves testify to that. You are between your families and kinsmen, and we bless the soil that you walk upon."

"This was translated to practice," the magazine said, "when the leaders of the Taleban refused to even discuss the matter of handing him over (to) the Saudis when they visited their country to obtain recognition of their government."

The leadership role that bin Laden and the "Afghan" Arabs, as well as all the other foreigners who later joined the terrorist camp network run by al-Qaeda in Afghanistan came to acquire in the following years, grew as the dependence of the Taleban on the relatively better fighting abilities of the former became a crucial factor in the desperate fight to conclusively defeat the United Front forces and complete the occupation of the country. The dependence was manifest within the first one month of the fighting that erupted after Operation Enduring Freedom was launched. "The Arabs and not the Afghan Taleban fighters are controlling important parts of the country and fighting major battles on frontlines," a Pakistani newspaper reported.[9]

Talking to the people of Kandahar and those close to the Taleban revealed that Arab troops had taken control immediately after the bombings by the United States and allied forces started. "The power centre shifted to the Arabs as they were the main fighters," a Kandahar resident was quoted saying. The Taleban still had all the liberty to frame their own rules and apply these on the locals but not on the Arabs themselves. "The Arabs are the real fighters who are repulsing the attacks of the (United Front) and United States allies on Kabul and Mazar-i-Sharif," the newspaper quoted a foreign non-Arab fighter who, for the past three years, had worked as a cook for the Arabs. Before the attacks (under Operation Enduring Freedom), the newspaper account held, the Taleban "had all the powers", but the scenario changed thereafter, and the Arabs emerged in Afghanistan "as the real rulers". Sheikh Osama bin Laden "had the last word on all matters and no one could disobey his orders". "During my visit to Kandahar city," wrote the news correspondent, "it was observed that the spying network of the United States was very strong and working quite efficiently. The majority of the sites attacked by the United States forces were those that were used by the Taleban or the Arabs in recent days."

The newspaper provided an interesting peep into the psychology of the Taleban under the impact of Operation Enduring Freedom. "The Taleban too are very sensitive about spying and they do not tolerate strangers," the report said. "Any suspicion on any person and he is immediately hanged, no questions asked." There were, however, saboteurs from the United Front and the Soviet era communist parties who ostensibly swore by the Taleban but were actually passing on vital information to the United States. "(The) attacks on Mullah Omar's home, jeep and on a building that he had left just (a) few hours ago were some examples of these insider jobs," the correspondent said, without divulging his source of information.

The extent of the influence of al-Qaeda and bin Laden on the Taleban-ruled Afghanistan was well-reflected in a confidential memo that the Russian government submitted to the United Nations on 9 March 2001.[10]

According to the memo, bin Laden ran at least fifty-five bases or offices involving over 13,000 men of various nationalities, ranging from Arabs and Pakistanis to Chechens and Philipinos. Besides, there were 3,500 fundamentalist Pakistanis as well as Pakistani soldiers and diplomats who were working as advisers to the Taleban. The memo contained the names of thiry-one Pakistani "advisers" to the Taleban.

Most of the facilities run by bin Laden were concentrated in or around the main cities of Kabul, Kandahar, Jalalabad and Mazar-i-Sharif. The bases were set up using the former Afghan army bases, on large farms previously owned by the state and in caves in rugged mountain regions. There were about 150 fighters based in Bagh-i-Bala, a hilltop restaurant that was once the most fashionable place to dine for sophisticated Kabul residents.

The memo identified the Seventh Division base of the former Afghan army at Rishkhor, south of Kabul, as the main al-Qaeda base. Run by bin Laden's deputy Qari Saifullah Akhtar, there were 7,000 fighters at the base in March 2001, including 150 Arabs and Pakistani fundamentalists "as well as a Pakistani army regiment." In a nearby camp, there were instructors from Libya, Tunisia and Egypt. Further south in Charasyab, at a former base for the mujahideen when they fought the Soviet occupation, Taleban fighters counted among themselves fifty Philipinos and forty Uighurs from Xinjiang province of western China. The memo claimed that at least 2,560 Chechens were either serving in or training with al-Qaeda. An unknown number of Czechs and Bulgarians were reported to be active at a well-defended base in Logar province, south of Kabul. The memo indicated that there was no military installation in Kandahar, the seat of Taleban supremo Mullah Omar. In the strategic Jalalabad province, the bin Laden units were based in Jalalabad city, in two large Soviet-built state farms and at former army posts close to the border with Pakistan.

According to the memo, Pakistanis were running as many as nineteen camps. There were six Pakistanis who held senior posts in the Taleban military, and a former royal palace in southwestern Kabul functioned as the "headquarters of the commander-in-chief of the Pakistani forces in Afghanistan." One Pakistani AWACS reconnaissance plane, originally provided by the United States to monitor Soviet and Afghan air activity during the jihad, was based at Mazar-i-Sharif specifically to survey the Afghan borders with Turkmenistan and Uzbekistan.

The elaborate terrorist infrastructure (the majority of the training camps were churning out graduate terrorists to work all over the world; few were joining the Taleban fighting force) thus built up by bin Laden within Afghanistan lies destroyed in the aftermath of Operation Enduring Freedom and Operation Anaconda. However, it is important to note that the gradual, and still muted, rebirth of the Taleban-al-Qaeda network within the country provides a clear indication that some of the infrastructure were either never destroyed in the United States-led bombings or have since been repaired and revived. This became apparent when the United States, facing rising Afghan resentment over the accidental bombing of a marriage party in southern Afghanistan on 1 July 2002, in which the Afghan government said forty-eight civilians were killed, went to great lengths in order to clear its name. The outcome of the painstaking United States probe will be helpful in appreciating the enduring dangers from the surviving Taleban-al-Qaeda network within Afghanistan.

The probe was carried out by the United States Central Command headquartered at MacDill Air Force Base in Tampa, Florida. According to the report, the Deh Rawod area of Afghanistan is considered the "home" of the Taleban and *remains an area where the Taleban enjoy popular support.* The extended families of both Mullah Omar and Mullah Berader, the former "Senior Military Commander" of the Taleban, reside in the area.[11]

Coalition aircraft have regularly been the target of hostile fire from the Deh Rawod area, the probe report points out. While ineffective, the fire was *clearly intentional and directed toward coalition forces. Two weeks prior to Operation Full Throttle, covert reconnaisance of the area was conducted. Gunfire from various calibre weapons was observed throughout the day and at night, including mortars and anti-aircraft fire. The Deh Rawod area appeared to support enemy military training.*

The operation was undertaken in order to render the Deh Rawod area unsuitable for an enemy sanctuary. Afghan forces were involved in the execution of the mission.

Two days before the incident (in July 2002), additional reconnaissance teams were inserted into positions where they could observe the specific objectives and the approaches that coalition ground and airborne forces would take to execute their missions. *Hostile fire was directed at coalition helicopters conducting these insertions, forcing at least one to land at an alternate site.* During this period of increased and focused reconnaissance, every time a coalition aircraft appeared overhead or could be heard at night, ground fire was directed at it. These fires were traced back to their source locations on the ground. From the nature and characteristics of the fires, it was clear that these were anti-aircraft fire and not small arms.

Several compounds in the Deh Rawod area were positively identified as sources of this anti-aircraft fire. The anti-aircraft fire had emanated from these compounds on repeated occasions over the previous two days and the source of the fires did not change. In all cases, the locations of these compounds were such that they could range and threaten coalition ground and airborne forces that were to execute Operation Full Throttle. On-call close air support assets were assigned to Operation Full Throttle to counter these threats, should anti-aircraft guns in these compounds become active in the moments immediately preceding the introduction of coalition forces into the area.

As coalition ground and airborne forces approached the area, fire erupted from some of the compounds. By firing, these anti-aircraft batteries established that they were manned, armed and operational. *Their proximity to the objectives, landing zones and blocking positions made them a threat to inbound coalition forces. Consequently, these sites were valid targets and AC-130 aircraft were directed toward them.*

Significant efforts were made to ensure that only the compounds that were the sources of fire were targeted. At the first targeted compound, the apparent location of most of the deaths and injuries, anti-aircraft fire was directed at the AC-130 as it approached. At one location, however, the AC-130 arrived at a target and found it to be "cold" and decided not to strike at it.

The AC-130 was not able to observe the anti-aircraft weapon itself. Rather, the ground location of the source of the fire was identified and fires were directed to that area. Just as the weapon itself is not seen, it is also not possible to determine if the fires from the AC-130 have damaged or destroyed the weapon. Consequently, personnel at the weapon's location were the primary targets. Unfortunately, it is also not possible to distinguish men from women or adults from children.

The dead and wounded later observed by coalition forces were mostly women and children. Coalition medical personnel treated the wounded. Four wounded children were medically evacuated by helicopter. A search of the first targeted compound, about two to four hours after the AC-130 had departed, revealed bloodstains and evidence of the AC-130 weapons' impact. These were no weapons or spent cartridges of any type readily observed within the compound. Further, the local Afghans maintained that most of the dead had already been buried, although no fresh grave sites were observed.

Near the second compound that had been targeted, coalition forces established a checkpoint. The checkpoint identified approximately twenty injured personnel being transported to local medical facilities. Of the twenty, two were male adults.

Villagers had initially claimed 250 dead and 600 injured, but a village elder later admitted that the real numbers were only about twenty-five per cent of those figures. The Afghan government presented a report listing forty-eight dead and 117 wounded. Coalition forces could only confirm thirty-four dead and approximately fifty wounded. *An exact number will never be able to be confirmed.*

Although the AC-130 struck six anti-aircraft sites, the local Afghans claimed that all of the dead and injured were located at only the first two compounds. Both of these targets were east of the Helmand river, while the other four targets were on the west side. Due to the difficult terrain, safety and other limitations, neither coalition forces immediately following Operation Full Throttle, CJTF-180 representatives during the fact-finding mission on 3-4 July 2002, nor Investigation Board members during their visit to the area on 24 July 2002, were able to visit any of the sites on the west side of the river. The visits to the two compounds did not reveal the presence of any anti-aircraft weapons or even a significant presence of shell casings from any weapon. The fact-finding team found two small piles of RPK (squad machinegun) rounds (about twelve total shells), but also noted that the two compounds showed no signs of having been occupied and had recently been raked. By the time the Board members visited the area, they were only able to confirm the existence of battle damage at the two compounds consistent with fires from an AC-130. Local Afghans continued to maintain that all the deaths and injuries were confined to these two compounds and did not facilitate visits to the other compounds.

In the period immediately following the incident, village elders admitted to coalition forces that people within the village regularly had fired at aircraft using AK-47s, RPKs (squad machineguns) and DShKs (heavy machineguns), but not with a weapon larger than 23 mm. In fact, village elders acknowledged holding a local shura (town meeting) the day prior to the incident to discuss firing weapons into the air during weddings and firing at aircraft. Also, two freshly completed drawings on the walls of the local pharmacy/ hospital depicted people firing at helicopters and fixed-wing aircraft.

The enquiry report says that there were people within this area of Oruzgan province that regularly aimed and fired off a variety of weapons at coalition aircraft. These weapons represented a real threat to coalition forces. As Operation Full Throttle commenced, anti-aircraft weapons were fired and, as a result, an AC-130 aircraft, acting properly and in accordance with the rules, engaged the locations of those weapons. Great care was taken to strike only those sites that were actively firing that night. *While the coalition regrets the loss of innocent lives, the responsibility for that loss rests with those that knowingly directed hostile fire at coalition forces.* The operators of those weapons elected to place them in civilian communities and elected to fire them at coalition forces at a time when they knew there were a significant number of civilians present.

Explaining the background of the incident which had sparked a major row between the United States and Afghan governments, Chairman of the Joint Chiefs of Staff, Air Force General Richard Myers told the ABC-TV interview programme "This Week" on 8 September 2002, "The terrorists have hidden behind civilians before. And they will do it in the future." He said the follow-up investigation showed that the aircraft were intentionally fired upon. There are coalition and Afghan eyewitness accounts to the hostile fire from both the ground and air. He termed it very unfortunate that innocents were killed when coalition forces returned fire on 1 July 2002.

The American investigation into the incident, as indeed the other probes carried out by the Afghan government, Afghan intelligence and the United States-led coalition into various other incidents since the beginning of this year, indicate two developments with serious repercussions for Afghanistan: one, that the Taleban-al-Qaeda network has been largely destroyed but there are survivors and pockets of support within the country who are now regrouping and have already become active; and, two, that their aim is to seek to destabilise and discredit the Transitional Islamic Government of Afghanistan and slow down the reconstruction process to the extent possible. In both cases, the inspiration and, obviously, material help has come from the al-Qaeda network which, as the United Nations Monitoring Group report shows, has not only survived the global war against terrorism but is up to all sorts of tricks.

The wider terrorist network, which had preceded the Afghan jihad and was instrumental in strengthening the Taleban in taking over almost the entire Afghanistan, is thus once again playing a crucial role in keeping alive its Afghan segment. The post-Taleban Afghanistan, therefore, turns out to be yet again a test-case for the success or failure of the international community's coordinated efforts to counter international terrorism. By faciliting an adequate reconstruction of the devastated country, the world community can act decisively in defeating at the very least the Afghan agenda of international terrorism.

Speaking at the seventh summit of the 10-member Economic Cooperation Organisation in Istanbul on 14 October 2002, President Karzai made the point that "we want to be a model of tolerance and prosperity rooted in the rich heritage of Islamic civilisation." He said that the people of Afghanistan truly believed in the teachings of Islam and rejected any misuse of the holy name of Islam by extremist groups to justify violence, death and destruction. His point was that the fight against terrorism would only be won decisively if Afghanistan could be turned into a country of peace and prosperity. "The consolidation of peace and stability depends on regional cooperation and the international community's sustained engagements in the reconstruction of Afghanistan," he said. "Rebuilding highways, creating transport and transit arteries and road networks in Afghanistan is an important undertaking with significant economic and political impact for Afghanistan and the region. We will soon start the project of rebuilding our highways with the generous assistance of the USA, Japan, the European Union, Saudi Arabia, Pakistan and Iran. The completion of this vital project will significantly enhance transit and transport facilities among members of the Economic Cooperation Organisation. We have already established the Judicial Commission to rebuild the Afghan judicial system as well as a civil service commission to reform the entire administration and impose a merit-based system and a human rights commission to protect human rights, women's rights and civil liberties."[12]

In retrospect, it would appear that the 11 September 2001 terrorist attacks on the American soil, which led promptly to the launching of the global war against terrorism, would not have taken place without the Afghan factor. The Afghan factor worked in this regard in two different ways: one, the Taleban rule facilitated greatly the growth of the international terrorist network by providing sanctuary for training, arming and despatching Islamicist terrorists to other countries, which apparently enabled al-Qaeda eventually to strike at the United States with the stupendous force of the 11 September attacks; and, two, it was the persistent Taleban refusal to hand bin Laden over to the Americans, for trial for his alleged role in the bombings of the United States embassies in Nairobi and Dar-es-Salaam on 7 August 1998, that set the process leading to the imposition of the United Nations sanctions on the Taleban, thus exacerbating their relations with the United States and the United Nations. The steadfast Taleban refusal also led to the United States strikes at the terrorist training camps in Afghanistan on 20 August 1998.[13, 14] It is this persistence of the relevance of the Taleban-ruled Afghanistan to global terrorism that makes the reconstruction of the country all the more vital for the safety of today and tomorrow.

****

Endnotes

1. Saeed, Hafiz Muhammad,chief of Lashkar-e-Toiba, in an article posted on www.jamatdawa.org in early September 2002.
2. Roy, Dr Olivier, interview on Azadi Afghan Radio, 4 November 2000.
3. Quoted by Bodansky, Yossef, *Bin Laden...* p.10.
4. ibid., p.11.
5. Rashid, Ahmed, *Taliban...* p.84.
6. ibid., pp.84-88.
7. Bodansky, Yossef, *Bin Laden...* pp.25-26.
8. *The Nida'ul Islam* magazine, 18th issue, April-May 1997.
9. Anwar, Masood, "Arabs have taken over fighting from Taliban", datelined Kandahar, *The News*, 6 November 2001.
10. The Russian memo was first publicised by Reuters on 26 September 2001.
11. Extracts from the unclassified executive summary: "Investigation of civilian casualties, Oruzgan province, Operation Full Throttle", released on 10 September 2002 by the Public Affairs office of the United States Embassy in New Delhi.
12. Associated Press of Pakistan despatch from Istanbul, 14 October 2002.
13. Bodansky, Yossef, *Bin Laden....* describes vividly the United States strikes and thereafter. "Barely forty-five minutes after Ayman al-Zawahiri (the Egyptian professor who joined the jihad) ended his conversation with (Pakistani journalist Rahimatullah) Yusufzai on 20 August 1998, at 10 p.m. local time, the cruise missiles struck the terrorist camps in the Khost area. Bin Laden, Zawahiri and the terrorist elite were not there. Teheran was the first to provide a clue about their safety. On 21 August, Mullah Omar explained why bin Laden was not hurt. 'Osama bin Laden (had) been moved to a safer place before the United States struck on his bases,' he told the official Iranian news agency, IRNA. The next day,

22 August, the Taleban issued a formal reaction to the American strikes. 'The American strike was nothing but proof of the United States' enmity against Islam and the Muslim world.' Reiterating the pledge never to forsake bin Laden, the Taleban emphasised that he was safe. 'Before the attack, Osama (had) been transferred to a safer place and no force and no attempt can force Afghanistan to hand him over to the American government,' Taleban announced. 'Osama is a guest of the Afghan people who has assured that he will not act from the territory of Afghanistan against any country.' On 21 August, at around 11 p.m. local time, Zawahiri called Rahimatullah Yusufzai again, using the same satellite phone. Zawahiri confirmed that he was together with bin Laden 'somewhere in Afghanistan', where they were all 'safe and sound'. The main purpose of Zawahiri's call was to deliver bin Laden's warning in English, 'The war has just started. The Americans should wait for the answers... Tell the Americans that we aren't afraid of bombardment, threats and acts of aggression. We suffered and survived the Soviet bombings for ten years in Afghanistan and we are ready for more sacrifices.' Zawahiri then reiterated bin Laden's call to all Muslims to continue the jihad against the Americans and the Jews as well as liberate Islamic holy places. 'The whole Ummah must change its attitude and fight the challenges posed by America and its agents. We should strengthen bin Laden's hands in this struggle.'"

14 In a statement issued on 28 July 2000 and published in the first issue of the Taleban magazine, *The Islamic Emirate*, the Taleban "Supreme Leader" Mullah Muhammed Omar ruled out any change in the Taleban policy about Osama bin Laden, saying that his expulsion would be tantamount to "leaving a pillar of our religion". "Our stand on this issue, as with any, is based on Islamic law, and we call on all to abide by the Sharia. There is no possibility of us changing our position on this, but we remain open to try Osama or any other individual under the Sharia if sufficient evidence is brought to warrant a trial. Therefore, it is for the accusers

to back up their claim. We see, as the only possible means of resolving the problem, a conference that would be composed of Islamic scholars from Afghanistan, Saudi Arabia and a third country which would decide the issue in accordance with the Sharia."

5
Two Days in September 2001

History seldom provides the luxury of indulging in hypothesis and speculation. The history of the world since 9 September 2001, however, does provide some space for such indulgence. The hypothesis is that 9 September 2001 did happen and that 11 September 2001 did not happen. The scope for speculation in such a scenario would be limitless. For, there is a consensus that the events of these two days changed the world and Afghanistan for ever.

Commander Ahmad Shah Massoud, the defence minister of the Islamic State of Afghanistan and the military genius who had stood like a colossus blocking the advance of the Taleban in Afghanistan, was assassinated on 9 September by two Tunisians (and not Moroccans, as all early reports had conveyed) posing as TV journalists. Massoud's death was one of the most violent one could think of; the bomb placed inside the TV camera burst close to Massoud, whose entire body was blown up. His friend and fellow-mujahideen, the Burhanuddin Rabbani government's ambassador in New Delhi Masood Khalili was burnt almost all over the right side of his body. The upper portion of the TV camera man's body was blown away and the Afghan translator also died. The TV interviewer, who had just declared that he was no journalist and belonged to the Islamic centres (by implication, a member of the Islamic terrorist network), survived the blast and was put in a room close by, from where he escaped and was shot dead while he reached a river embankment a few hundred yards away.

While one eyewitness account later said that Massoud must have died within thirty seconds of the blast, with two pieces of metal lodged in his heart, most of the fingers of his right hand blown off, every inch of his skin ruptured in open wounds and white gauze stuffed into his eye sockets, Khalili has survived miraculously, though he continues to suffer from terrible pains with shrapnel still embedded in his body. His right eye, which was almost lost, is relatively functional after several high-calibre operations.[1]

The assassination of Massoud removed overnight the main roadblock that the Taleban-al-Qaeda forces and Pakistan were facing in completing their conquest of Afghanistan. The period between 26 September 1996, when Kabul was captured and 9 September 2001, when Massoud was felled, had been spent in ceaseless combat and decidedly without the fruits of victory for the fundamentalist rulers and international terrorists.

Apart from completing the takeover of the country, the removal of Massoud also facilitated the northward advance of the Taleban-al-Qaeda forces across the Afghanistan-Tajikistan border. Thus, the 9 September assassination had, in one stroke, paved the way for the ultimate destination of the Taleban-al-Qaeda rule: subjugation of Afghanistan and sealing its fate as the nursery for international terrorism and for Pakistan's long-cherished strategy of creating a "strategic depth", a secure western border that would facilitate greatly all future overt and covert operations against the eastern neighbour, India. As far as al-Qaeda was concerned, the felling of Massoud also meant that the time for the thrust towards Central Asia, to expand the establishment of the Ummah, had finally arrived.

But neither happened. For, within forty-eight hours of the assassination of Massoud, thousands of miles away in the West, four hijacked aircraft deviated from their routes and created mayhem and havoc, staging the first assault against the American government and the American people on the American soil.

Jon Lee Anderson, in his excellently researched article, "The Assassins: Who was involved in the murder of Ahmed Shah Massoud", describes how the news of the attacks on the World Trade Centre and the Pentagon evoked reactions in the Taleban-al-Qaeda network. "On 11 September, at around 8 p.m. in Afghanistan, Mullah Omar, who was in Kandahar, called the Taleban foreign minister in Kabul. According to Afghan intelligence sources, who intercepted the call, Mullah Omar said, 'Things have gone much further than expected.' It was 11.30 a.m. in New York, less than three hours after American Airlines Flight 11 had crashed into the north tower of the World Trade Centre, and an hour and a half after the south tower had collapsed. Mullah Omar told the foreign minister to call a press conference to say that the Taleban had not been involved in the attack. The press conference took place at 9.30 p.m. in Kabul. The foreign minister assured reporters that Afghanistan had not attacked the United States, and he read a statement by Mullah Omar saying that Osama bin Laden was not involved: 'This type of terrorism is too great for one man.' Among the calls intercepted that night was one from Kabul to Kandahar. 'Where's the Sheikh?' the caller asked. Sheikh was the code name that senior Taleban officials used for bin Laden. Again, according to Afghan intelligence sources, someone in Mullah Omar's house told the caller that bin Laden was there. 'Then, afterward,' an intelligence officer said to me, 'there was a chaos of phone calls back and forth between Kandahar and Kabul.'"

Anderson quotes Massoud's younger brother Wali (who, at the time of the assassination, was the chargé d'affaires at the Afghan embassy in London and presently has launched a Massoudist party called the National Movement of Afghanistan) speculating that Massoud's murder was the first step in a larger plot and that the 11 September attacks were the second consecutive step. "Look at the logic," he quotes Wali arguing, "They wanted to do what they wanted to do on the eleventh, but provided there was no Massoud." The expectation of the plotters was that Massoud's death would finish the United Front off and that if, in the aftermath of the attacks in New York and Washington DC, the United States desired to retaliate, it would not be helped by any Afghan ally on the ground. The build-up of Taleban troops on the front lines in the late summer and early fall was thus a preparation for Massoud's assassination. "They were waiting for something," an Afghan intelligence official said. And, as evident from Mullah Omar's telephone conversation, the attacks on the United States were not expected to be as catastrophic as they turned out to be. "They were expecting a reaction," the intelligence official said. "But they thought it would be a Clinton-type reaction. They didn't anticipate the kind of revenge that occurred."

In retrospect, Wali Massoud's speculative analysis appears to be substantive; for, it is possible that the Taleban-al-Qaeda network calculated the probable United States reaction basing on their experience of the American missile attacks of August 1998 in retaliation of the bombings of the embassies in Nairobi and Dar-es-Salaam. Essentially, in their reckoning, the United States would have acted alone, and the retaliation would again have been of the technological type with American service personnel exposed to the least risk. The rousing of the entire American people in grief and anger and the unprecedented sympathy and cooperation that the entire international community spontaneously bestowed on the United States must have caught the Taleban-al-Qaeda terrorist network by complete surprise.

To return to our hypothesis, however, if the 11 September attacks had not occurred, the supreme opportunity that the international terrorist network and Pakistan had been waiting for, the removal of Massoud from the battlefield, would have opened up vast possibilities for them. The civil war in Afghanistan would have conceivably come to an end, if not immediately but certainly after a few more battles. The only impediment to this scenario would have been a joint military action by Massoud's backers, Russia, Iran, Tajikistan and India. But would the United States have allowed these four countries to get militarily involved in Afghanistan? The terrorist network might possibly have counted on such an American reaction to any major military move by the four countries. On the other hand, the Taleban-al-Qaeda forces, backed by Pakistan, would have shortly begun to take Tajikistan on. This too could possibly have drawn both the backers of Massoud and the United States into the region for an essentially policing act, by seeking to restrain the Taleban-al-Qaeda forces from making serious forays into Tajikistan. China too could not have sat impassioned in the face of such a development; after all, Uighur terrorists were getting trained in bin Laden's camps and participating in the battles between the Taleban-al-Qaeda and Massoud.

More than anything else, however, the events of 9 and 11 September 2001 emphasised once again the supremacy of al-Qaeda and the international terrorist network over the

Afghan Taleban. They also underlined a trend which had for some years been apparent: drawing sustenance from the Taleban rule in Afghanistan, the international terrorist network was able increasingly to instigate anti-establishment terrorist acts in various Islamic countries. In other words, while Arabs and other foreigners who had come to Pakistan and Afghanistan to participate in the jihad against the Soviet occupation had gradually attained a position strong enough to turn their attention back to their own countries where they wanted to overthrow the reigning governments and despatched men and materials to achieve the goal.

By the mid-1980s, Bodansky writes, Afghanistan had become a magnet for militant Islamists from all over the world. In the early 1980s, it hadn't taken long for Egyptian and other Arab Islamist groups to begin using Peshawar as a centre for their headquarters in exile. As a result of their growing cooperation, they established an "international jihad organisation" using Pakistan and Afghanistan as their springboard for operations back home. For example, one of the first jihad movement bureaus was opened in 1984 by Dr Ayman al-Zawahiri, for the Islamic jihad movement of Abbud al-Zumur, a lieutenant-colonel in Egyptian military intelligence and a senior clandestine military commander of the Islamic jihad who was arrested on the eve of President Anwar Sadat's assassination. Zawahiri escaped from Egypt in the mid-1980s.[2]

By the late 1980s, he notes, the world of international terrorism was changing. The camps of the Afghan resistance in Pakistan actually became the centre of radical Islamist terrorism, with Sunni Islamists constituting the majority of the fighters. Traditionalist radical Islam was rising throughout the Muslim world as a popular reaction of the believers to the pressures of the modern world and especially relations with the West. The building frustration of the Muslim masses led to the emergence of a dedicated militant vanguard with an unprecedented commitment to the cause of reviving traditionalist Islam. In their religious zeal, these believers became so devoted to their cause that they disregarded their own lives, the extent of carnage they inflicted on their victims, and the overall consequences of their actions.[3]

To return to the year 2001, a year in which, had the 9 and 11 September events not happened, Commander Massoud's European tour would have ranked as a highlight. In fact, the United Front concluded in the aftermath of the assassination that one of the factors that the Taleban-al-Qadea network considered was the emergence of Massoud as an outstanding diplomat and statesman during his visit to the European Union, a development which appeared to have firmed up the decision already reached by the international terrorist network to kill Massoud. Even before Massoud had embarked upon his tour, the Taleban expressed their unhappiness over the decision of the European Parliament to extend an invitation to him. On 5 April 2001, the Taleban slammed the European Parliament's invitation to Commander Massoud, saying that this would encourage him to step up his fight against the ruling militia. "To invite him personally for this meeting is a tyranny against the Afghan people, because this will encourage him to fight more," Deputy Interior Minister Haji Mullah Khaksar said. Massoud did not deserve the invitation because he held less than ten per cent of the country whereas the Taleban controlled the most, including the capital Kabul. The trip would not help Massoud. "To be invited to a meeting in Europe cannot make one popular with the nation," Khaksar said. "One becomes popular when the people accept him. His trips to Europe and other places are futile exercises. The Taleban Foreign Minister Wakil Ahmed Muttawakil also accused the European

Parliament in stoking the war in Afghanistan. He said that the European Union should be more concerned about sending badly needed humanitarian aid to the war and drought-ravaged country instead of inviting the opposition leader. Meanwhile, Commander Massoud said in Paris on 4 April 2001, after meeting with the French Foreign Minister Hubert Vedrine, "Faced with the aggression of Pakistan, I give myself the right... to seek aid everywhere." He also accused the Taleban of being directly propped up by Pakistan and bin Laden. Khaksar, however, denied Massoud's allegations, saying that the Taleban did not allow outside interference in the running of the Afghan government. "Pakistan cannot interfere in Afghanistan's affairs, nor does it need to do so. We are against interference," he asserted.

While the European visit provided Massoud with a tremendous opportunity to highlight the Afghan civil war and the role played by Pakistan in its prolongation by constantly propping up the Taleban militarily, it was the Pakistan factor that almost marred the visit, though the United Front has always been reluctant to talk about this aspect of the visit. Brice Lalande, a former French minister and a close friend of Massoud, was instrumental in arranging the visit to Europe in the summer of 2001. Talking about the visit later, he told the author that the visit was spoilt by French President Jacques Chirac's refusal to receive Commander Massoud. "Chirac was scared that if he received Massoud, Pakistan, which had placed valuable orders for supply of military hardware, would be displeased and might cancel the orders, and he, therefore, decided not to be associated with the visit at all. Even Prime Minister Lionel Jospin fell in line with the President and declined to receive Massoud. Finally, the day was somewhat saved by Foreign Minister Vedrine who hosted a luncheon in honour of Massoud and held talks and later a joint press conference."[4]

Lalande and several other French and Italian politicians recalled the scandal that was caused by the French government's role in delivering a virtual snub to a man who was widely considered in the European continent as a hero and a living legend. European journalists, both print and electronic, had been writing about Massoud for years, especially his lone stand against the Soviet occupation forces on the Afghan soil and, thereafter, his struggle against the Taleban who were fully backed by Pakistan and the international Islamicist terrorist network. There was both appreciation and sympathy for him in Europe, and it was this knowledge which had prompted Massoud to embark on the tour. The fact that Massoud was French-speaking had also endeared him to the French people; he was equally popular in Italy. But the behaviour of Chirac and Jospin shamed and infuriated the people in both France and Italy.[5]

The popular indignation at the treatment meted out to Commander Massoud was so strong that a group of right and left-wing members of the French Parliament set off a letter to President Chirac, roundly criticising him for his silence about the visit of a man they described as "a friend of France and a freedom fighter".[6]

The Taleban were unhappy over the visit principally because they knew that Massoud enjoyed remarkable popularity in Europe. Since it would be Massoud's endeavour to get the European Union member-countries actively involved in seeking a political solution to the Afghan crisis that the Taleban were naturally apprehensive; they were happy with the continuing American indifference and certainly did not want any fresh European interest in Afghanistan. It was at this juncture that the Pakistan factor worked in their favour. Both President Chirac and Prime Minister Jospin decided to keep Massoud at an arm's length because they did not wish to antagonise Pakistan, which had become a valuable purchaser of French defence hardware.

However, Vedrine's hospitality not only proved to be a face-saver but also a major opportunity for Massoud to educate the people of France and other European countries about the situation in his country and the need to get involved so that the overwhelming presence of Pakistan in the Afghan civil war could be counterbalanced. He made several important declarations and observations at his press conference in Paris on 4 April 2001, which the post-Taleban Afghan government has been largely following in the task of restoration of normalcy and improvement of life and governance to facilitate development.

He said, "We believe that the future government should be formed by means of general elections, via the people's ballot, through the vote of both women and men. The only form of government able to ensure social justice and equality between Afghanistan's various ethnic groups is democracy and the people's vote. Our future government and the Taleban will be incomparably different. We have always opposed and continue to oppose any kind of extremist or radical movements, even if they claim to be Islamic, and we do not believe they are good for Afghanistan, the region or the world. As I have repeated earlier, we believe in elections with the participation of both women and men. We fully respect human rights, we support it, we will protect it. We prescribe against the cultivation and trafficking of illegal narcotics; we believe they are haram (forbidden by Islam), and they are detrimental to all humankind, and destructive to our own country. As during the jihad, we fully oppose terrorism and terrorist activities. *No one had ever witnessed a terrorist attack by the mujahideen, even when the Russians were in Afghanistan.* Terrorism is wrong and we are against it. We not only support women's education, women working and women's participation in society, but we encourage it. Women can play an instrumental role in rebuilding the country after these many years of war."

One reason why the United Front later felt that the decision of the Taleban-al-Qaeda network to kill Massoud was hastened was his success in highlighting the role of Pakistan in the Afghan civil war and the necessity for the Europeans to pressure Islamabad to let go its hold and allow a political process to be initiated. For, Massoud firmly believed that the Taleban on their own, without the assistance of Pakistan, would not be able to withstand the combined assault by his forces and a general uprising among the people, particularly among the Pushtuns of southern Afghanistan. "As I have repeated many times," he told the press conference, "a major way in which other countries and the international community can help to establish peace in Afghanistan and end the fighting and bloodshed is to bring adequate pressure on Pakistan. This has been mentioned in talks with the French Foreign Ministry and it will be mentioned in talks with others. It is then up to these officials to make a decision."

Massod's diplomatic foray, proving effective at least in focusing attention on Pakistan's role in perpetuating the Taleban rule, was preceded by a significant exercise with a seminar held by the United States-based Association for Peace and Democracy for Afghanistan, entitled "Loya Jirgah and a Political Solution to the Afghan Problem", at Annandale, Virginia, on 25 March 2001.

The resolution adopted at the seminar read in part: "We, the participants of the seminar... after comprehensive discussions and deliberations, determine that the convening of an emergency Loya Jirgah, based on the peace plan of His Majesty the former king of Afghanistan Mohammad Zahir Shah, is the only mechanism capable of achieving a just peace and making possible the realisation of the will of the people of

Afghanistan. Thus, we call on the United Nations, Organisation of Islamic Conference, United States, European Union, and interested nations to assist the people of Afghanistan in implementing this peace plan; affirm that *the foreign-imposed war in Afghanistan is the result of the direct and indirect interference of Pakistan military circles and religious fanatic groups,* and call for the immediate cessation of this intervention." Thus, what Commander Massoud was asking the Europeans to listen to and accept and act upon was also echoed a few days earlier by the seminar held by representative Afghans in the United States. The call for Pakistan to vacate its vested interests in Afghanistan was also pouring in from various quarters, most notably from long-time Afghanistan watchers. Equally significantly, the seminar also urged the United States government to adopt "an independent and clear" Afghan policy conducive to a just peace in Afghanistan, a nation that had sacrificed "over one million martyrs" for the cause of freedom and liberty (a reference to the forgetfulness displayed by Western governments and, especially the United States government, that the break-up of the Soviet Union began with the defeat at the hands of the mujahideen in Afghanistan). The reference to an "independent" Afghan policy was a dig at the widely held perception amongst the expatriate Afghans that Washington's policy was being influenced to a great extent by Islamabad. The point was emphasised later by Commander Massoud in his Paris press conference. In response to a question, he said, "... Hitherto the Americans have (had) no clear or distinct policy. My message to Mr Bush is that if attention is not given to bringing peace in Afghanistan, and the people of Afghanistan are not assisted on the road toward achieving peace, then verily this crisis will continue to plague not just the people of Afghanistan, but also spread to America and other countries." Uncannily, his warning to a willfully negligent Washington turned into a terrible reality within a mere span of five months.

Massoud's European tour also served to highlight the continuing American coldness towards the only bulwark that was still standing against the advancing Taleban, who had come to represent the most repressive regime in the post-Cold War world. In an illuminating analysis, Dr Elie D. Krakowski of the American Foreign Policy Council, Washington DC, commented, "The invitations to address the European Parliament, to meet with Western foreign ministers, even more than what Massoud said, holds an important lesson for United States policy. Putting pressure on the Taleban shall entail a desire to maximise chances of success. That, in turn, means making use of available means. The 'Islamic State of Afghanistan' is precisely such a means. Support for it does not mean an endorsement of all its positions. It simply increases the leverage of the United States. The Europeans have understood that. So have the Taleban, if their anger and protests are any indication. Such symbolic acts as reopening the (Afghan) embassy (in Washington DC) and allowing the Afghans to resume their rightful place can only play a positive role. But we should go further. Commander Massoud should also be invited to present his case in the United States and meet with high United States officials. Congress might want to consider following in the footsteps of the European Parliament. Washington should consider extending political and diplomatic support to Massoud's government."

Meanwhile, several important developments were taking place in the first week of July 2001. In an interview to *Jane's Defence Weekly*, Commander Massoud said that he was confident of checking and even rolling back anticipated advances by the Taleban in the summer of 2001. His comments were made in the backdrop of a restoration of cohesion within the anti-Taleban alliance and a decision to concentrate on military resistance. Massoud said that the financial position of the opposition forces had improved, in comparison to the previous year's "particularly bad financial position", with the assumption of greater control over mining and marketing of gems. "Some ten days after my return from Europe," he told the weekly, "Pakistani military chiefs held a meeting in which it was decided to press ahead with the war." He argued that continued military resistance to the Taleban was essential if the militia was to be brought to the negotiating table and the way opened for a political settlement. The weekly noted that there had been an increase in the United Front's capability, including acquiring new Soviet-era T-55 and T-62 main battle tanks and armoured fighting vehicles following the meeting in Dushanbe in October 2000, between Russian Defence Minister Igor Sergeyev and Commander Massoud.

The turning of fortune in the battlefield was reflected in a 3 April 2001 despatch sourced from the Islamic State of Afghanistan. The despatch said, "The Pakistan-backed Taleban failed to make any gain in the first phase of their summer campaign in Takhar province. They are now preparing to launch the second phase of their campaign. The casualties of the Taleban and Pakistanis in the Takhar front were 500 dead and wounded. Among those killed were Mustafa, the commander of the 998th Commando Regiment of Cherat. He was a resident of the Wah Cantonment in Punjab (Pakistan). Mullah Dost Mohammad, another Pakistani officer who was in command of the armoured units of the Taleban, was also killed. His body was airlifted to the Weash area of Chaman in Baluchistan of Pakistan. He was the commander of the 4th Division of Herat. Two prominent commanders of Sipah-e-Sahaba, an extremist religious party in Pakistan, Sardar Sekandar from Parachinar and Eshfaq Ahmad were also killed in Takhar. Mullah Rahmatullah Sangarmal, a prominent commander of the Taleban, was severely wounded and was flown to KHizbarachi for treatment. The Taleban and their Pakistani supporters were confident of their victory in Takhar and even Pakistan's former Chief of Army Mirza Aslam Baig wrote to the Pakistani newspaper, *Jang*, that the final victory of the Taleban was imminent and close. The Taleban had wrongly claimed the capturing of the Farkhar gorge and reaching Kalafghan. The mujahideen defence of the Farkhar gorge was remarkable. The Taleban launched successive attacks on the gorge, and on one occasion, fighting continued for sixteen hours. The counter-attacks launched by the mujahideen in the Farkhar gorge, Chal, Eshkamish and Khawja Ghar demoralised the enemy troops forcing them to adopt a defensive posture. They are waiting for the arrival of fresh Pakistani troops before resuming their attacks against the mujahideen. The Taleban are also press-ganging people in the areas they control to send them to fight in Takhar."

At around the same time, 4 July 2001, the United States Deputy Secretary of State Richard Armitage said in Washington DC that his government could launch military retaliation against the Taleban if bin Laden attacked United States interests. He was commenting on a warning given to the Taleban by the American ambassador to Pakistan William Milam during a meeting in Islamabad on 29 June 2001. The Taleban, who were sheltering bin Laden, were told that they would "bear responsibility" for any attacks on United States interests. This was revealed by a Taleban official to the Reuters news agency. Armitage told Reuters in turn, "What it means is that Arabs in these terrorist camps (in Afghanistan) could be responsible for putting Afghans and the Afghan government, in the person of the Taleban, in a very difficult position." He said it was "conceivable" that the United States military could target the Taleban in such a scenario.

The same day, the Taleban had an outburst against the United States government for the renewal of trade sanctions against them as a punishment for refusing to hand over bin Laden for his alleged role in various terrorist acts, including the 7 August 1998 bombings of the American embassies in Nairobi and Dar-es-Salaam and the attack on the guided missile destroyer USS Cole on 12 October 2000, in Aden, Yemen. Rejecting the American action as tyrannical, Taleban Foreign Minister Wakil Ahmed Muttawakil said that the continuation of the sanctions was oppression which would harm the Afghan people. He repeated the Taleban's position that they would not allow bin Laden to use Afghan territory as a base for action against any country. This was in response to United States President George Bush's statement to Congress that bin Laden was continuing to plan and commit violence against the United States and its nationals from inside Afghanistan.

On 3 July 2001, an Algerian convicted of trying to carry out a terrorist attack in Los Angeles on the eve of the millennium celebration testified that he had received money and training at camps in Afghanistan that American officials said were run by bin Laden. Ahmed Ressam, the Algerian, described in detail his training in light arms, explosives, assassinations and techniques for blowing up "the infrastructure of a country". After more than six months of training in Afghanistan in 1998, Ressam testified, he returned to Canada with $12,000 in seed money to plot terrorist attacks against the United States, Islam's "biggest enemy". While not naming bin Laden but in describing the origins of his plan to set off a bomb at the Los Angeles International Airport, he confirmed the key outlines of the picture drawn by American intelligence of bin Laden's operations. He described a network of camps in which Algerians, Jordanians, Germans and others were trained and indoctrinated for terrorist missions around the world. Ressam's testimony offered a rare insider's look at the design and attempted execution of a terrorist plot. His account depicted a decentralised structure in which militants were trained and given considerable latitude in selecting targets and missions.

Between July and early September 2001, while the military stalemate largely held, both the Taleban and United Front forces continued to test each other out by making forays into the other's territory, drawing fire and retreating. There were intelligence reports in the summer of 2001 that a large number of Taleban and al-Qaeda fighters (as many as 16,000, according to some accounts) were massing along the northernmost frontier for the United Front; among the fighters were Arabs, Pakistanis, Uighurs, Uzbeks and Tajiks. According to Anderson, Commander Massoud felt that the number was exaggerated and dismissed it as of little consequence. In early September, Massoud reconnoitered the area by helicopter and his officers photographed it; Massoud later planned the deployment of his troops basing on the aerial photographs.

Then came the morning of 9 September 2001. The whole previous night and right up to the early morning of the 9th, Massoud, Khalili and a few others stayed awake, reading Persian poetry sitting on a hilltop. One verse that Massoud recited is remembered vividly by Ambassador Khalili: "There will not be another night like this, my friend, you will never see another night like this again," the verse ran. Anderson describes what happened thereafter: a few minutes after Massoud went to sleep, his personal secretary, Jamshid, who was also his nephew and brother-in-law, received a telephone call from a United Front commander Bismillah Khan, saying that the Taleban had attacked the Shamali front. Jamshid woke Massoud up and Massoud and Khan talked the matter over until day-break. Then Massoud retired once more for sleep.

Around 7.30 a.m. Jamshid learned that the Taleban were retreating; Massoud slept undisturbed until 9 a.m.

It was after breakfast, when Massoud was about to leave on a reconnaissance trip that he decided to see the two Arab journalists who had been waiting for nine days to interview him. Ambassador Khalili takes up the story at this point: "Massoud came into my room and seeing my passport lying on the bed, he asked why I was not having it on my breast pocket. It was such a beautifully bound passport. I said that I did not need the passport as long as I was at Khoja Bahauddin and that I would certainly put it in my breast pocket when I would be going back to Delhi. No, he insisted, I should put the passport in my breast pocket right then. Okay, I agreed and did so. Many days later, I would realise that I survived the terrorist bomb blast because the passport stopped shrapnel from entering my heart."[7]

The reason for Massoud to grant an interview that morning could be the word from the Arabs that they would be leaving Khoja Bahauddin the same day, 9 September. The Arabs had come for the interview with a letter of introduction from the director of an organisation called the Islamic Observation Centre in London; besides, Jamshid had received a call from an associate of Abdul Rasul Sayyaf, commander of an anti-Taleban force, informing that the Arabs were Sayyaf's friends. Anderson quotes Jamshid saying that Massoud agreed to grant an interview because he thought that he could convey a message through them to the Muslim world saying that those who were fighting the Taleban were also Muslims and not kafirs (unbelievers) and that "we don't have Russians and Iranians fighting here".

When the interview began, what struck Khalili (who was translating the English questions into Persian for Massoud) as odd was the preponderance of questions about the United

Front's attitude toward bin Laden. There were questions like "What will you do with bin Laden if you take power?" and "Why do you call him a fundamentalist?" Khalili found the questions tendentious and asked the Arab the name of the newspaper he worked for. What the man said in reply must have stunned Khalili. "I am not a journalist," he said. "I am from the Islamic centres. We have offices in London and Paris and all over the world." Khalili then turned to Massoud and whispered, "Commander, they are from those guys (al-Qaeda)." In response, Massoud nodded and said tersely, "Let's just get through with it."

The end came soon thereafter. Anderson records that the Arabs had moved a table and some chairs that were between Massoud and their camera, which they had positioned on the lowest level of the tripod (according to Khalili, the camera was on the table). Fahim Dashty, an Afghan journalist who was running a documentary film making company called Ariana in the Panjsher Valley and used to film most of Massoud's interviews, had begun filming. He was adjusting his backlight when, as he recalled later, the room seemed to have exploded. Khalili remembered that he saw a thick blue fire was rushing toward him. Anderson quotes Dashty recalling, "I felt I was burning," and he rushed out. There he saw Jamshid and asked him to take him to hospital. Instead, Jamshed asked where Massoud was, and in response Dashty recalled he went back to the room and saw Massoud very badly injured "all over his body, his face, his hands and legs".

Two bodyguards carried Massoud to his car; Dashty, also badly injured, got in and the car was driven to the helicopter pad. Khalili followed in another car. All the three were flown to a hospital, run by Indian doctors, inside Tajikistan. As the helicopter was flying, Khalili later told the author, his consciousness returned, he opened his eyes and saw Massoud's horribly bloodied face close to his own face. He lost his consciousness again.

As the Burhanuddn Rabbani government had already decided to keep the assassination of Commander Massoud a secret, the first media reports said that he had been injured but had survived and that he was under treatment. In Delhi, there was widespread concern over the fate of Ambassador Khalili as well, and enquiries poured into the Afghan embassy. The embassy routinely fobbed off all queries by insisting that both Commander Massoud and Ambassador Khalili were injured and being treated.

A typical example was the following AFP story dated 12 September 2001. Mahmoud Khalili, the son of Ambassador Khalili, was quoted claiming that both his father and Commander Massoud were being treated for wounds suffered in the attack. "Father is burned, he is alive, he will be okay," a relative in New Delhi quoted Mahmoud as saying by telephone from Dushanbe. The relative told the AFP in New Delhi that Masood Khalili had seen Massoud after the suicide bombing. "My father told me he saw him (Massoud)," Mahmoud was quoted saying. "He is in good condition."

"Afghan opposition spokesmen have insisted," the story ran, "that Ahmad Shah Massoud is alive despite numerous reports he had died in the alleged suicide bombing."

Reuters reported from Kabul on 11 September 2001 that the Taleban had launched a fresh push against the United Front forces in the north as "mystery surrounded the fate of their main rival, Ahmad Shah Massoud, following Sunday's suicide bomb attack. With the Taleban themselves denying any role in the assassination attempt on Massoud, his opposition alliance reported a fresh push by Taleban forces to dislodge its fighters from positions north of Kabul. The sound of fighting could clearly be heard in the city on Tuesday (11 September).

Members of (Massoud's) alliance both inside and outside the country say he was wounded in the blast, but insist he is recovering. Other reports suggest that he died in the blast. 'Massoud is still under treatment in a hospital in neighbouring Tajikistan,' Bismillah Khan, one of Massoud's top commanders said over satellite phone from a location to the north of Kabul."

On 11 September 2001, Pakistan officially denounced the assassination attempt on Massoud's life, saying that Pakistan was opposed to violence in Afghanistan, which might be aggravated by such acts of terrorism. "Pakistan desires to see peace and national reconciliation in Afghanistan where people have long suffered the ravages of the foreign military intervention followed by more than a decade of civil strife," a spokesman for the Pakistan Foreign Office said in a statement in Islamabad.

The United Front, however, firmly believed that Pakistan was very much in the know of the al-Qaeda plot to assassinate Massoud. Ambassador Khalili told the author in New Delhi after his return from treatment in Germany, "We received information at the time that there was some sort of a celebration at the ISI headquarters on 9 September. While we are fairly convinced of the authenticity of this report, there was another report, which is unconfirmed, saying that General Pervez Musharraf had attended the celebration."[7] Jon Lee Anderson writes, "Wali (Massoud) and other Afghans I talked to insisted that Pakistan was also involved in Massoud's murder. Massoud had never established close links with the Pakistanis, even in the seventies and eighties, when many Afghan Islamists went into exile in Pakistan. (He was legendary as a fighter in part because he stayed in Afghanistan, in the field.) The ISI supported the Taleban early on. An intelligence officer who was close to Massoud said that on the night of 9 September, the President of Pakistan Pervez Musharraf held a party to celebrate the assassination. He said that this information came from General Fahim, who is now (the) Minister of Defence in the Interim Afghan Government. I asked Fahim if there had been such a party, and he was evasive. 'Maybe,' he said. But he confirmed that Musharraf was at (the) ISI headquarters that evening, meeting with Hamid Gul, who had just returned from northern Afghanistan."

The news of his death was, however, finally announced, along with the announcement of the preparations for his funeral. During this author's visit to the Panjsher Valley in June 2002, Massoud's father-in-law Khokho Tajuddin explained that the news of his instant death had to be suppressed as, otherwise, there would have been a violent reaction in the valley and amongst United Front officers and men. It was basically to maintain control over the situation that the United Front leadership decided, without wasting time, to let the news of Massoud's death percolate slowly.

In hindsight, this was an eminently sensible decision. Judging by the fact that his colleagues and followers wept openly at his memory one year later, at the first International Conference on Massoud Studies, held in Kabul on 7-8 September 2002, it was not difficult to appreciate the depth of emotion that his sudden death had caused amongst his people. Standing in front of his mausoleum on the top of a hill in the Panjsher Valley, many Tajiks told the author, one year after his death, that they did not believe that he was dead.

Roughly forty-eight hours after the violent assassination of Commander Massoud at the remote Khoja Bahauddin close to the Afghanistan-Tajikistan border, the unthinkable happened, and the World Trade Centre, the veritable symbol of the financial clout of the United States, collapsed as the two hijacked jet planes crashed into the twin towers killing over 3,000 people and a third plane attacked the Pentagon, the seat of the military powers of the sole superpower in the 21st century. A fourth plane which could have expanded the macabre theatre of terror, crashlanded in the solitude of rural Pennsylvania because its intrepid passengers challenged the hijackers.

It was at the Emma E. Booker Elementary School in Sarasota, Florida, where President George W. Bush was informed that a "small, two engine plane" had hit the North Tower of the World Trade Center (WTC), New York. "This is pilot error," Bush later recalled saying. "It's unbelievable that somebody would do this." Conferring with his White House Chief of Staff Andrew H. Card Jr., he said, "The guy must have had a heart attack." But the patently wrong notion soon had to give way to the stunningly painful realisation that for the first time in its history, the United States had been attacked in a very major assault by an enemy. For, at 9.05 a.m. United Airlines flight 175, also a Boeing 767 like the first hijacked plane in American Airlines flight 11, smashed into the South Tower of the WTC. Bush, at that very moment, was sitting on a stool in a classroom of the school he was visiting; Andrew Card whispered, "A second plane hit the second tower. America is under attack." Bush later recalled his precise thought at that moment, "They had declared war on us, and I made up my mind that we were going to war."[8]

Two days later, on 13 September 2001, the Bush administration was in the thick of building up an international coalition to fight terrorism. The State Department focused on Pakistan, regarding it as the linchpin of the plan that was evolving. Pakistan was the first country to have recognised the Taleban as the rulers of Afghanistan and the Taleban, as the State Department looked at it, had a substantial following within Pakistani territory. Besides, after turning an overtly nuclear weapons state, the risk of a nuclear war with India had increased significantly. Secretary of State Colin Powell told Bush that no action could be taken against the terrorists without Pakistan's support. But the Pakistanis would have to be put on notice, and with the President giving a free hand to him, Powell did precisely that by telling General Pervez Musharraf that he would have to accept each of the seven demands the United States was making on Pakistan. The demands were:

- First: Stop al-Qaeda operatives at your border, intercept arms shipments through Pakistan and end *all* logistical support for bin Laden;
- Second: Give blanket over flight and landing rights within Pakistan to the United States;
- Third: Give access to Pakistan naval bases, air bases and borders to United States forces;
- Fourth: Provide to the United States immediate intelligence and immigration information;
- Fifth: Condemn the 11th September attacks and "curb all domestic expressions of support for terrorism against the (United States), its friends or allies";
- Sixth: Cut off all shipments of fuel to the Taleban and stop Pakistani volunteers from going into Afghanistan to join the Taleban; and
- Seventh: Should the evidence strongly implicate Osama bin Laden and the al-Qaeda network in Afghanistan and should Afghanistan and the Taleban continue to harbour him and this network, Pakistan will break diplomatic relations with the Taleban government, end support for the Taleban and assist the United States in the after-mentioned ways to destroy bin Laden and his al-Qaeda network.

Deputy Secretary of State Richard Armitage called Pakistani intelligence chief Gen. Mahmoud Ahmad to the State

Department and told him that the demands were not negotiable. "You must accept all seven parts," he said. At 1.30 p.m., Powell called Musharraf "as one general to another" and said, "We need someone on our flank fighting with us. Speaking candidly, the American people would not understand if Pakistan was not in this fight with the United States." Musharraf said that Pakistan would support the United States with each of the seven demanded actions.[9]

Despite President Musharraf's ready acceptance of the American demands, considerable bad blood was generated between the two sides during the follow-up discussions on working out a strategy. The Pakistanis were clearly irritated by the publicity given to the forthcoming collaboration, and this was well reflected in a statement a Foreign Ministry spokesman, Riaz Mohammed Khan, made on 26 September 2001. There was "no joint operation or specific contingency plans that have been placed before the Pakistan government," he said. He also added for good measure that the fight was not against Afghanistan or its people but against terrorism. "Pakistan cannot and can never join in any hostile action against Afghanistan or the Afghan people," he said. "We are deeply conscious that the destinies of the two people are intertwined." It should be remembered that in the initial phase of Operation Enduring Freedom, the United States-led operations were extremely unpopular in Pakistan, especially in the western parts and also in Karachi. Not unexpectedly, apart from joining the war against the Taleban-al-Qaeda regime with which collaboration was still continuing, Pakistan found it particularly galling to being obliged into a situation where collaboration with the United Front, which was till then an enemy, was an imminent factor. Besides, Musharraf was not at all confident of the consequences of tough measures against Islamic jihadi groups active within Pakistan. His desire was to go slow so that his government would not be landed with a sudden flare-up of popular emotion and discontent. As it was, he was already being accused of surrendering before the Americans and acting against the interests of Muslims. He was also extremely hesitant about meeting the Americans' demand for opening up Pakistani airfields and air bases for use of the American defence forces. In fact, his government would continue to deny that any such concession had been granted to the United States well after American planes had begun to fly into and out of Pakistani facilities.

The demands that the United States made upon Pakistan made it clear that Washington's move for forging a global coalition against terrorism was aimed single-mindedly at eradicating the Taleban and al-Qaeda from Afghanistan and Pakistan and from other countries where they could have established their network. Logically, therefore, as far as the Pakistan-inspired terrorism in the Indian state of Jammu and Kashmir was concerned, this coalition was not aiming at it. This point was well-ventilated by former Indian Foreign Secretary Salman Haidar who said when Operation Enduring Freedom was about two months old, that "The Afghan operation has made little dent in the curbing of terrorism in other parts of the region, and India's concern about cross-border violence remain unmet. Expectations that Pakistan, source of this activity, would be a prime target of the international coalition against terror, have been disappointed. Indeed, Pakistan is being viewed as a long-time partner of the anti-terror international effort and not just an auxiliary for the military campaign. Gen. Musharraf is regarded by his Western allies as an important bulwark in the anti-extremist fight, a moderate who needs to be supported and fortified. *Thus, we are not likely to see decisive action against terrorist centres in Pakistan-occupied Kashmir. At best, there may be pressure for restraint and no Nelson's eye for Pakistani mischief in Kashmir."*[10]

When this unpleasant truth dawned on New Delhi, the latter took it up with all seriousness with Washington DC (India's urgency was heightened further by the 13 December 2001 terrorist attack on Parliament House, which was the most audacious terrorist attack on Indian soil till date). During the flurry of diplomatic and military visits between the two capitals in the first half of 2002, the Americans were obliged to assuage the troubled Indian feelings by assuring that they were treating all sorts of terrorism, including the cross-border terrorism peculiar to Jammu and Kashmir, at par and that every government included in the global coalition shared this view. Even Pakistan was obliged, under pressure from the Americans, British and other coalition partners, to tow the line and disinherit any relationship with terrorist groups active in the Indian state. Indian diplomacy gained substantially through the deliberate Indian act of escalating tension on the international border with Pakistan by deploying the largest ever peace-time army there. Pakistan followed suit and for days since December 2001, global attention shifted from Afghanistan-Pakistan to India-Pakistan, much to the dismay of the Americans who were determined to concentrate it in the military operations then in progress in Afghanistan.

The Kargil conflict had convinced India that the Taleban-al-Qaeda terrorist network had spread its tentacles into Jammu and Kashmir and, when Operation Enduring Freedom was launched to wipe this evil entity out, it expected that by logical extension, the aspect of cross-border terrorism from Pakistan into India would be part of the military campaign. New Delhi's misgivings first arose when Pakistan was allowed to take out the trapped Pakistani officers and men, along with non-Afghan foreign fighters, from Kunduz in November 2001, in the thick of the battle.

The international media, reporting on 23 November 2001 from Angi, northern Afghanistan, said that according to United Front sources, Pakistani airplanes had "once again" flown into the besieged city of Kunduz to evacuate "Pakistanis who have been fighting alongside Afghan Taleban forces trapped there". The planes arrived as United Front leaders prepared to accept a partial surrender of Taleban forces in the last northern city they held. But contradictory signals continued to reflect the fate of the town. "Earlier in the week," one report said, "(United Front) officials said they had been told by a Taleban leader in Kunduz that at least three Pakistani Air Force planes had landed in recent days on similar missions. Two more planes landed Thursday night, according to the latest report. One (United Front) official said that a group of people had been observed today waiting for another plane to arrive at the Kunduz airport. None of the sightings could be confirmed. American officials, who have been evasive on this subject, say they do not have information on the planes. Pakistani officials today declined comment." An explanation was available when a report posted on truthout.com noted with wry humour, "The United States is indebted to Pakistan for its support of the war against terrorism, but it has said it wants any foreign fighters trapped in Kunduz captured or killed. Pakistan has made it clear that it is deeply concerned about some of its agents and soldiers trapped in the town."[11]

The deliberate American policy of ignoring the escape of the trapped Pakistani and non-Afghan Taleban and al-Qaeda fighters from Kunduz convinced the Indian government that the Bush administration was not really concerned over the India-Pakistan angle except for preventing by any means a military confrontation between the two nuclear weapons adversarial neighbours. The Indian frustration at this deliberate neglect of the most serious problem faced by New Delhi was expressed in no uncertain terms by the Principal Secretary to the Prime Minister and National Security Adviser Brajesh Mishra at the 38th Munich Conference on Security Policy on 2 February 2002, when he asked, "Where are the thousands of foreign fighters and advisers of the Taleban who were trapped in Kunduz in the final phase of the military campaign but found a providential escape route?" The disappearance of the Taleban and al-Qaeda leaders and activists after the military campaign was "a matter of immediate security concern. Anyone who looks (at) the map of the region would understand why for India, this is a matter of immediate security concern. This is also why, India would like to see concrete evidence of a diminution of terrorism from across its borders before it acts on military de-escalation."

To return to Washington DC, where in madly hectic nine days since the cataclysmic morning of 11 September 2001, the plan for Operation Enduring Freedom had been evolving. It was on 20 September that President Bush, addressing a joint session of Congress, declared a "war on terror". On September eleventh, he said, enemies of freedom committed an act of war against (the United States). Americans had known wars – but for the past 136 years, they had been wars on foreign soil, except for one Sunday in 1941 (the Japanese attack on Pearl Harbour). Americans had known the casualties of war – but not at the centre of a great city on a peaceful morning. Americans had known surprise attacks – but never before on thousands of civilians. All of this was brought upon (the Americans) in a single day – and night fell on a different world, a world where freedom itself was under attack. "Americans have many questions tonight. Americans are asking: Who attacked our country? The evidence we have gathered all points to a collection of loosely affiliated terrorist organisations known as al-Qaeda. They are the same murderers indicted for bombing American embassies in Tanzania and Kenya, and responsible for bombing of the USS Cole. Al-Qaeda is to terror what the mafia is to crime. But its goal is not making money; its goal is remaking the world – and imposing its radical beliefs on people everywhere."[12]

Bush said that the terrorists practised a fringe form of Islamic extremism that had been rejected by Muslim scholars and the vast majority of Muslim clerics – a fringe movement that perverted the peaceful teachings of Islam. The terrorists' directive commanded them to kill Christians and Jews, to kill all Americans, and make no distinctions among military and civilians, including women and children. "This group and its leader – a person named (Osama) bin Laden – are linked to many other organisations in different countries, including the Egyptian Islamic Jihad and the Islamic Movement of Uzbekistan. There are thousands of these terrorists in more than sixty countries. They are recruited from their own nations and neighbourhoods, and brought to camps in places like Afghanistan where they are trained in the tactics of terror. They are sent back to their homes or sent to hide in countries around the world to plot evil and destruction."

Pointing out that the leadership of al-Qaeda had great influence in Afghanistan and supported the Taleban regime in controlling most of that country, Bush said, "In Afghanistan, we see al-Qaeda's vision for the world. Afghanistan's people have been brutalised – many are starving and many have fled. Women are not allowed to attend school. You can be jailed for owning a television. Religion can be practised only as their leaders dictate. A man can be jailed in Afghanistan if his beard is not long enough."

He said that while the United States respected the people of Afghanistan, it condemned the Taleban who were not only repressing their own people but they were also threatening people everywhere by sponsoring and sheltering and supplying terrorists. "By aiding and abetting murder, the Taleban regime is committing murder." Bush followed his rhetoric up with making the following demands on the Taleban: Deliver to (the) United States authorities all the leaders of al-Qaeda who hid in Afghanistan; release all foreign nationals – including American citizens – you have unjustly imprisoned, and protect foreign journalists, diplomats, and aid workers in your country; close immediately and permanently every terrorist training camp in Afghanistan and hand over every terrorist, and every person in their support structure, to appropriate authorities; and give the United States full access to terrorist training camps, so the United States can ensure that the camps are no longer operating. "These demands are not open to negotiation or discussion," Bush warned. "The Taleban must act and act immediately. They will hand over the terrorists, or they will share in their fate."

Being only too painfully conscious that the declaration of war on the Taleban could be considered as an assault on the Muslims, Bush also chose to address the Muslim world directly. He said, "I also want to speak tonight directly to Muslims throughout the world. We respect your faith. It is practised freely by many millions of Americans, and by millions more in countries that America counts as friends. Its teachings are good and peaceful, and those who commit evil in the name of Allah blaspheme the name of Allah. The terrorists are traitors to their own faith, trying, in effect, to hijack Islam itself. The enemy of America is not our many Muslim friends; it is not our many Arab friends. Our enemy is a radical network of terrorists, and every government that supports them. Our war on terror begins with al-Qaeda, but it does not end there. It will not end until every terrorist group of global reach has been found, stopped and defeated."

As *The Washington Post* research team later found out, almost in the very first few hours of the evolution of the American response to the 11 September terrorist attacks, the Bush administration had zeroed in on two vital segments of the policy to be adopted: Pakistan and the United Front. According to the reconstruction of the evolution of the United States response, it was on the 13 September 2001 morning that Central Intelligence Agency Director George Tenet said in the White House Situation Room, in the presence of Bush, that the United States could begin to go after bin Laden and the Taleban by invigorating the (United Front), the primary opposition force in Afghanistan, where bin Laden was hiding and operating. The Front's roughly 20,000 fighters were decidedly a mixed bag dominated by five factions, but in reality probably twenty-five sub-factions. It was a strained coalition of sometimes common interests, Tenet said. On the top of that, its most charismatic leader, Ahmad Shah Massoud, had been assassinated by two suicide bombers posing as journalists on 9 September, in what was believed to be an al-Qaeda operation. Without Massoud, the (United Front) was more fractured and leaderless than ever. (This impression persisted for sometime, for unfortunately, the view of Barnett Rubin, one of the foremost Afghanistan scholars, was not taken seriously. Rubin told the BBC emphatically on 11 September, "The opposition to the Taleban is not only the work of one man, no matter how important his skills were. It represents the views of a lot of the Afghan people. One way or another, the opposition will continue, even if not in the form of military actions by the United Front." Despite the obvious military weaknesses of the opposition forces, Rubin argued, "what they have managed over the past year or so is to hold onto territory in north-east Afghanistan through which the supplies flow, and some other leaders have returned to the country and managed to start military activities on a small scale.")

Continuing to build his case for associating the United Front with any military action that the United States would initiate, Tenet said that despite the "fractured and leaderless" state of the opposition forces, "...with the CIA teams and tons of money", the alliance could be brought together into a cohesive fighting force. The research team also found out that *the President and war cabinet members knew (that) the CIA was giving very limited financial and technical covert support to the (United Front) – several million dollars a year – under a previous intelligence order. The agency's paramilitary teams had periodically met clandestinely with alliance leaders over the past four years.* Tenet said that he could insert paramilitary teams inside Afghanistan with each warlord. Along with Special Forces teams from the United States military, the paramilitary forces would provide "eyes on the ground" for further American military action. American technological superiority would give the (United Front) a significant edge. The newspaper also revealed that the CIA had been on the ground in Afghanistan for years and had engaged in developing a more aggressive approach toward bin Laden and the Taleban prior to 11 September. The Pentagon, on the other hand, had not been asked or encouraged to do any planning as part of the pre-11 September process and, as a result, its thinking about fighting bin Laden turned out to be far more conventional, which frustrated Defence Secretary Donald H. Rumsfeld because Bush at that time was only looking for the unconventional.

The United Front was soon approached by the Americans, which could only be a welcome development for the former; at long last, Commander Massoud's fervent appeal to the United States for help was being heard, but the logic was quite different. The Americans had begun to woo the United Front only because there was no alternative to this opposition force.

A *New York Times* story of the period (24 September 2001) typifies the dichotomy displayed by the Americans. After describing how the "tiny, long ignored" Rabbani government's embassy in Dushanbe was suddenly buzzing with diplomatic activity, with American diplomats and Russian generals "coming, courting, testing the mettle of the new commander" of the United Front, General Muhammad Fahim, the story said, "While alliance officials here put on a brave face, doubts exist about its military abilities. The killing this month of Ahmad Shah Massoud could prove crippling. The alliance has also been accused of drug and gun-running and human rights violation, including summary executions, the burning of houses and looting. Most of the targets were ethnic Pushtuns, a base of Taleban support. *If it gains power, there are fears that the vicious internecine war that followed the Soviets' departure in 1989 could rekindle."* It was this expression of lack of confidence in the good intentions of the United Front that would pursue the opposition force even when it was entering Kabul as the victorious army.

The extent of dire predictions that journalists and scholars indulged in in this particular genre would be considered amazing in the context of another country.[13]

The height of presumptuousness that occurred was, of course, the stern Bush admonition to the United Front not to march into Kabul after the Bagram air base had fallen, which was done at the behest of Pakistan. To its credit, the United Front decided to ignore the warning and went ahead with taking Kabul over; for once, the Bush administration chose to ignore the slight administered by a weakling.[14]

Once Operation Enduring Freedom was launched with massive bombing expeditions and the United front forces, reinforced by American troops and logistical support, the preparations for forging a new government in the post-Taleban period (which was foreseeable) began. Reports from Rome said that former king Zahir Shah was ready to return to Afghanistan though he was not keen on a restoration of the monarchy. He sent signals about setting up a Loya Jirgah of tribal elders, Islamic intellectuals and other influential figures, to discuss the future of the country. *The Washington Post* quoted his youngest son, Mirwais, saying that the former royal family wished to see Afghanistan "have peace and for the people to decide their government in a democratic manner, with free elections." Reports also conveyed the former king's determination to see that the Afghan people were allowed complete freedom to choose their future.

Washington DC took due notice of this sentiment, which had emanated from other Afghan sources as well. The spokesman for the State Department Richard Boucher told a press conference on 3 October 2001 that "the future of Afghanistan, the decision on what kind of government they want to have, is for the Afghan people to decide, and we have worked with the United Nations, with other governments, with other groups, to try to understand that and try to work together with people to allow Afghanistan to eventually have a broad-based government." There was a direct question at the press conference concerning the former king, "Does the Administration think he has legitimacy to be the ruler of Afghanistan again?" To which, Boucher gave the following reply, "I'm going to answer this question the same way I have for the last week. And that is, we believe that Afghanistan needs, the Afghan people deserve, a broad-based government. We believe they deserve peace and stability. We have been the leading donor of assistance to the Afghan people. We have done a lot to see that they get that. But it is not for us to decide the future government of Afghanistan. And Afghans themselves will have to make that decision, and we work with the United Nations and others to try and help that process along."

By the first fortnight of October 2001, discerning observers reached the conclusion that the Taleban's days were numbered. In fact, Pakistani President Pervez Musharraf used this very language to describe the plight of the fundamentalist force his government had nurtured over the years. Reports began to appear that warlords had started deserting the ruling militia; but doubts lingered in many minds, especially as media reports over the years had created the impression that the Taleban were an irresistible force (since few media reports ever discussed or mentioned or probed the extent of Pakistan's and Arab and other non-Afghan fighters' role in the military victories of the Taleban). While some analysts felt at the time that the United Nations was projecting the former king as the head of the new government to be set up after the exit of the Taleban (judging by the remarks of the personal representative of the Secretary-General Francis Vendrell on 27 September 2001, in Islamabad, to the effect that he had found Zahir Shah in good health and willing to work for the betterment of his people), others thought that with even the United Front sending a delegation to meet him and extending support to him, his chances had certainly brightened.

Two parallel developments occurred around this time; Iran was apprehensive that the United States was trying to hoist a monarchy back on Afghanistan, which was next door to Iran, which could be followed up by a similar design for Teheran as well. On the other hand, the Pakistan government was fully engaged in churning up a "moderate" Taleban government to replace the existing one in order to hold on to its domain of influence. Some reports suggested that President Musharraf had planned to stage-manage a coup to topple Mullah Omar and replace him with a "moderate" Taleban leader who would be acceptable to the international community and to the Afghan minority communities as well. There was yet another school of thought which felt that for some years to come, after the exit of the Taleban, Afghanistan should be declared a United Nations-administered state, during which period a full-scale political process could be developed.

The United Front lost little time in calling the bluff of Pakistan. "There is no such thing as moderate Taleban elements," declared Dr Abdullah Abdullah, who was the foreign minister in the Burhanuddin Rabbani government and continues to be the foreign minister of the independent Afghanistan. "The Taleban will not be in the future government of Afghanistan," he emphasised. Dr Abdullah's firm 'No' came in the wake of suspicions in the United Front that the United States could be instrumental in brokering a deal between the former king, the Taleban and Pakistan, thereby seeking to marginalise the main opposition front representing the minority communities. All this was happening in the backdrop of a visit to the former king by President Musharraf's emissary Sayed Ahmad Gailani, a former mujahid and a leading religious figure. Gailani told the media in Rome, "We have met the king and we have reached total agreement. To let moderate Taleban inside Afghanistan's future government has always been our position and the former king has agreed with us." The former king himself, however, was emphatic in his utterances about two things: that the Taleban must be replaced, describing the fundamentalists as "degenerates" and "an occupying force" and that it was the people of Afghanistan who would choose their new rulers at a Loya Jirgah. "Most important for me at my age is not something that could happen to me but a happy Afghanistan that could get rid of the cruelty imposed upon it," he said in an interview to the BBC. Hamid Karzai, who had returned to Pakistan at the time, told *The Daily Telegraph*,

"Hundreds of the Taleban are sending their families to the countryside or to Pakistan and are ready to defect the moment the king gives an order for a national uprising. We believe that the ground will soon be ready to hold a Loya Jirgah inside Afghanistan with the help of international powers, the United Nations and the Organisation of Islamic Conference. The American forces cannot just come in, do their job and go. They must help the Afghan people restore Afghanistan's independence so that we create a government that is part of the international community."

International diplomacy was heightened to an unprecedented extent as the war against the Taleban-al-Qaeda regime intensified. Clearly, every major government wanted to have a say in the future of Afghanistan, leading to a situation in which acrimony between governments got exposed almost on a daily basis. France, Germany and the United Kingdom held a closed door meeting on the future of Afghanistan a couple of hours ahead of the European Union summit being held at the time in Ghent, Belgium, opening on 19 October 2001. When Italy came to know of this exercise of exclusivity and backdoor diplomacy, it flared up. "Earlier this week," Italian diplomats told the media, "the French Foreign Minister Hubert Vedrine was making joint statements in Rome about the political future of Afghanistan. Today, Italy has not even been invited to this meeting. This kind of behaviour is damaging." President of the European Union and former Italian Prime Minister Romano Prodi said that the meeting was damaging to European unity. Turkish Prime Minister Bulent Ecevit said that Western nations had so far failed in their efforts to find a solution to Afghanistan's future. While Arab nations welcomed Turkey's intervention as part of a United Nations mediation effort, British Foreign Secretary Jack Straw said, "I sought the advice of Prime Minister Ecevit about the future of Afghanistan bearing in mind the key political, geographical and historical role of Turkey's relations in Central Asia and Afghanistan."[15]

Around this time, on 26 October 2001, came a piece of news which may not have attracted adequate attention at the time but helps explain the situation today, when remnants of the Taleban-al-Qaeda network continue to elude the coalition forces trying to detect and eliminate them and also manage to carry out fairly serious terrorist attacks within Afghanistan, including the 5 September 2002 assassination attempt on President Hamid Karzai.

According to this story, Taleban "infiltrators" who were sneaking into Pakistan from the heavily bombed eastern and southern Afghanistan were quietly "colonising" Pakistani border areas and setting up a logistics base, which was being boosted by volunteers, medical treatment, cash and food. "United States warplanes roar overhead on their way to Afghanistan but they cannot touch the Taleban networkers who are successfully tapping religious, tribal and family ties, making the wild, sun-baked plains of Baluchistan province a sanctuary from the bombing. Several times a week, ambulances deposit wounded fighters at hospitals in Quetta, the province's biggest city, and in the opposite direction new recruits and former veterans, including doctors, make the six-hour car drive to Kandahar," the report said. Daily donations collected at mosques, bazaars, homes and offices exceeded ten thousand sterling pound, according to Said Sanan, a Taleban officer who defected to Pakistan two weeks earlier. "Baluchistan is important to the Taleban. They are soaking up the support," he told the British newspaper.[16]

The report quoted analysts saying that Baluchistan could become a rallying point from which militants could launch a guerrilla campaign against a post-Taleban government should they be ousted from Afghanistan. Read in the context of the recent parliamentary elections in Pakistan, in which the religious coalition Muttahida-Majlis-e-Amal (MMA) has gained superiority and will shortly form governments in the two provinces of Baluchistan and North West frontier Province, what the Taleban-al-Qaeda network accomplished a year ago assumes both significance and urgency. There is little doubt that the remnants of the network, who were relatively in the doghouse in the aftermath of the emergence of a popular government in Kabul and the continued global war against terrorism, must have received more than a psychological boost with the electoral victory of the MMA, which has quite unambiguously declared its anti-Americanism and its opinion that the present Afghan government is nothing more than a puppet regime of the Bush administration. Significantly, the Karzai government too came out with comments which betrayed its sense of uneasiness at the stunning electoral victory of the Islamist coalition in Pakistan.

On the battlefront, Operation Enduring Freedom was obviously taking longer time than popular imagination would allow. Media reports suggested, when the campaign was a month old, that it was not at all going the way it should have; allowing no room for the obvious uncertainties involved in the unique nature of the campaign, in relation to the terrain in particular. Toward the end of October 2001, there were unconfirmed reports that like Commander Abdul Haq, who had been caught and executed by the Taleban for attempting to raise a rebellion within the Pushtuns in southern Afghanistan, another rebel Pushtun leader Hamid Karzai had been caught and executed. On 6 November 2001, however, United States Defence Secretary Donald H. Rumsfeld scotched the rumour and that United States Special Forces had pulled Karzai out of southern Afghanistan for consultations and denied that he had ever been caught and put in custody by the Taleban. "To my knowledge," he said, "he was not detained or held by the Taleban. It was a very sensible arrangement whereby he requested to be extracted for a period, and we cooperated. As for Haq, one of the few Pushtuns who were actively fighting the Taleban on behalf of the opposition United Front, it was soon revealed that he was apprehended while he was on a mission to instigate a localised rebellion against the Taleban in southern Afghanistan."

The author, however, wrote about the true circumstances of Haq's death. "Abdul Haq, the one-time commander of Kabul, who was arrested on spying charges and executed on 26 October by the Taleban, was a victim of his own perceptions of the 'moderate' Taleban and the culpability of the ISI of Pakistan." Haq's tragic end should serve as an eye-opener to those who were talking of "moderate" Taleban who could be converted into potential allies in forming a broad-based government to fill the vacuum when the Taleban were removed. As the circumstances of Haq's misadventure inside Afghanistan were being speculated upon, the available intelligence suggested that the astonishing extent of his exploits was based necessarily and unfortunately on the premise that the Taleban would not kill a fellow-Pushtun (this impression persisted despite the experience of the assassination of former President Najibullah, who also believed that there would be no danger for him from his community).[17]

Prior to October 2001, Haq returned to active politics and thus re-entered the tortuous history of Afghanistan. The mission he took upon himself was to facilitate the return of former king Zahir Shah from Rome to Kabul. During this period, he moved back and forth ceaselessly between Washington DC, London, Rome, Islamabad and Dushanbe, talking in turn to the Bush administration, the Labour government, an initially indifferent Italian government, the Musharraf regime, the ISI and Commander Massoud. According to the United Front, Massoud advised Haq to continue his efforts to get the former king back in saddle but cautioned that the coalition comprising the Taleban, the Pakistan government, the ISI and Osama bin Laden and al-Qaeda would not abdicate in favour of Zahir Shah despite the ethnic link. Massoud also told Haq that he would not be interested in setting up an exiled government outside the territory of Afghanistan and pointed out that the United Front continued to control nearly thirty per cent of the territory. The sources said that Haq's proposal to work together to bring the former king back and strive for forming a broad-based government with him at its head came at a time when the United Front and the ousted Burhanuddin Rabbani government were virtually completely absent from the radars of the western governments. Despite the bleak prospects, Commander Massoud conveyed to Haq that he would not be interested in joining a Loya Jirgah "outside Afghanistan" even though "all of us are working for a Loya Jirgah". Massoud emphasised that the Loya Jirgah should create a king or leader and not the other way round. Thus, even though he advised Haq to continue his efforts to bring Zahir Shah back, his underlined message was that "Do not expect much from your efforts because these are flawed." The ethnicity of Zahir Shah would not really wash with the Taleban.

As the subsequent developments showed, Haq went about his mission with undiminished zeal, facilitated to a large extent by the Pakistan government's gift of a spacious bungalow and armed bodyguards. The CIA had by then adopted the suave and accomplished ex-mujahideen politician as its engine to propel the supposed "moderate" Taleban elements into an adequately cohesive group to initiate a move to dislodge the Taleban from the seat of power. The strategy relied for its success essentially on the assumption that the Pushtun ethnicity would help win the day.

"The rest is history," the author wrote. As the Musharraf regime and the ISI watched benignly, Haq sneaked into Afghanistan with a band of trusted men without apparently realising that the very men he had been confiding in, the so-called "moderate" Taleban (his faith reinforced by Islamabad's certificate about the moderation of these men) had already betrayed him. Kandahar was, therefore, ready to strike and it did. Quite unintentedly, Haq passed into history.

At the 6 November 2001 press conference, Rumsfeld also talked about the uncertainties of the war against terrorism in the backdrop of growing doubts over the military capabilities of the United Front forces. He said that there was no telling how long it would take for the anti-Taleban forces to succeed. As one report put it, he declined to say whether the opposition forces in northern Afghanistan would ultimately succeed.

The war was now about seven weeks old and, not excluding the Bush administration, there were plenty of doubts about the goals and strategies of the campaign, all of which were adequately reflected in the media. "Beware of unsavoury Afghan allies," warned the *International Herald Tribune* in its 11 October 2001 edition in a contributed article. "As it supports local commanders, the United States should consider carefully the dismal human rights records of some of its new allies. From 1992 to 1997, forces that are now part of the alliance shelled civilian neighbourhoods in Kabul and looted, raped and killed civilians there and in other parts of the country. No Afghan commander from this period has been held accountable for violations of international humanitarian law. Nor has the alliance indicated any willingness to bring to justice any of its commanders. Now accountability appears to have taken a back seat to expediency as America hastily assembles and supports a broad opposition to the Taleban."

A more sensible effort by *The Washington Post*, "Lessons from Somalia for War in Afghanistan" in its 31 October 2001 edition, felt that "...as in Somalia, the Bush administration has let the political and military tracks diverge – the bombing may be precisely targeted on the Taleban, but it has no political endgame to guide it. The political talks that are under way are ambitious, seeking to include every faction and ethnic group under a United Nations umbrella, but already there is talk of turning security over to non-American foreign forces, which as in Somalia would stand no chance of beating off a challenge from any one of the many warlords." With the benefit of hindsight, one would say that the article, based on interviews of two Americans previously involved with Somalia, ambassador Robert Oakley and United Nations commander Jonathan Howe, was not as terribly off the mark as the IHT one, quoted above. The International Security Assistance Force, a multinational force, is about to complete one year in Afghanistan; yes, some of the Afghan warlords have been quite a headache; but no one would say that the security situation is worse than a year ago. Afghanistan has by now proved to be no Somalia.

In a 27 October 2001 editorial, *The New York Times* was almost in panic over the possibility that the United Front forces might actually march into Kabul any moment in the (then) near future. It also displayed fetching sympathy for Pakistan's interests in Afghanistan. "A government that marginalises Pushtuns would be unacceptable to Pakistan and would undermine its leader, General Pervez Musharraf, who has taken political risks to align himself with the United States," the venerable NYT advised. Therefore, even if you cannot prevent the United Front forces from entering Kabul, kindly ensure that a coalition government is put in place "that reaches well beyond the discredited warlords of the (United Front)."

In the midst of all the doubts and uncertainties, a completely new element emerged to confound the confusion, the risk that Pakistan's nuclear arsenal might fall into rogues' hands. The IHT said on 2 November 2001 that American policy-makers were casting a wary eye towards their "troubled, nuclear-armed ally, Pakistan. Quoting a *New Yorker* story by Seymour Hersh, it said that elite United States and Israeli units were being trained to take out Pakistan's nuclear weapons to make sure that the warheads did not fall into the hands of renegades, if Musharraf were toppled by Islamist opponents." This particular line of thought at the time gave rise to considerable acrimony and denial on the part of the Pakistan government and media.

While it might seem improbable today, there were actually cries to halt the coalition bombings when the campaign was barely one month old. A typical letter published in the IHT on 31 October 2001 said, "The United States and Britain will have a disaster on their hands in Afghanistan if they do not cease bombing and start a food and shelter programme for millions of ordinary Afghans immediately... the relentless heavy bombing tells a different story (from the one, according to which the war was against terrorists and their protectors). It is the ordinary Afghans who are suffering. They are the ones who have been subjected to terror and hunger. ...Prolonged bombing of an impoverished country is turning even the most liberal minded people in Pakistan, and indeed the whole world, against the United States' policies of bombing."

Sanity and wisdom also prevailed as opinions were expressed around the world thick and fast. "This war can't be won if Pakistan dictates the rules," said a 30 October 2001 article in *The Weekly Standard*. "The Bush administration has pursued a Pakistan-centred policy toward the war in Afghanistan," it said. "It seeks a political solution that will not offend an ally, Pakistan's nimble leader Pervez Musharraf or his allies, the Pushtun tribes that have supported the Taleban. This policy has been driven in part by the spectre of a nuclear-armed Pakistan descending into an Islamic revolution and by a fear that General Musharraf is the last wall against the fundamentalist hordes. If the West allows itself to be blackmailed because of fear of chaos in a nuclear-armed Muslim country, then it will surely get blackmailed repeatedly. The Talebanisation of Pakistan will stop only when the Taleban in Afghanistan have been extirpated."

There was lament that efforts to build a political alternative to the Taleban were proving to be in disarray. "It's a disaster," said a Western diplomat, unnamed, according to a story in *The Washington Post*. No powerful leader had emerged to unify Afghanistan's largest ethnic group, the Pushtuns, who dominated the Taleban leadership. Rifts were also developing in a recent partnership between the United Front and former king Zahir Shah.

The United States precision bombing was at this time striking "systematically" a network of caves and tunnels in eastern Afghanistan where Osama bin Laden was thought to be hiding. United States planes also began to airdrop ammunition to opposition forces facing the Taleban front line north of Kabul. United States Defence Secretary Donald Rumsfeld said that some second-level al-Qaeda leaders had been killed since the campaign began on the 7th October. "To our knowledge," he said, "none of the very top six, eight, ten people have been included in that." The United Front said that it had agreed to launch a major offensive on Mazar-i-Sharif. American attacks began to focus increasingly on the "engagement zones" where Taleban-opposition faced each other. Explosions numbering between twenty and twenty-five rocked several Taleban positions north of Kabul. While the area was pummelled by American bombers on 27 October, the attacks were "less robust" on the following day. American warplanes appeared to be targeting Taleban forces on positions overlooking the United Front-held Bagram airfield north of Kabul. "It was unclear," one report said on 30 October 2001, "whether the attacks on caves and tunnels meant that the United States military was closer to locating bin Laden."

The world's imagination was taken up with the image of Afghanistan's caves and tunnels which had sheltered warriors even during Alexander the Great's invasion two thousand years ago. The added novelty of the highly sophisticated war machinery of the United States, inclusive of devices which could pinpoint people hiding in caves by the courtesy of geostationary satellites and thermal imagery, heightened the excitement. "When the Soviet Union took on Afghanistan in 1979," recalled an article in the *Los Angeles Times* (31 October 2001), "its troops found themselves crawling, terrified, through a vast network of mountain caves studded with knives and booby traps, pursuing mujahideen fighters who seemed to melt into mountainsides like the night itself." Defence officials, according to the article, acknowledged that there were hundreds, if not thousands, of caves, tunnels, aqueducts and bunkers in the mountains and deserts of Afghanistan, the legacy of centuries of warfare and of an ancient farming technique that relied on underground water supplies. But if fighters loyal to the Taleban and bin Laden holed up inside mountains to escape United States troops and the bitter Afghan winter, reconnaissance planes equipped with thermal-guided cameras could spot them sitting around fires. Laser-guided missiles on Talon gunships could be trained on them. "The meticulous preparations being made by United States military planners to weaken the defences of the Taleban and the al-Qaeda terrorist network suggest that they have learned from Soviet mistakes.

With the vastly more sophisticated technology at their disposal," the article said quoting unnamed analysts, "Finding the enemy in the highlands of Afghanistan is still likely to be difficult, but far from impossible."

For more than ten days (since around 20 October) United States warplanes went on dropping 5,000-pound laser-guided 'bunker buster' bombs developed for the Gulf War. To detect the caves, the CIA's Gnat and the United States Air Force's Predator and U-2 unmanned reconnaissance aircraft were equipped with high-accuracy ASARS- radars. The Pentagon planned to outfit low-flying helicopters in the winter with thermal-guided cameras designed to detect and photograph hot spots underground. Then AGM-130 missiles could be directed into tunnel mouths. "You can basically imagine the gunships just going out at night looking for warm spots on mountainsides," the article quoted a security expert saying. "They can detect a group sitting around a fire, just by the body heat and the heat of the fire."

On 8 November 2001, the United Front, about seven kilometres away, announced that they were about to capture Mazar-i-Sharif. "God willing," said a deputy to senior commander Atta Mohammad, "we will soon enter Mazar-i-Sharif. Very soon you will hear the good news that we have liberated it."

The same day, in Washington DC, Rumsfeld and the United States commander for operations in Afghanistan, United States Army General Tommy Franks pronounced themselves satisfied with the way coalition operations had progressed to date. Franks told the media, "We like the progress we have had up to this point." Responding to criticism of a tardy progress, he said, "Frequently, we will undertake military operations at the same time we build capacity." Rumsfeld elaborated, "Because they don't have armies and navies and air forces, and because we're not really arrayed the way one is in a traditional, conventional conflict, what you're going to see... ultimately, is the effect of all the pressure that's being put on, through law enforcement, through intelligence gathering, through financial freezing of accounts, as well as the air war and the work that's being done on the ground. And what will happen is life will become so difficult for al-Qaeda and the Taleban that people would decide they'd prefer not to have them in their country at some point."[18]

Franks confirmed that ground combat operations by the United front forces against the Taleban – he called it a big fight – were occurring near Mazar-i-Sharif, but he declined to pronounce an outcome to the battle. He also noted that securing the city would be useful in order to "provide a land bridge... up to Uzbekistan, which provides us, among other things, a humanitarian pathway for us to move supplies out of Central Asia and down into Afghanistan." Franks reiterated that the use of ground troops – United States or coalition members – had not been ruled out. He refused to speculate on the size and extent of Taleban casualties or remaining troop strength.

It was at this juncture of the war against terrorism that one of the most curious events took place. Less than a day after the United Front captured Mazar-i-Sharif, both the United States and Pakistan warned the victorious opposition force not to move on Kabul. This was followed by an anti-Taleban Pushtun leader, Haji Mohammed Zaman, urging the United Front not to take Kabul, arguing that time should be allowed for political efforts involving former king Zahir Shah. The BBC, quite appropriately, reported on 11 November 2001 that the fall of Mazar-i-Sharif had caused "unease" in Pakistan, which had long opposed the United Front and which was too close to India. Besides, the United Front was virtually unrepresentative as far as the Pushtuns, the majority community, was concerned. While Pakistan also argued that after all, it was Commander Massoud's forces which were mainly responsible for the mayhem that occurred during the mujahideen rule in Kabul, the BBC noted what was historically correct, namely, that much of the bloodshed was caused by the bombardment of Kabul by Gulbuddin Hekmatyar who was backed by Pakistan.

It was on 11 November 2001 that Bush indicated that while the United Front would be encouraged to move south, the United States would not want its forces to enter Kabul. "We share a common view," Bush said, "that in order for there to be a country that is stable and peaceful on this good leader's western border, that any power arrangement must be shared with the different tribes within Afghanistan. A key signal of that will be how the city of Kabul is treated." His comments were made after his first-ever meeting with Pakistan President Pervez Musharraf on the previous day. Reporting on the talks between the two presidents, *Dawn* wrote in its 12 November 2001 issue, "This (Bush's admonition to the United Front not to capture Kabul) was described as the most specific comment so far by the United States president on the direction of the war in Afghanistan and apparently backed the assessment of Gen. Musharraf, who said his view that Kabul should not be taken by the opposition force was based on the past experience of mayhem in the Afghan capital." Doing so could trigger "the same kind of atrocities being perpetrated against the people there" after the Soviet Union left Afghanistan more than a decade ago. Bush praised Pakistan's efforts in the fight against terrorism which, he said, benefited the entire world and linked Pakistan more closely with the international community. "The United States wants to help Pakistan build these linkages. I've authorised a lifting of sanctions, and over $1 billion in United States support. I will also help debt relief for Pakistan."

Bush's unambiguous corroboration of Musharraf's demand that the United Front should not march into Kabul as the victorious army appeared to have reassured Pakistan considerably. *The News*, in its 12 November 2001 issue, quoted a Pakistani government official saying Pakistan's stand that the United Front had a despicable record of brutalities and atrocities in power and should not be allowed to take over Afghanistan, had been unambiguously accepted by President Bush during his meeting with President Musharraf in New York on 10 November. "With Bush's acceptance of Pakistan's views, Islamabad stands vindicated," he said. "We are quite satisfied with the development. The (United Front) represents only a minority in Afghanistan." The Pakistani official went to the extent of suggesting that Pakistani soldiers would form part of the international peace-keeping force for Afghanistan, which would in any case mainly comprise troops from Muslim countries. And "Pakistani troops will be in a better position to help the United Nations peace-keeping force in Afghanistan because of (the) Pakistani people's long-standing affinity (with Afghanistan)." Around that time, Pakistani army officers and men were still helping the Taleban forces to fight the United Front.

Musharraf told *The Washington Post*, when asked whether the takeover of Kabul by the United Front would start a civil war, "Yes, certainly. The problem is there are different ethnic groups – the Uzbeks, the Hazaras, the Tajiks and the Pushtuns. The taking of Kabul by the minority groups – the (United Front) is composed of minority groups – will be fiercely opposed by the Pushtuns and will lead to anarchy." Still canvassing for the "moderate" Taleban to get a foothold in any future government, through whom Islamabad would hope to retain some of its influence on Afghanistan, Musharraf said, "The moderate Taleban are willing to bring about change. They should be accepted in a future coalition." (Earlier on 1 November 2001, he told *Asahi Shimbun*, "Participation of moderate Taleban members in a new Afghan government is indispensable.") Denying the charge that the Taleban were created by the ISI, Musharraf denied vociferously any Pakistani culpability, saying, "No. The Taleban are homegrown. After the Soviets left, the ethnic groups were fighting, and gave rise to the Taleban. They are not a creation of Pakistan at all." Denying that the Pakistani military was sympathetic toward the Taleban, he said, "Not at all. We had diplomatic relations with the Taleban for a reason: They represented the Pushtun community and controlled ninety per cent of Afghanistan. There are Pushtuns on our side of the border. There was no alternative but to have diplomatic relations. It was not wrong then or now." He also set no score by the Indian allegation that terrorists trained in camps in Afghanistan had entered the Indian state of Jammu and Kashmir by crossing Pakistan. "That's the Indian view," he said, "but it's not the case at all."

It was during this visit to New York that Musharraf pitched in with his suggestion that bombings should be stopped during Ramadan, a holy month in the Islamic calender. The suggestion had emanated from several other sources as well. Asked by anchorman Ted Koppel if he still felt that bombings should cease, Musharraf said, "…I've always been saying that preferably the operation had to be short, and it would have been much desirable that the operation terminated before Ramadan. But then, I've been saying that strategic objectives have to be achieved. One understands that. But then, I'm very conscious that sensitivities of the month of Ramadan must be considered." Pressed further to spell out his precise worries if bombings were continued, he said, "Well, I can't be very positive about it, but I said that it will have negative effect on the Muslim world. Now I don't think it's going to be such that to take it over-seriously, but it will have a negative effect." Further on, Musharraf almost conveyed his deep unhappiness over the bombings, "...an operation which is focused against terrorists, their supporters, and their abettors, on the television all around, it's being – it has got a projection as if this is a war against Afghanistan, against the poor and innocent people of Afghanistan. That's the unfortunate part. So it is having an effect that way of people being against the bombing of Afghanistan is increasing all around the world, I would say. But that doesn't mean that they are not conscious of the tragedy of the 11th September."[19]

United States Deputy Secretary of Defence Paul Wolfowitz called Musharraf's bluff when he said, in response to a question at a press conference in Washington DC on 9 November 2001, "We're not going to write a blueprint for Ramadan. We know that Ramadan is a special time. I think it's a time to concentrate even more than we do anyway, which is a lot, on things like humanitarian operations. But let's also remember that the people are suffering up north because of Taleban oppression, because of Taleban cutting off humanitarian assistance, that those people suffering and dying are Muslims, and I don't think stopping the war and leaving them under Taleban oppression for an extra month is doing any favour to Muslims anywhere." A tough, but eminently sensible, stand, indeed.[20]

In an interesting footnote, the Iranian media reported on 11 November 2001 that around 200 Pakistani fighters had been killed in Mazar-i-Sharif on 9-10 November after its capture by United Front forces on 8 November. Haji Mohammad Muhaqiq, heading the faction representing the Shia Hazara community and also the political committee of Hizb-i-Wahdat, told the Iranian *Entekhab* newspaper that the opposition forces had encircled some 1,200 Pakistanis in the Maktab Soltan Raziyeh area who were "not able to flee" with the Taleban. "We gave them warnings to surrender," Muhaqiq was quoted saying. "They asked us to send representatives over several times, but unfortunately they shot them. So far, six of our men have been killed. Finally, we gave the order to attack them and the clashes are still continuing. Some 200 of Pakistanis have been killed."

As far as Musharraf was concerned, the longer the war continued, the greater were the dangers of further exposures of Pakistan's close association with the Taleban-al-Qaeda regime. Hence, his insistence that the war should be short and be over before Ramadan, while its objectives should be achieved. The two interviews, however, conveyed an impression that he was not quite hopeful about the fulfillment of the objectives of the war. It took Koppel considerable efforts to get the Pakistani president admit that the Americans had presented evidence which had linkages with Osama bin Laden. "Yes, we were shown proof, and there were – we saw that there were linkages leading to Osama bin Laden," Musharraf said in response to persistent questions by Koppel. At the same time, however, the president was at pains to emphasise that his government had not examined the evidence "judicially". Asked if the linkages were definitive, he said, "Fairly definitive. But we didn't go in to do analysis of all this, and we didn't like to sit in judgment on this, on the evidence. Therefore, since a lot of circumstantial evidence was leading to that, and the proof that was shown to us was leading – having linkages with them."

Quite correctly, Koppel viewed Musharraf's answer as implying that the evidence about bin Laden's culpability was not definitive and he asked him again to be specific. This apparently alerted Musharraf who did not obviously wish to be seen as expressing doubts over the authenticity of what the Americans were asking him to accept, and he, therefore, answered, "Well, it is (definitive) – it is. I said we haven't analysed it judicially, or we haven't been that analytical about it. We were shown proof, and we thought that it is adequate, the evidence is leading to a linkage with Osama bin Laden."

It was four days after Mazar-i-Sharif fell to the United Front that on 13 November 2001 Kabul was captured. All the warnings issued by Bush and Musharraf were apparently swept aside and the victorious United Front forces marched into the capital, driving the Taleban out after a five-year infamous rule. Nearly a month and a half earlier, Mullah Omar had warned that the Taleban would retreat to the mountains and wage a long war against any successor government if his government was toppled in an attack on Afghanistan. "Taleban are an organised force," he had thundered. "Theirs is not a government like that of Zahir Shah whose government was toppled and his forces surrendered before another authority. If the Taleban government is toppled, they would retreat to the mountains." Omar went to the extent of warning former king Zahir Shah who, at the time, appeared close to being persuaded to return and head a Taleban-less dispensation, "Don't be mistaken. People will come after you and kill you." Interestingly, it was Mullah Omar who first talked of the possibility of "moderate" Taleban playing a role in a future set-up, a line that was taken up with considerable enthusiasm by Pakistan.

Pakistan viewed the developments as a complete reversal for its policies, but doggedly pursued its aim of not allowing the United Front more space in the future administration than absolutely unavoidable. With this purpose in mind, it held parleys with Iran, Saudi Arabia and the United States to ensure that there would be a "broad-based" government implying that the new set-up would have adequate pro-Pakistani Pushtun representation. Musharraf held on to his familiar plea that on the first count, the majority Afghan community should be adequately represented in the new government; and, on the second count, unless the Afghan Pushtuns were mollified, Pakistan would face fresh turmoil in its frontier provinces where the ethnic Pushtuns dominated. He counselled with senior government officials and two corps commanders on 16 November 2001, and confabulated with United States special envoy for Afghanistan James Dobbins twice on the 17th, both agreeing on the need to support the United Nations process to restore normalcy in Afghanistan.

Pakistan's nervousness kept on increasing as United Front leaders and their men began to occupy various ministry buildings in Kabul and former President Burhanuddin Rabbani came out with a statement that foreign troops, and even those from other Muslim countries, were not necessary for maintaining peace. Speaking to *Vremya Novostei* on 21 November 2001, he said that he would only welcome foreign humanitarian missions in his country. "The people of Afghanistan are tired of the roar of bombers and the pounding of artillery guns. They want calm," he added. On 16 November, the Indian government stated that the positioning of a peace-keeping force should be based on a "consensus" and must be implemented in a manner that was "acceptable to the country involved". Around the same time, the Russian government found it necessary to warn "certain countries" against pushing their narrow interests in Afghanistan. Foreign Minister Igor Ivanov was quoted by the Russian news agencies on 17 November, saying, "We believe (that) this is a dangerous attempt which can aggravate contradictions within Afghanistan," since differences among other countries could lead to a new civil war in Afghanistan. Russian government sources explained that the minister was addressing Pakistan directly through his statement.

In the very first spat between the victorious United Front and other governments, the former objected to the arrival of 100 British marines without a prior consultation with the Afghans. The objection from Kabul followed a statement by the Rabbani regime's envoy in London Ahmad Wali Massoud, who said, "We were not told (that) the British troops were arriving at Bagram. We do not know why they are there. Foreign armies should be careful about going into Afghanistan." The British government, however, countered the United Front objection by claiming that the marines had been sent only after the Front had been informed about the development "at the highest level". While it added that more British troops would be leaving for Afghanistan soon, Prime Minister Tony Blair sounded ecstatic over the major role that British troops would be playing in the country in the days to come.

The closure of the lone Taleban embassy in the world, the one in the hitherto enormously hospitable Islamabad, came on 22 November 2001, hours after the United States declared on the previous day that the only way to avoid a confrontation in Kunduz province – where the majority of Taleban supporters were holed up at the time – was for the Taleban and their supporters to surrender to the United Front. The American ultimatum was followed swiftly by another from the United Front, which named the following day as the date for the ultimatum to expire.

A spokesperson for the coalition Kenton W. Keith told a media conference in Islamabad on the day that there was little anyone could do in Kunduz if the Taleban refused to surrender. Pakistan President Pervez Musharraf, desperate even at this late hour to salvage whatever he could of the Taleban and Pakistanis, identified with the fundamentalist militia, pleaded with Blair and Powell that the offer of surrender by some of the persons "previously aligned with the Taleban" should be considered on humanitarian grounds. The coalition spokesperson, however, pleaded ignorant of any such offer and said that the matter of surrender had to be settled purely between the United Front and those who might be surrendering.

Putting the situation in Kunduz in the right perspective, he said, "It is important to remember that those who are hiding in Kunduz are a group of the most hardened fighters. They are not only heavily armed but are also using them. As we see it, the easy way to stop the conflict in Kunduz is by the surrender of these forces. I can assure that those who surrender would be treated with dignity."

Interestingly, the spokesperson also sought to allay the commonly held fear that the United Front was a bunch of blood-thirsty hooligans, an impression constantly underlined by the likes of Musharraf and several Western commentators. He said, "We have been observing the situation. The (United Front) is not only a disciplined force but it acted in moderation while taking over Mazar-i-Sharif and Kabul. The Taleban (are) a threat to the whole world. To make a comparison between the Taleban of today and the (United Front) of yesterday is not correct." It may be recalled that both Musharraf and various Western commentators had predicted dire consequences for the Taleban and residents when opposition forces would capture Mazar-i-Sharif and Kabul.

Meanwhile, a spokesman for Mullah Omar said at Spin Baldak that the Taleban had decided not to abandon Kandahar and would fight to defend the five southern and eastern provinces still under their control. Claiming that the Taleban had lost all contact with Osama bin Laden, the spokesman said, "You should forget the 11 September attacks because now there is a new fighting against Muslims and Islam, and the international terrorists like America and Britain are killing daily our innocent people." The spokesman also asserted that Mullah Omar would never leave Kandahar.

India was also watching the Kunduz situation, as there were credible reports of the presence of at least 1,000 Pakistanis amongst the 4,000 or so of Taleban fighters, besides a fairly large number of other non-Afghans. As New Delhi considered the situation, it felt that if the Taleban fighters did not surrender and escape, especially the Pakistanis, the outcome could be grave for India since most of them would in all probability land in the Pakistan-held Kashmir and continue to fight Indian forces by infiltrating into Jammu and Kashmir. Unfortunately, this fear proved to be true when, with clear American connivance, Pakistani officers and men along with scores of other non-Afghans, were allowed to be airlifted and ferried to safety in Pakistan.

However, as the Taleban held on to Kandahar and parts of southern and eastern Afghanistan, an Indian delegation led by special envoy S. K. Lambah visited Kabul and met with President of the Islamic State of Afghanistan Burhanuddin Rabbani, Defence Minister Gen. Mohammad Fahim, Foreign Minister Dr Abdullah Abdullah and Interior Minister Yonus Qanooni on 21 November 2001. The fact that the United Front was in the forefront of government-making in the post-Taleban Afghanistan apparently placed India in an advantageous position as New Delhi had steadfastly supported the opposition coalition throughout the Taleban period. Returning to New Delhi, Lambah told mediapersons that "The visit was very useful. It enabled us to meet Afghan leaders and get a first-hand information about the situation." The resumption of relations between New Delhi and Kabul was seen at the time as a kind of poetic justice, for it symbolised a major defeat of Islamabad's Afghanistan policy, namely, to keep India out of Afghanistan altogether, which it successfully carried out during the five years of the Taleban rule.

As the United Nations process for normalisation of Afghanistan, which was under way for some time, began to gather steam, global attention was focused on the main contenders that were emerging on the scene. Broadly speaking, they were Burhanuddin Rabbani (Tajik), Gen. Fahim (Tajik), Abdullah (Tajik-Pushtun), Rawan Farhadi (Tajik), Gen. Rashid Dostum (Uzbek), Mohammad Atta (Tajik), Mohammad Mohaqiq, Hamid Karzai (Pushtun), Gul Agha Sherazai (Pushtun), Gen. Abdul Malik Pahalwan, Ismael Khan (Tajik), Karim Khalili (Hazara), Abdul Rasul Sayyaf (Pushtun), Gulbuddin Hekmatyar (Pushtun), Younis Khalis (Pushtun), Pir Sayed Ahmad Gailani (Pushtun), Abdul Qadeer (Pushtun), Zahir Shah and Abdul Wali (Pushtun).

It was on 25 November 2001 that Kunduz, the last Taleban-al-Qaeda held city, fell to the advancing army of the United Front, effectively ending resistance in the north. The capture of the city, which continued to prove to be incomplete with pockets of resistance offering fight, followed the surrender of a large number of Afghan and non-Afghan fighters, including the top Taleban commander Noorallah Noori. Doubts, however, persisted over the attitude of al-Qaeda fighters, mostly Arabs, Chechens and Pakistanis. The Afghan Taleban who had surrendered were segregated from the non-Afghans, and the United Front force under Gen. Daoud Khan stayed ready for any eventuality, since the uprising of foreign fighters in Mazar-i-Sharif, leading to a bloody massacre, after the surrender remained fresh in memory.

A *PTI* (*Press Trust of India*) story datelined Islamabad and dated 25 November portrayed a visibly dismayed Pakistan at the surrender in Kunduz. "A senior Pakistani official watched in dismay on Saturday as the television in his office showed Taleban fighters streaming out of Kunduz in Afghanistan to surrender to the (United Front)," it ran. "'I am sorry to put it in this way,' he said, switching off the set. 'But Rumsfeld's been extremely callous.' Pakistan has been mesmerised by the situation in Kunduz. There were reports that as many as 1,500 Pakistanis were with the Taleban garrison at Kunduz and that extremists in the Taleban were threatening to execute any one who tried to surrender. The Kunduz drama has captured the frustration and anger of many Pakistani officials who entrusted their interests in Afghanistan to the United States after 11 September, when the Bush administration demanded that Pakistan join in the war against terrorism."

On the same day, delegates to the United Nations-sponsored conference of all Afghan factions to chart out the future governance began to arrive in Bonn, the venue being the secluded hilltop castle of Petersberg. The conference began on 27 November 2001, chaired by the United Nations special envoy for Afghanistan Lakhdar Brahimi, who had spent many frustrating years in trying to solve the Afghan puzzle and had at one time conceded defeat and retreated. Seeing all the factions sitting and negotiating together in Bonn must have given him unique pleasure.

The negotiations proved to be quite tortuous, which was completely anticipated, but the sunny side of it was that the talks finally led to an accord, which was signed on 5 December 2001, by which a roadmap was laid out before the Afghans to begin with the setting up of an interim administration for the first six months, then the holding of a Loya Jirgah to elect a transitional government for the following eighteen months, at the end of which general election would be held to elect a parliament and a popular government. An editorial in *The Times of India* reflected the collective sigh of relief that went up around the world as the participants signed the Bonn Accord. Entitled "Bonn Homie", the editorial said, "After more than a week of hectic parleys, behind-the-scene feints and assorted arm-twisting by interested third countries, the make or break multi-party talks on Afghanistan's post-Taleban political future have finally yielded an accord. While those familiar with the fractious nature of Afghan politics will keep their fingers firmly crossed on the eventual implementation of the deal on the ground, there is reason to be cautiously optimistic... The ambitious political blueprint, however, will have little meaning for ordinary Afghans if the interim government in Kabul does not undertake immediate reforms in the Talibanised social sector, including education, healthcare and, not least, women's rights."

Despite the last-minute defiance shown by Mullah Omar who had declared that he would not leave Kandahar come what may, the Taleban abandoned the southern stronghold and their spiritual centre on 6 December 2001, one day after in distant Bonn the Afghan factions arrived at and signed the peace accord. Operation Enduring Freedom, which had been succceded by Operation Anaconda aimed specifically at weeding out the Taleban and al-Qaeda remnants from their mountain hideouts, came to a nominal end.

Chairman of the interim administration Hamid Karzai, who was rescued from within Afghanistan a little over a month ago when he was almost captured by the Taleban-al-Qaeda network, arrived back in Kabul on 13 December 2001 to prepare for the installation of the interim government and the passing of Afghanistan from the Taleban to the post-Taleban period on 22 December.

The initial pages of this book have recorded the beginning of the process of normalisation with the installation of the interim administration, followed by the Loya Jirgah in June 2002 and the establishment of the Transitional Islamic Government of Afghanistan in the same month.

As far as the war against terror in Afghanistan is concerned, it is not yet over; as a matter of fact, with growing indications of a regrouping of the Taleban-al-Qaeda forces, albeit severely decimated, reflected in sporadic but increasingly serious incidents, such as the 5th September 2002 assassination attempt on President Karzai, the job of mopping up the evil terrorist force will obviously have to be continued. The border areas of Pakistan are proving to be uncomfortably hospitable for the revival and regrouping of the Taleban-al-Qaeda network. Besides, the network continues to be alive in the majority of the sixty countries where it had spread prior to 11 September. The October elections to the National Assembly and provincial assemblies of Pakistan have thrown up relatively disturbing results, with the fundamentalist Muttahida Majlis-e-Amal (MMA) emerging with a surprisingly vigorous performance. All these point to several seemingly unanswerable questions, such as, will Pakistan witness a revival of Islamic fundamentalism again with conceivable impact on Afghanistan? Will the present and future Afghan governments be able to withstand any fresh fundamentalist onslaught in the future? Only one thing appears to be fairly clear: that there will never be another Taleban-like regime in the country again. And that certainty should be a strong enough catalyst to steer the country towards uninterrupted peace and development, and ultimately, prosperity. Amen.

****

Endnotes

1. Anderson, Jon Lee, "The Assassins: Who was involved in the murder of Ahmed Shah Massoud?", *The New Yorker*, 10 June 2002.
2 & 3. Bodansky, Yossef, *Bin Laden...* p.15 and p.26.
4 & 5. The author's conversation with Brice Lalande and several other Europeans familiar with Afghanistan, in Kabul during 2-8 September 2002.
6. BBC report of 3 April 2001, datelined Paris.
7. In conversation with the author in New Delhi after ambassador Masood Khalili returned from hospital in Germany where he was under prolonged treatment following the assassination of Commander Massoud, in which incident Khalili was severely wounded but survived.
8. Balz, Dan and Woodward, Bob, "America's Chaotic Road to War", Bush's global strategy began to take shape in first frantic hours after attack, *The Washington Post*, 27 January 2002, p.A09.
9. Balz, Dan; Woodward Bob and Himmerman, Jeff, "Afghan Campaign's Blueprint Emerges", *The Washington Post*, 29 January 2002, p.A01.
10. Haidar, Salman, "Afghan Shadow on Kashmir", *The Hindu*, New Delhi, 11 November 2001.
11. Mukarji, Apratim, "Advent of the Northern Alliance in Afghanistan: US Policy Examined", Himalayan and Central Asian Studies, Jan.-March 2002.
12. Official text: The White House Office of the Press Secretary, 20 September 2001, Address to a Joint Session of Congress and the American People.
13. A typical example was the following piece of journalism. Entitled "Gods and Monsters", and written by Jake Tapper, 10 November 2001, it read, "Hooray! The Northern Alliance has announced that it captured Mazar-i-Sharif! With the first good news on the war front, America turns to the northern notch of Afghanistan to see whom we should now be saluting.

Speaking by satellite telephone to CNN-Turk television, Uzbek warlord General Abdul Rashid Dostum claimed that the northern Afghan city that had once been under his control – until the Taliban chased him into exile in 1998 – had finally fallen after several days of fighting. Dostum said that Northern alliance forces had killed 500 Taliban soldiers. Hooray for General Dostum! Hooray for Jabha-yi Muttahid-i Islami Milli bara-yi Nijat-i-Afghanistan! Hooray for the United National Islamic Front for the Salvation of Afghanistan aka "the Northern Alliance"! "In a short period of time we entered Mazar-i-Sharif and we are in Mazar-i-Sharif," Dostum said. "Yes, we have everything, including the airport." "Who is our new hero, General Dostum, and his brave Junbish fighters,with whom the US military has been working?" www.salon.com

14 Speaking about how the United Front arrived at the decision to ignore President Bush's warning, ambassador Khalili told the author that once his government was certain that the warning had been issued at the behest of Pakistan,which had publicly warned against the United Front taking Kabul over, "there was unanimity that the advice not to march into Kabul could be ignored". At that moment of supreme triumph,not so much for the victorious United Front but for the people of Kabul and Afghanistan,it was felt that it was absolutely irrelevant to listen to such motivated and ill-considered advices.

15 News report, "Coalition will include moderate Taliban elements", *The Hindu*, New Delhi, 20 October 2001.

16 Carroll, Rory, "Taliban building logistics base in Pakistan on the sly", *The Guardian*, 26 October 2001.

17 Mukarji,Apratim, "Afghanistan: The Execution of Abdul Haq", *Mainstream*, New Delhi, 3 November 2001.

18 Backgrounder dated 9 November 2001, issued by the Public Affairs office of the United States Embassy, New Delhi.

19 "President sees Taleban ouster soon", *The Nation* online edition, 11 November 2001.

[20] News transcript released by the Department of Defence, Government of the United States, Washington DC.

Appendix 1(a)

As Fighting Nears Kabul, Two POWs Tell *Time* that Pakistan Sent Soldiers to Help the Extreme Islamists

Edward Barnes/ Panjshir Valley
4 November 1996

The 26 men sit in grim isolation, huddled in a darkened cell of a former Soviet-built prison deep in northern Afghanistan's Panjshir Valley. They are sequestered from nearly 600 other prisoners, but even if they were allowed to mingle, they would still stand apart. The style of their clothes, the color of their skin, their very language mark them as outsiders. They are not Afghans. They are Pakistanis, captured while fighting against the forces of the Afghan government that was driven from the capital five weeks ago by the group of Islamic fighters known as the Taliban. The presence of these foreign supporters of the Taliban, claim officials at the prison, is hard proof that Pakistan, a U.S. ally, has arrogated for itself a more extensive role in Afghanistan's war than has ever been acknowledged.

Even before the Taliban's victorious drive on Kabul, the ousted government had long insisted that the student-led band of Muslim warriors were actively backed by Pakistan's Inter-Services Intelligence Agency (ISI) and by some members of the country's powerful military. The motive: gaining some influence over a neighbor with whom it shares a long and exceedingly porous border. Prime Minister Benazir Bhutto has denied any involvement, but in late September, Naseerullah Babar, Pakistan's Interior Minister, flew to Afghanistan to work out a settlement between the Taliban and the most powerful of the Afghan warlords. While that seemed to support suspicions, the stories told by several of the prisoners in the Panjshir, if true, would constitute the first direct evidence that Islamabad's involvement with the war-riven nation to the west extends to recruiting Pakistanis and paying them to fight alongside the Taliban.

Khalid Mohammed Zai, 22, was a member of an Islamic paramilitary unit, based in Kulty Chawni in Pakistan's Punjab province. He says his unit was under the control of the ISI, and his mission, as it was explained to him and 1,000 other Pakistani fighters he says entered Afghanistan during the past two months, was to "go as a fighter and rise to a high position of influence." He was transported across the border by Pakistani military vehicles and, once in Kabul, received orders and money from the senior Pakistani officer in Kabul, a man named Naser. Zai was in the forefront of the Taliban troops who swept into Kabul on Sept. 27 and pushed the armies of Ahmad Shah Massoud, the former government's army commander, into the hills surrounding the capital. Zai was captured Oct. 13 near the Salang Pass, the high-water mark of the Taliban effort to drive Massoud's forces from the region. The campaign turned disastrous when Massoud retreated until the Taliban had stretched their lines dangerously thin. Then the Lion of Panjshir turned and abruptly struck at their flanks, a tactic he has used many times against the Soviets.

The momentum of this counterattack carried Massoud's forces through the village of Charikar, where Mohammed Zahid Pashtun, 26, another Pakistani fighter, was stationed.

Appendix 1(a)

A devout Muslim and former engineering student, Zahid says he signed up for combat duty with a Pakistani intelligence officer and was given 40 days of training. He eventually reached Charikar, where Afghan civilians, who initially welcomed the Taliban, revolted after just 11 days of repressive rule, outraged by a draconian regime that bars women from working outside the home. Also outlawed are movies, music and chess. Captured, he now says he regrets his role. "I heard and saw how the Taliban treated people. If I get home again, I will tell people that the Taliban are not true Islam."

While Massoud is eager to drive them out, the Taliban have sworn they will not leave Kabul. Massoud, an ethnic Tajik, is aided by the Taliban's plummeting popularity, but the key to his offensive is his tenuous alliance with Abdul Rashid Dostum, a powerful Uzbek warlord, who is with Massoud's forces battling the Taliban near Kabul. The tribal nature of the conflict has always complicated the fighting. Last week the Taliban, mostly ethnic Pashtun, were going house to house in Kabul in search of Tajiks and Uzbeks. Pakistan's meddling can only worsen the hostilities, and the lines of refugees will stretch deep into the winter.

–With reporting by Meenakshi Ganguly/ New Delhi and Lewis M. Simons/ Washington

Appendix 1 (b)

The Not So Hidden Hand
How Pakistanis help the Taliban crusade
Anthony Davis/ Baharak

Back in the Dark days of the mid-'80s, the village of Baharak in Afghanistan's northeastern Panjshir valley won fame far beyond its modest size as a major Soviet base. From its stony wheat fields, artillery and tanks pounded the surrounding mountains and the elusive mujahideen guerrillas they sheltered.

Today, Baharak once again plays host to foreigners who went to Afghanistan to fight. This time they are Pakistani. Since the fundamentalist Taliban swept the Burhannudin Rabbani regime from Kabul in September, fighting has spread from the capital, north to the mouth of the 100-km-long Panjshir. Last month the forces of Rabbani's military chief Ahmadshah Massoud counter-attacked and the war shifted back towards Kabul. Apart from the 350-plus who died or were wounded, more than 700 Taliban fighters were taken prisoner and locked up in the Panjshir. Among them are 37 men who concede that they are Pakistani citizens. "If you want proof that Pakistan is actively interfering in our country, go to Baharak," a Massoud aide told Asiaweek. "Talk to them. They will tell you."

Clad in a shalwar kameez and checkered head scarf, Hasan abu Hamid's sturdy build and dark complexion mark him as unmistakably Punjabi. As with several of his compatriots, Hasan's road to Afghanistan was smoothed by Jamiat Ulema

Islami (JUI), a Pakistani religious party. Son of an alim, or religious scholar, Hasan studied under a local JUI leader named Maulewi Mahmoud. "He told us that in Afghanistan and Kashmir, shariah law was not being enforced and it was our duty to fight. After Afghanistan and Kashmir, we would ensure that shariah was properly enforced in Pakistan." Earlier this year, the 24-year-old underwent training in a camp in southeastern Afghanistan near the town of Khost. "There were about 40 of us in the group," says Hasan. "We were trained by a Pakistani man called Safiullah and two assistants in the use of small arms – pistols, rifles, rocket-propelled grenades."

Ultimately, Hasan's newfound military skill was of little use. In mid-October, he and six other Pakistanis operating with a force of some 60 Afghan Taliban were ambushed by Massoud's troops on the winding Salang Highway. "We were attacked from two sides as darkness fell," recalls the tall Punjabi. "We abandoned the armored vehicles and ran. We moved at night across the mountains and next morning came down and surrendered." Captured in the same group was 22-year-old Khalid, a Pakistani of ethnic Pushtan stock from Baluchistan. Having graduated from Koranic studies in southern Punjab, he went on to join a small militant faction, Jamiat-ul-Mujahideen. He received military training for four months in a camp in Pakistan-run Azad Kashmir, for many years a springboard for volunteers eager to wage holy war in Indian Kashmir. Khalid was himself an instructor for two years until last August, when he was ordered to Afghanistan. The Panjshir POWs are clear proof of what has long been rumored – that several Pakistani religious parties, such as the JUI, are solidly behind the Taliban crusade and encouraging young Pakistani zealots to fight with them. It is also clear that Pakistan authorities know exactly what is going on; JUI leader Maulewi Fazlur Rahman was a member of Benazir Bhutto's ousted government. And Fazlur Rahman is known to have worked closely with former interior minister Maj.-Gen. (Retired) Naseerullah Babar, Bhutto's pointman on Afghanistan.

The former Kabul authorities have found it less easy to present clear evidence of the involvement of Pakistan's military intelligence. The Inter-Services Intelligence Directorate (ISI), for years the sharp end of Pakistan's Afghan policy, also is believed to have helped the Taliban logistically and advised them on strategy. Shortly before the fall of Kabul a Taliban military transport landed in Massoud-controlled territory. On board were five Pakistanis. Today they are being held in Panjshir under suspicion that they are ISI officers. The leader of the group, Omar Faruq, a gray-bearded man in his early 50s, insists that he is a religious teacher. His group, he says wearily, was merely visiting a shrine in Afghanistan and were the victims of a frame-up. But analysts are in little doubt that ISI has links with Pakistani religious parties that provide volunteers for jihad in both Kashmir and Afghanistan. "It is part of a privatization of an enterprise earlier run by the ISI for the Kashmir conflict," says a Western source. "Beyond that, these religious factions are sending youth to fight and the authorities have done nothing to stop it." That certainly gels with what the Panjshir POWs have to say. "When groups finished training for Kashmir," says Khalid, the former instructor, "ISI officers would issue them with weapons, ammunition and 2,000 rupees [$50] a man."

Source: *Asiaweek*

Appendix 2

Veiled in Fear

Military action in Afghanistan has brought to power a more fundamentalist Islamic group known as the Taliban. After this background report, three native Afghans discuss the Taliban's rise.
9 October 1996

CHARLAYNE HUNTER-GAULT: Afghanistan's new rulers are called the Taliban, and they've begun to enforce a strict Islamic social code which, among other things, severely limits women's activities. The decrees are so harsh that even Iran's rulers have criticized the Afghan rulers. And the UN Secretary-General has warned he might stop all UN programs there. The Taliban have taken over a country wracked by nearly 20 years of internal conflict and civil war, including military occupation by the Soviet army from 1979 to '89. We start with a report from Afghanistan by Mark Austin of Independent Television News.

MARK AUSTIN, ITN: On a hill overlooking Kabul, these are Afghanistan's new soliders of God, praying they say for peace and stability in a country that's known only conflict for nearly two decades. But below them is a battle-torn city where the fear of war is fast being replaced by a fear of repression. It's symbolized by the white flag of the Taliban militia, heavily armed religious students who patrol the streets, enforcing their vision of Islamic law. The penalties for disobedience flogging or even death. Their first edict, women must not work, must not be seen uncovered on the streets. Men must grow beards and pray five time a day. The only sounds from the radio, Islamic prayer and poetry. All music and entertainment is banned here. Television shops are being closed down, TV's and video recorders destroyed, tapes hung from trees.

SPOKESMAN: We will confiscate it and destroy it stage by stage.

An extreme brand of Islam?

MARK AUSTIN: At the gates of the presidential palace, we took tea with one group of militia men who told us their goal was a pure Islamic society, free of crime and corruption. But when we toured the palace, itself, they proudly showed us works of art they destroyed.

SPOKESMAN: The painting is against Islam

MARK AUSTIN: After 17 years of war and suffering, what this city is now experiencing is the most extreme brand of Islam anywhere in the world. The Taliban takeover may have brought temporary peace of a kind, but for the people of Kabul, it's peace at a price.

These are the child victims of the Taliban assault on Kabul, appalling injuries caused by shelling and rocket fire. But their tragedy is compounded by the imposition of strict Islamic laws. Eighty percent of the nurses and 40 percent of the doctors here are women, and now most are too frightened even to leave their homes. These are the hands of one of the city's top surgeons. She won't risk being identified but says it's almost as if women no longer exist.

SURGEON: I can't go to my job. I can't help my people because they said that the woman must sit in the houses, and they can't go outside. It's really bad for us. I'm very sorry, and I want to leave this country.

MARK AUSTIN: Many are already leaving Kabul. Aid workers say more than 100,000 have fled in the last few days. Reports of arrests and beatings abound in this city, and for the women here, the veil conceals the fear that children do not hide. The Taliban are urging people to stay, but there's a sense of panic, and the exodus continues, leaving those who remain to come to terms with life under new rulers with new rules and an existence that many women here say is taking them back to the dark ages.

Appendix 3

Terrorist Details His Training in Afghanistan

Laura Mansnerus and Judith Miller
4 July 2000, *The New York Times*

An Algerian convicted of trying to carry out a terrorist attack in Los Angeles on the eve of the millennium celebration testified yesterday that he had received money and training at camps in Afghanistan that American officials say were run by Osama bin Laden.

Ahmed Ressam, the Algerian, described in detail his training in light arms, explosives, assassinations and techniques for blowing up "the infrastructure of a country." After more than six months of training in Afghanistan in 1998, Mr. Ressam testified, he returned to Canada with $12,000 in seed money to plot terrorist attacks against the United States, Islam's "biggest enemy."

In his testimony yesterday in Federal District Court in Manhattan, Mr. Ressam did not mention Mr. bin Laden, the Saudi exile charged with conducting a jihad, or holy war, against the United States and its allies.

But in describing the origins of his plan to set off a bomb at Los Angeles International Airport, he nonetheless confirmed the key outlines of the picture drawn by American intelligence of Mr. bin Laden's operations. He described a network of camps in which Algerians, Jordanians, Germans and others were trained and indoctrinated for terrorist missions around the world.

Appendix 3 255

Mr. Ressam testified at the trial of Mokhtar Haouari, an Algerian accused of providing money and support for the plot to blow up the airport. In Los Angeles in April, Mr. Ressam was convicted of trying to bring explosives into the United States. He has since agreed to cooperate with prosecutors; his sentencing has been postponed to July 25.

Mr. Ressam's testimony, translated from Arabic by an interpreter, offered a rare insider's look at the design and attempted execution of a terrorist plot. His account depicted a decentralized structure in which militants were trained and given considerable latitude in selecting targets and missions.

In his testimony, Mr. Ressam said the camps were run by Abu Zubaida, the nom de guerre of a Palestinian whom American officials have identified as an important lieutenant to Mr. bin Laden.

American officials say Abu Zubaida reports directly to Mr. bin Laden and is in charge of recruiting for the camps. Mr. Ressam said Abu Zubaida arranged for his trip from Montreal to Afghanistan, providing him with Afghan clothes and an Afghan guide to take him from Pakistan to a camp called Khalden.

Mr. Ressam also described how, at the camps, he and others were made aware of orders to kill Americans that had been issued by Sheik Omar Abdel Rahman, the blind Egyptian cleric who was convicted in 1995 of conspiring to blow up the United Nations and other landmarks in the United States. He is now serving a life sentence in federal prison.

Mr. Ressam recounted how and why he selected the Los Angeles airport as a target and how he planned to rehearse and carry out the bombing. The plot went awry on Dec. 14, 1999, when a border guard in Port Angeles, Wash., questioned him in a routine check. Mr. Ressam, who does not speak English well, panicked and tried to flee. He was arrested and the authorities found more than 100 pounds of explosives in his car.

Mr. Ressam said he had planned the operation for more than a year but was forced to improvise when two other Algerians in his terrorist cell were detained in Britain and others then backed out. He said he selected the Los Angeles airport because he had passed through there on a flight from Pakistan.

Mr. Ressam testified that he wanted to test security at the airport by leaving a luggage cart with a bag unattended.

Mr. Ressam said he was trained at two camps in Afghanistan, Khalden and Darunta. Both have been identified by American officials as integral parts of al-Qaeda, a terrorist group founded by Mr. bin Laden that is an umbrella organisation for anti-American militants around the world. There was no mention of al-Qaeda in the testimony yesterday, but Mr. Ressam was asked whether Abu Zubaida belonged to a "terrorist organisation."

"Yes," he replied.

The United States has been pressing Afghanistan, most of which is ruled by the Taliban, to close down the camps and evict Mr. bin Laden. The Afghans have refused and American officials recently warned the Taliban that they would be held responsible for any attacks against the United States organised from their country.

A senior Bush administration official said Mr. Ressam's account "demonstrates that Afghanistan, in fact, has turned into the most threatening terrorist sanctuary in the world today."

Mr. Ressam said he was among 50 to 100 men at the camp in Afghanistan. He described his training in light weapons and explosives and instruction in "urban warfare." Among the possible targets among "enemies' installations," he said, were power plants, airports, railroads and large corporations.

Appendix 3

Later, he said, he went to another camp for training in explosives, and returned to Canada with ingredients including hexamine, a booster used in bombs, and glycol. He said he bought other components in Vancouver and made his own timing devices.

When asked why he chose an airport as a target, he said, "An airport is sensitive politically and economically."

After Mr. Ressam had outlined his plan, he was asked if he realised that many civilians would die. "Yes, I would try to avoid that as much as possible," Mr. Ressam replied.

"But no matter how you did that, many would die," said Joseph F. Bianco, an assistant United States attorney.

"Yes," Mr. Ressam said.

Mr. Ressam is the star witness against Mr. Haouari, whom he met in Montreal through friends in a circle of Agerian émigrés. He agreed just a few weeks ago, as his sentencing date approached, to cooperate with the government.

Mr. Haouari is charged with providing money and support to Mr. Ressam, as well as bank fraud.

In testimony yesterday, Mr. Ressam, 34, began the story of a career that took him from a job in his father's coffee shop in Algeria to his arrest in 1999 with a cache of explosives in his rental car.

He described a life of petty crime in Montreal, where he arrived as an illegal immigrant in 1994 "to improve my life situation."

"I lived on welfare and theft," he said. He said Mr. Haouari was dealing in stolen checks and passports and sometimes worked with him.

Mr. Ressam said that when he returned to Montreal from Afghanistan, he had been assigned to work with several other Algerians from the camps on general instructions to meet in Canada, rob banks and use the money to finance "an operation in America."

When his comrades failed to arrive in Canada, he testified, he worked mostly on his own.

He said that at the time, he and Mr. Haouari were working on a plan for Mr. Ressam to open a shop as a way to get information for counterfeit credit cards. He had told Mr. Haouari about the terrorist training camp, he said, and Mr. Haouari expressed interest in going, too.

He testified however, that he did not give Mr. Haouari details of the plan or identify the target.

"No, no, for security reasons I didn't want to tell him," Mr. Resam said.

Appendix 4

The Taliban and The Media

During the night of 26 September 1996, the Taliban militia entered the Afghan capital of Kabul and took control of the city.

One of their first moves was to lock up the premises of national television and ban all TV broadcasts.

Four years after they took power, the Taliban and their allies control more than 90% of the country.

Their most recent military victories mean they are likely to gain permanent control of the valleys held by the opposition, particularly the Panjsher valley, currently held by Massud.

Law and order reigns in Kabul. Afghanistan is now known as the Islamic Emirate of Afghanistan and Sharia (Islamic law) has been brought into force.

The Taliban have introduced radical reforms, particularly concerning the status of women.

Press freedom, which was already threadbare under the Taliban's predecessors, has totally disappeared. All television broadcasts have stopped and the TV building is being used as a barracks.

This sole radio station, which covers the whole country, puts out only religious programmes and official propaganda – even music has no place on the Taliban's airwaves.

The printed press – no more than ten publications throughout Afghanistan – is under government control.

Only foreign media, working with the help of dozens of Afghan journalists living in exile, are trying to supply impartial news to a population manipulated by the "theology students". The Taliban have shown no qualms about murdering Afghan journalists who have fled to Pakistan.

Many more have been threatened after writing reports criticising the Taliban's domination of that country.

These attacks on press freedom are underpinned by the religious precepts taught in the madrasas, Pakistan's Quranic schools.

The danger that Pakistan, and particularly North-West Frontier Province, may also come under the Taliban's influence is increasing as Pakistani religious movements engage in a power struggle with the military government over cable television. Newspapers have all but disappeared in Afghanistan.

Since the fall of King Zahir Shah in 1973 and the end of the "decade of democracy", the press has been in the hands of the government.

After coming to power in 1978, the (communist) Democratic Party introduced a media system based on the Soviet model.

About 100 publications, all dependent on state institutions, were scrupulously vetted by the security ministry's "seventh committee", which was in charge of censorship.

When the Mujahideen took control in 1992, 90% of publications disappeared, either because they were banned or because they had been stripped of their material resources.

The Taliban victory of 1996 marked the start of a complete takeover of the press: journalists fled the country by the dozen and new teams, made up of militiamen, "Pakistani advisers" and former journalists, were brought in to replace them.

The Taliban arrested many journalists who had not managed to escape or go into hiding.

Appendix 4

Khalil Rostaqi, an intellectual and journalist with the newspaper Mayan, was arrested a week after the taking of Kabul and held for six months.

Around the same time Abdulhanan Rahimi, a national television reporter, was arrested at his home. Accused of spying for General Massud and compilling "reports hostile to the Taliban", he was kept in a cellar for five months with three other people. Before he was released, one of his captors warned him: "If you're arrested a second time, you're as good as dead." At the moment, fewer than ten publications appear regularly in Afghanistan for 21 million inhabitants: the English-language weekly Kabul Times, a showcase for the government abroad, the Pashto-language magazine Nangarhar and the Farsi-language newspapers Hewad (Fatherland), Anees (Companion) and Shariat. In the provinces, a few publications controlled by the local authorities appear irregularly.

Their content is meagre, with no photos, illustrations, readers' letters or editorials.

All the news printed comes from ministries and the official news agency.

Working conditions for journalists are very harsh: they have to take orders from the Taliban representatives assigned to editorial offices, and the state pays little and irregularly.

Most journalists earn about 12 euros per month. On the other hand, the dean of Kabul university insists that journalism courses are still taught "according to the criteria of international media and professional ethics".

He claims that what goes on outside the university does not concern him, and he refuses to comment on the Taliban's attitude to press freedom.

Needless to say, the university admits only male students. In July 2000 the Taliban launched The Islamic Emirate, an English-language monthly published in Kandahar, to "counter the biased information put out by the enemies of Islam".

The first issue's front page carried the headlines "No terrorist camps in Afghanistan" and "Extraditing Osama ben Laden would be scorning a pillar of our religion".

The Taliban have also set up a web site, afghan-ie.com, to push for recognition of their regime by the international community – even though they have banned Afghans from having internet access. In their government media, the Taliban frequently demand Afghanistan's seat at the United Nations, which is still officially occupied by the "government" of former president Burhanuddin Rabbani. One Afghan journalist who recently returned to Kabul was categorical: "There are no journalists left in Afghanistan today.

They are working as religious officials.

They are formally forbidden to write anything." Another journalist, living in exile in France, took a similar view of those working for the country's only radio station, Radio Sharia: They put out 12 hours of programmes per day with no journalistic content whatever, and no songs. Sermons alternate with religious debates and propaganda in which they insult Massud and the Americans." It is forbidden on pain of death to take photographs of the Emir of Afghanistan, Mullah Mohammed Omar.

Foreign journalists who have been covering Afghanistan since 1996 tell how nervous the militia are of still and video cameras, which they call "the Devil's boxes".

"If we had had our cameras with us, they would have killed us", said Salim Safi, a Pakistani journalist from the news agency News Network International who was arrested in September 1999 along with another reporter.

After covering an opposition rally in the north of the country, he had decided to give his video camera to an Afghan friend to take to Peshawar.

The Taliban accused the two men of entering Afghanistan illegally and of "spying for the Iranians".

Salim Safi told how the militia had threatened him: "You're a well-known journalist.

So what? You'll be dead and no-one will know." The journalists were only released five days later, after their employers appealed to the Afghan foreign ministry. Even more recently, on 11 Asugust 2000, three foreign journalists were arrested on the orders of the deputy minister for the maintenance of the faith and the suppression of vice, who accused them of trying to take pictures of a football match in Kabul.

Pakistani Khawar Mehdi, who was with American freelance photographer Jason Flario and Brazilian reporter Pepe Scobar, said: "The religious police arrested us and interrogated us for two hours.

They confiscated the photographer's films, claiming we had broken their law, which forbids taking photos of living creatures." Khawar Mehdi went on to give his impressions of the regime: "The Taliban have an increasing tendency to regard foreign journalists as spies.

They don't like us and they suspect us of the worst intentions when we go to Afghanistan." Zaheer, am Afghan photographer aged about 60, commented: "Photography is dead in Afghanistan." Another photographer, based in Peshawar, admitted that he had not been to Afghanistan since 1998.

"It has become impossible for us to work and, what's more, they tell us we have to grow beards", he said. As for television, the Taliban do not seem ready to authorise the broadcasting of programmes again.

Abdul Hai Mutmaeen, minister of information and culture for the eastern province of Kandahar, told a foreign journalist in August 2000 that there was "no question of lifting the ban on television".

And yet, last July, during a seminar organised by the ministry and devoted to "the role of the media", certain officials hinted that TV broadcasts might resume.

The problem, according to the minister, is that "you can't control what people watch".

It is also noteworthy that since they arrived in Kabul, the militia, have systematically destroyed any broadcasting equipment they came across, publicly burning films and videotapes and smashing television sets, cameras, video cameras and hifi equipment. Ever since the communists came to power, it has been very difficult to find western newspapers in Kabul.

On the other hand, publications from neighbouring countries, particularly Pakistan and Iran, found their way onto the Afghan market when the Mujahideen were in charge.

On 27 February 1997 the information and culture minister announced a ban on the sale of books and magazines published abroad.

Since then, Afghans have been deprived of Pakistani newspapers such as The Frontier Post, The News International and the Pashto-language Wahdat.

More than 3,000 copies of Wahdat crossed the border in the mid-1990s to be sold in Afghanistan's major cities.

The Taliban have put an end to sales of all newspapers published in Pakistan and Iran.

One circulation official for a Pakistani daily said the militia kept a close watch on deliveries.

"The driver of the delivery van has been threatened on several occasions", he said.

"He is only authorised to take copies of the newspaper to institutions approved by the Taliban." In practice, that means only a few ministries, diplomatic representatives, foreign journalists and international organisations are allowed to receive the newspapers.

"In any case, there are no news-stands left in the country's big cities", the official added.

Some Afghans still try to get hold of foreign newspapers. Wahdat is said to be handed round secretly.

A Pakistani who recently returned home from Jalalabad said: "I have seen students stuffing newspapers down their trousers so that they won't be caught.

They know they are taking a major risk." The only newspaper authorised by the Kabul authorities is Zarb-e-Momin, an Urdu-language weekly published in Karachi which supports the Taliban cause.

An Afghan journalist in Peshawar said the Kabul government took a kindly view of the newspaper because it opposed "western propaganda against the Taliban". Paradoxically, Afghan officials prefer to get their news from the Palistani press.

"They have no choice: they can't ban all the media", a Pakistani journalist commented wryly. The Pashto-language daily Wahdat, published in Palistan, did try to maintain a correspondent in Jalalabad, eastern Afghanistan, but Asadullah Hisar Shahiwal was forced to resign under pressure from the authorities.

He was arrested several times because of reports published in Wahdat.

The daily still has a correspondent in Kabul, Danish Karukhel, but an editorial executive based in Peshawar said he had very little room to manoeuvre.

"His work as a journalist is restricted to interviewing Taliban officials.

One critical report would be too dangerous for him." The Taliban frequently attempt to justify their ban on foreign media by claiming that their reporting on Afghanistan is "subjective".

The Kandahar information and culture minister said that "the Americans are against the Taliban" and "their media give a distorted view of the situation". The Taliban have never hesitated to attack or threaten foreign journalists. Scarcely a month after they entered Kabul, militiamen stopped and beat up two Argentine journalists because they had tried to interview women.

In November of the same year Dorothée Olliéric, a reporter with the French TV channel France 2, was prevented from working because she was not wearing a veil.

In all, more than 25 foreign journalists have been arrested by militiamen since September 1996. In August 2000 the authorities introduced strict regulations to cover the work of foreign reporters and special correspondents.

On arrival in Kabul, they are given a list of "21 points to be respected".

The first is to give a true account of "what is really happening in Afghanistan" and not to "offend the people's feelings".

Next comes a long litany of recommendations which might amount to no more than bureaucratic harassment in other countries but which testify to the Afghan authorities' distrust of the foreign press and their determination to maintain strict control of reporters on Afghan soil.

A document published by the information and culture department states that foreign journalists are not allowed to "go into private houses", "interview an Afghan woman without the department's permission" or "photograph or film people".

Journalists are also supposed to tell the department when they travel outside Kabul and to respect the country's "no-go areas".

The authorities also insist that foreign correspondents work only with interpreters and other local assistants who have been approved by the department, register all their professional equipment with the relevant ministry and renew their work permits every year.

Finally bureau chiefs representing international media are obliged to attend government press conferences and to check that only the name "Islamic Emirate of Afghanistan" appears in their reports.

No penalties for the infringement of these regulations are specified in the documents issued by the authorities. Some Pakistani journalists have condemned official control of the interpreters assigned to foreign reporters.

"Almost all of them are affiliated to the government", a Peshawar journalist said.

"People are afraid to say anything in front of them because everybody knows they will report back to the information and culture department.

I've heard interpreters tell a foreign journalist the exact opposite of what the person being interviewed actually said." Another means of keeping a close watch on foreign journalists: they are only allowed to stay at Kabul's Intercontinental Hotel.

They are banned from staying with ordinary citizens.

An Afghan family who took in a Pakistani journalist was harassed by Taliban militia, said Jan Agha, an Afghan businessman living in exile in Peshawar. In Kabul, foreign press correspondents are few and far between.

Only the BBC and Agence France-Presse still have foreign correspondents living in the capital, although the authorities recently gave permission for the television channels CNN and Al-Jazeera to open offices.

Kate Clark of BBC radio and Amir Shah of the American news agency Associated Press have often spoken about the pressure to which they are subjected.

Kate Clark said security was so tight that "we have to work discreetly and very fast".

She added: "We have to grab the news and run away for fear of being victims of dirty tricks." Some Pakistani reporters who are used to covering the Afghan conflict have the greatest difficulty obtaining visas in Peshawar to go to Afghanistan.

Ilyas Khan, a reporter with the Pakistani monthly The Herald, complained: "Western journalists obtain visas easily, whereas we, who speak the Afghans' language, are prevented from entering their country." He said this was a deliberate policy aimed at shielding the rapid deterioration of the situation in Afghanistan from the world's gaze.

"A foreign journalist with an interpreter cannot fully grasp developments and find the right information." Shamin Shahid, Peshawar bureau chief of the daily The Nation, has had 20 visa applications refused by the Afghan consulate since February 1999. Journalists in exile threatened after the Taliban took Kabul and Jalalabad, most journalists fled either to parts of the country under opposition control or to Pakistan, Iran or Tajikistan.

Of the 15 editorial staff of Subh Omid (The Morning of Hope), a fortnightly launched in March 1995, only two stayed in Kabul.

Latif Pedram, one of its founders, went into hiding when the Taliban arrived for fear of being "beheaded".

"Exile has become the only way to survive when you're an Afghan journalist", he said.

The United Nations High Commission for Refugees has helped about ten journalists to go to western countries from Peshawar. Dozens more have reached a host country under their own steam.

Afghans fleeing the Taliban have met up with others who left the country to escape the communists or the Mujahideen.

Some have launched new media, while others are working for the five international radio stations that broadcast programmes in Farsi.

Their broadcasts, and particularly those of the BBC, are extremely popular in Afghanistan.

Latif Pedram said: "The international stations are the only mass media Afghanistan has ever known.

They are both a lifeline and a window opening up to the rest of the world." These journalists are not out of danger just because they have left the country.

Two Afghan reporters have narrowly escaped murder attempts in Pakistan since 1996.

At least five others have been attacked or received death threats.

Investigations by the Pakistani police, which are often slapdash, have provided no clues to the identity of the attackers. On 2 October 1998 two men fired at Abdul Hafiz Hamid Azizi as he was on his way home in Peshawar.

A writer and regular columnist for the Afghan dailies Sahaar and Wahdat, Hamid Azizi, who is of Tajik origin, had received anonymous death threats.

One of the letters warned him "not to publish articles and not to write political analysis.

Otherwise you or your family will be punished by death, kidnapping or dishonour, as an example to others".

Three days later Najeeda Sara Bid, a reporter with the BBC's Pashto-language service in Peshawar, escaped a murder attempt near her home.

Like Hamid Azizi, she had received anonymous death threats.

"They insulted me in the street and threatened me on the phone or by email", she told Reporters Sans Frontières.

A few weeks before the murder attempt, a group of Afghans stopped her in the street.

Sara Bidi recalled their threats: "How long will you go on writing and defending women's rights? Why don't you stay at home? Afghanistan has an Islamic government and we will prevent you from working, even in Pakistan." The journalist is sure that the Taliban are behind the harassment.

By way of evidence, she produced a threatening letter written on Afghan interior ministry headed notepaper.

A few months later Sara Bidi went into exile in Europe. On 2 November 1998 Mohammad Hashim Paktianae, a journalist with the official press under communist rule and a cousin of former president Najibullah, was murdered at his home in Hayatabad.

No inquiry has come up with any clues, but members of the journalist's family believe it was connected with his work for the Afghan opposition. In August 1998 Walliulah Saleem, head of the independent Afghan news agency Sahaar, based in Peshawar, received death threats for which he blamed the Taliban and went into hiding for four months.

More recently, on 4 july 2000, Inayat-ul-Haq Yasini, a journalist with the daily Wahdat living in Peshawar, received anonymous phone calls threatening him with "the worst consequences". In its 26 June issue, Wahdat had published the findings of an opinion poll of Afghan refugees living in camps in north-west Pakistan.

The caller also complained that the article was too favourable to General Al-Maroof Shariati, who heads the National Afghan Council for Peace, an opposition party working in exile. According to Afghan journalists questioned by Reporters Sans Frontières, the threats come both from the Taliban and from Pakistani religious groups, and even from "Pakistani secret services working hand in glove with the masters of Kabul".

The journalists said they had been summoned by Pakistani secret service officials who had asked them to fax the service all articles prior to publication, and not to work for Radio Tehran.

One experienced Afghan reporter noted that several of his colleagues avoided writing reports criticising the Taliban for fear of being threatened or banned from entering the country. The Kabul authorities are even thought to have drawn up a blacklist of Afghan journalists regarded as "undesirable" – a way of punishing them for writing "hostile" reports about the Taliban.

One such journalist, Jamal Kotwal, left his country in 1993 after working for various media controlled by the communist regime.

Now living in Peshawar, he has worked for the Iranian government station Radio Tehran, which has resulted in further attacks by the Taliban.

"They have let me know, indirectly, that it was dangerous for me to continue to work for the official radio of a country that was threatening Afghanistan", he said.

"I resigned out of fear.

Since then, I have stayed on the blacklist of journalists who are against the Taliban." Jamal Kotwal is now working as a correspondent for the international German station Deutsch Welle. According to one Afghan journalist, about 30 Afghan publications are currently being produced abroad.

Ten or so can be accessed on the Internet.

Published in Iran, Pakistan, Tajikistan, Germany or the United States, these newspapers are produced mainly by opposition groups.

A few dozen copies are smuggled into Afghanistan, where readers risk severe penalties.

In Pakistan the daily Wahdat, published in Pashto, has achieved great popularity with the refugee population.

Although its staff is composed mainly of Afghan journalists in exile, it also has a few reporters who support the Taliban.

Janullah Hashimzada, for example, said he travels to Afghanistan regularly and never has any problems with the authorities.

Describing himself as "pro-Taliban", the young reporter claimed the international press made "unfair attacks on Afghanistan". A "talibanisation" of Palistan? "We shall not hesitate to use all the means at our disposal to force the government to close down cable television channels in this country", warned Ehsan-ul-Haq, one of the leaders of the Islami Muttahida Inqilabi Mahaz movement, which groups 21 fundamentalist Moslem organisations in Pakistan.

In June 2000 the religious movements of this country launched a campaign against cable television operators, which were authorised by the federal government at the start of the year.

To stir up their supporters against "vulgar and obscene" TV programmes, the religious leaders issued a fatwa calling on all Moslems to "rise up against the Devil" represented by cable operators.

In April 2000, activists from the Islami Tehrike-e-Taliban group had destroyed broadcasting equipment, particularly videotapes, at the Miranshah market, just a few miles from the Afghan border. The campaign began in North-West Frontier Province, where the Taliban movement emerged.

On 13 June 2000 a group a religious leaders called on the district council in Hyatabad, south-west of Peshawar, to close down six cable operators who had recently opened for business in the region.

A district official asked the Peshawar police superintendent to close the operators.

Zakria Khan, one of the investors targeted by the campaign, took up the story: "On 13 June the police summoned me to appear in Hayatabad police station.

Appendix 4

The police official told me that he had been asked to wind up my company and confiscate my equipment, but he had no written documents to back up his claims." After talking to his lawyer, Zakria Khan decided to comply with the police official's ruling for fear of having "big trouble" otherwise.

He also told Reporters Sans Frontières how young fundamentalist activists had cut cables at night: "We managed to catch several of them, but the police let them go straight away under pressure from the religious leaders." On 21 June provincial governor Muhammad Shafique announced a ban on cable television operators in the region during a demonstration in Peshawar by several thousand religious campaigners.

The next day, his spokesman issued a retraction after the federal government reminded him that a governor was not empowered to take such a decision.

On 24 June Zakria Khan and five other cable operators filed an appeal with the Peshawar high court.

The conflict with the central government finally forced the provincial governor to resign on 13 August. The cable operators were given official permission to resume business on 5 July, but the religious movements continued their protests, publishing highly aggressive statements in the leading regional and national newspapers.

On 20 July one of the religious leaders said: "The Peshawar high court's ruling is not in line with the constitution and with Islam.

We will prevent the operators from working by force if the government does not do so by law." In response, the federal government pointed out that the cable operators had valid licences, and said it would not tolerate attacks on their companies. The fundamentalist movements threatened to continue their campaign against cinemas, and film magazines and posters.

Yet the Pakistani mullahs questioned by Reporters Sans Frontières retorted that the religious movements had no intention of violating press freedom, because freedom of speech was fully guaranteed by Islam.

Maulana Hasan Jan, a former member of the lower house of Parliament for a fundamentalist party, told a story to illustrate their point: "One day, Omar, the second caliph, decided to lower a dowry.

A woman protested, quoting a verse from the Koran.

The caliph immediately reversed his decision, in accordane with the woman's criticism." For religious leaders, the caliph's attitude shows how open Islam is to criticism. The Pakistani religious movements have the power to impose some of their points of view to the local authorities, alternating political pressure, threats, demonstrations and acts of sabotage.

The existence of a varied press, a basic element in Pakistan's liberal Islam, has never been publicly questioned by the religious leaders.

But there are fears that their pleas for stricter enforcement of Sharia law may result in censorship. Pakistan's religious political parties maintain close ties with the Taliban movement.

The parties, which have their roots in the religious schools of north-west Pakistan, helped the Taliban during their rise to power and are currently taking advantage of the success enjoyed by the masters of Kabul.

In return, they vaunt the advantages of the system in force in Afghanistan, especially in their newsletters. On several occasions, the Pakistani religious movements have urged their supporters to attack journalists.

In October 1996 members of Jamiat Ulema-i-Islam (JUI, a fundamentalist party) raided the premises of the daily Ummat and burned copies of the newspaper containing articles criticising the Taliban.

In December 1996, Fakhr Alam, correspondent of the newspaper The Muslim in Peshawar, was the target of a murder attempt.

His attackers ransacked and then set fire to the daily offices.

The Muslim had published a cartoon of the JUI leader dancing with both Afghan and Pakistani actresses. Fakhr Alam managed to identify one of the attackers as a leader of the JUI student wing, who was later arrested.

Under pressure from the JUI, however, he was released after six days in custody.

No one was sentenced by the Pakistani courts in connection with the attempted murder.

In September 1998 Saeed Iqbal Hashmi, correspondent of the daily Mashriq in Peshawar, was sentenced to death in a fatwa issued by religious leaders close to the JUI.

The reporter decided to go into hiding when JUI activists demonstrated outside the newspaper offices.

On 17 December 1998 two armed men went to his parents' home to murder him.

"The religious leaders accused me of being Jewish and of belonging to a Jewish lobby hostile to the Taliban's interests", he recalled.

"I've never seen a Jew in my life." In fact, the leaders were angry about one of his reports, about some sexual abuse of young boys at Quranic schools.

As the Pakistani authorities were unable to ensure his safety, Saeed Hashmi decided to go into exile in Europe in January 1999. Pakistani editorial writers have expressed concern about the "talibanisation" of the Peshawar region.

Ismail Khan wrote recently in The News International: "The idea of the talibanisation of North-West Frontier Province may still seem a bit far-fetched, but reality is staring us in the face.

Should we close our eyes and behave like ostriches? The time has come for us to take a firm stand." An editorial writer with the Frontier Post added: "These self-proclaimed guardians of the nation's morality ought to know that the population is not willing to accept their spiritual guides." Conclusion and recommendations: Afghanistan today is one of the countries where absolutely no press freedom exists.

The Taliban have extended and developed the policy of their predecessors, both the communists and the mujahideen.

They totally control all means of communication and – like nowhere else in the world – they have banned pictures.

This attitude deprives the Afghan people, scarred by more than 20 years of civil war, of seeing what their country and the world outside look like.

This phobia of representing humanity and nature explains the Taliban militamen's relentless attacks on foreign journalists, cameramen and photographers seeking a visual record of a country that seems to have been thrust back into the middle ages.

It is to be hoped that the Taliban's determination to be recognised by the United Nations as the legitimate power in Afghanistan will force them to cancel at least some of their restrictions on freedom of speech. Reporters Sans Frontières calls on the leaders of the Taliban movement: to recognise freedom of speech as a basic right of all Afghan people, to lift the ban on photographs and television, to end the restrictions imposed on foreign journalists working in Afghanistan. Reporters Sans Frontières calls on the Pakistani government: to provide protection for Pakistani and Afghan journalists who request it, to ensure respect for Pakistani laws on the press throughout the country, to sign and ratify, as soon as possible, the International Covenant on Civil and Political Rights, article 19 of which guarantees freedom of expression. Reporters Sans

Frontières calls on the international community: to make respect for freedom of speech a condition of recognising the Taliban government, to support initiatives from Afghan journalists living in exile in favour of diversity of information, to intervene with representatives of the Taliban movement in order to guarantee the safety of foreign journalists working in Afghanistan.

© Copyright 2000 *The Frontier Post*

Appendix 5 (a)

Masood: Democracy and the People's Vote is Only Way to Go, We Oppose Extremism, Terrorism, and Drug Trafficking

Continuing Omaid Weekly's coverage of the early April European tour of Ahmad Shah Masood, generalissimo of Afghanistan's national resistance force, the following is a summarized translation from the original Dari-Persian, as compiled by our senior correspondent Wais Nassery, of the transcription from the April 4 press conference, held at 11:30 a.m. in Paris.

(Ahmad Shah Masood) In the Name of God, the Compassionate, the Merciful. I appreciate and thank all the laides and gentlemen for coming. I am prepared to answer questions that relate to Afghanistan and the region.

Q: What organisation or entity do you represent?

A: I have come to France as a representative of the Islamic State of Afghanistan and as a representative of the United National and Islamic Front of Afghanistan.

I represent an independent and free State with [an ancient] and continuing history in Asia. Throughout history, this State has preserved its independence, existing with its own unique culture, its own unique traditions, and its own civilization. And it shall continue to exist an an independent State, with its own unique culture, traditions and customs.

Appendix 5 (a)

Q: Are your forces adequate to [continue to] resist the Taliban and prevent their advancement?

A: Alhamdulillah [hallelujah or "Praise be to God"], compared to previous years, our forces are in better condition. And undoubtedly, if it were not for the Pakistani intervention, Pakistan Army soldiers, other foreign elements like Osama [bin Laden] and Pakistani taliban [fighting in Afghanistan], there would be no need for our forces. I am certain that the nation of Afghanistan itself, the people of Qandahar, and ethnic Pashtoons are themselves sufficient to defeat the Taliban.

All things considered, similar to the era of jihad against the Soviet Union, in no way will the Taliban, Osama bin Laden, along with the Pakistanis be victorious in this war in Afghanistan. And sooner or later, there will be a general [nationwide] uprising by the people of Afghanistan, culminating in the decisive and final defeat of the Pakistanis, Osama and the Taliban in Afghanistan.

I should also like to mention that the Taliban are not just in conflict with our military forces. In fact, today the Taliban have been distanced from the people, and these foreign forces along with the Taliban are in conflict with the people of Afghanistan, which is why their military victory is impossible.

Q: ...What political agenda does the United Front have? That is, what type of government is desired after the inevitable fall of the Taliban? What differences do you have with the Taliban as regards women's rights...?

A: We believe that the futre government should be formed by means of general elections, via the people's ballot, through the vote of both women and men. The only form of government able to ensure social justice and equity between Afghanistan's various ethnic groups is democracy and the people's vote.

Our future government and the Taliban will be incomparably different. We have always opposed and continue to oppose any kind of extremist or radical movements, even if they claim to be Islamic, and we do not believe they are good for Afghanistan, the region, or the world. As I have repeated earlier, we believe in elections with the participation of both women and men. We fully respect human rights, we support it, we will protect it.

We prescribe against the cultivation and trafficking of illegal narcotics; we believe they are haram [forbidden by Islam], and they are detrimental to all humankind, and destructive to our own country.

As during the jihad, we fully oppose terrorism and terrorist activities. No one had ever witnessed a terrorist attack by the mujahideen, even when the Russians were in Afghanistan. Terrorism is wrong and we are against it.

We not only support women's education, women working, and women's participation in society, but we encourage it. Women can play an instrumental role in rebuilding the country after these many years of war. (Applause)

Q: What do you expect from Europe, and what is your opinion about the West's general position on Afghanistan?

A: We expect Europe to play a critical role in establishing peace in Afghanistan. In my opinion, the sacrifice of the people of Afghanistan against communism makes it obligatory for the world to help and assist the people of Afghanistan to achieve peace in their country.

Our major request is humanitarian assistance to the refugees, including helping to provide education and health care.

Appendix 5 (b)

Afghanistan's National Resistance Leader Stresses National Unity, Highlights Pakistani Intervention During the EU Visit

Summarised translation from the original Dari-Persian of Omaid Weekly's coverage of the visit of Ahmad Shah Masood, generalissimo of Afghanistan's national resistance force, on his tour of Europe at the invitation of European Parliament President Nicole Fontaine. News also reported by international news agencies is largely not included in this translation of this week's collective reportage by Omaid Weekly's European correspondents Messrs. Wais Nassery and Mahmood Monajemzada, and Editor in Chief Mohammad Q. Koshan.

Paris, Strasbourg, and Brussels, April 7 (Omaid): After arriving in Paris on Tuesday, April 3, Ahmad Shah Masood, supreme commander of the United Front, and a delegation comprising Generals Sayed Hussein Anwari, Piram Qol and Arif Noorzai, held discussions in the Plaza Athenee hotel with officials from various European countries and the United States.

Masood and his high-profile entourage also briefly met with individual Afghans who traveled to Paris from numerous European countries and the US to see him. On the same day, a party from the Rome peace process, which included Prof. Fazelly, Dr. Zalmai Rassoul, and Dr. Amin Farhang, spoke with and delivered a message from former Afghan King Mohammad Zaher Shah to Afghanistan's national resistance leader and his delegation. Cmdr. Masood thanked the Rome delegation for coming to see him, and expressed his readiness to meet with the former King when conditions were suitable.

The last event of the first day of Cmdr. Masood's visit to Europe was a meeting with seven Afghans from Britain and the US, including Omaid Weekly's Editor in Chief. [eds: A concise report on this particular gathering will be published in next week's issue.]

On April 4, Cmdr. Masood and delegation, including other Afghan officials held discussions with French Foreign Minister Hubert Vedrine and numerous high-ranking French officials. During a special lunch hosted by Mr. Vedrine, Cmdr. Masood and his delegation met with a number of Paris-based diplomats from various countries. Later, Cmdr. Masood was greeted by a long standing ovation by the French National Assembly, where he also met with National Assembly President Raymond Forni and other prominent French parliamentarians.

Midday Wednesday, Cmdr. Masood answered journalist's questions at a large press conference. Mr. Humayun Tandar, Chargé d'Affaires in the Geneva office of the Permanent Mission of the Islamic State of Afghanistan to the UN, served as translator.

In the packed press conference, Omaid Weekly's Editor in Chief asked Cmdr. Masood to comment on the so-called "Defense of Afghanistan Council" – formed in Akora Khattak by Pakistani extremist groups and Pakistani military intelligence officers in early January and nominally led by Mowlana Sami ul-Haq – and the responsibility of Afghans in exposing and defeating this and other conspiracies. In his lengthy response, Cmdr. Masood said that in this conspiracy, Pakistan is using a Muslim "scholar" to incite greater conflict between Afghan Muslims and Muslims from Pakistan and other parts of the world. He said the Akora Khattak plot is another dimension of Pakistan's war against Afghanistan, and

Appendix 5 (b) 283

that Afghans must recognize the Pakistani government as their nation's enemy.

In the afternoon, Cmdr. Masood and delegation spoke with Afghans in the Embassy of the Islamic State of Afghanistan. Later in the evening, Cmdr. Masood and delegation were back in the same hall where the press conference was held. There they were welcomed by over 600 Afghans, as well as a large number of French nationals, all of whom greeted Afghanistan's national resistance leader with praise. Cheering him as Afghanistan's national hero, Cmdr. Masood and delegation entered the hall with the Afghan's pronouncement of "Allahu Akbar" (God is Great), and the entire room stood up and applauded.

The audience was then addressed by Mr. Masood Khalili, Afghanistan's Ambassador to India, who introduced Cmdr. Masood's delegation: General Sayed Hussein Anwari, from central Afghanistan who belongs to the Shia branch of Islam, a leading figure in Harakat-e-Islami, member of the Jihad Council, and member of the Afghan government's Leadership Council; General Arif Noorzai, an ethnic Pashtoon, prominent commander from Qandahar, and member of the Afghan government's Military Council; General Piram Qol, an ethnic Uzbek from northern Afghanistan, and member of the Afghan government's Military Council; and a number of high-ranking Afghan government diplomats and officials. [eds: Cmdr. Masood, an ethnic Tajik from northeast Afghanistan, is Vice-President and Defense Minister of Afghanistan, and supreme leader of Afghanistan's United Front national resistance force.]

Gen. Anwari spoke about unity among Afghan government forces and the people of Afghanistan, and the need to continually increase efforts in thwarting the Taliban militia and the invading Pakistani troops and Arab terrorists.

He said morale is high and strengthening among the national resistance force in its defence against the foreign occupiers, and that the Taliban are more and more revealing their true nature as Pakistani puppets.

Next, Gen. Noorzai severely condemned the Pakistan-Taliban policies in Afghanistan. Gen. Noorzai served as a jihad-era commander against the Soviets and now continues to serve in the national resistance against the Taliban and their Pakistani patrons.

A famed commander during the jihad against the Red Army, and now a prominent commander in the national resistance force fighting the Taliban and Pakistanis, Gen. Qol emphasized the importance of unity and its ultimate role in defeating the foreign occupiers.

Thereafter, the supreme commander of Afghanistan's national resistance effort addressed the large gathering. In his extensive speech, often interrupted by sustained applause, Cmdr. Masood explained the reason behind his acceptance of the invitation by EP President Nicole Fontaine: foremost, to bring greater attention to Pakistan's direct and destructive intervention in Afghanistan; make clear that Afghans will continue their resistance unitl Pakistan withdraws its military and paramilitary forces, and ceases its direct intervention; urge the international community to pressure Islamabad to stop its direct intervention. Cmdr. Masood said it's most regrettable that Osama bin Laden and his allies have endangered the security and integrity of Afghanistan, which they are turning into a center for global terrorism.

Afghans are capable of solving their internal problems, Cmdr. Masood stated, but the Taliban and Pakistan are feverishly working to undermine national unity by provoking linguistic and regional conflicts. But, Cmdr. Masood reassured, the Leadership Council of the Afghan government

Appendix 5 (b)

and its United Front military force includes all of Afghanistan's ethnic and religious groups – namely Pashtoons, Hazaras, Uzbeks, and Tajiks, as well as Sunni Muslims and Shia Muslims. And, he added, his accompanying delegation is a reflection of the diversity and unity present in the national resistance.

Cmdr. Masood said the Taliban are not only in conflict with the national resistance force, but the militia is now fighting against the entire people of Afghanistan. He asserted that today the Taliban are facing increasing hostility in all regions, from east to west. And that resistance is gaining momentum in Kunar and even Qandahar. With their recent rampage against Afghanistan's cultural heritage, Cmdr. Masood said the Taliban have brought on themselves unanimous condemnation from not only Afghans but the international community.

When asked what he expected from the rest of the world, Cmdr. Masood cited Afghanistan's sacrifice in defeating Soviet communism and promoting freedom and liberty. He said the European Union should assist Afghanistan in regaining its sovereignty.

In a warning to the United States – the only Western nation to harbor a negative attitude toward Afghanistan's national resistance force and its supreme leader due to Washington's reliance on Islamabad to formulate its Afghan policy – Cmdr. Masood said that if the US fails to do more in helping to restore peace to Afghanistan, not only Afghanistan but the entire region [eds: and consequently long-term US energy and politico-military interests] will be in peril.

Addressing the Rome initiative, Cmdr. Masood said that His Majesty the former King can play a very positive role, the extent of which depends entirely on the former King's own willingness and ability to take decisive action.

At the end of his talk, Cmdr. Masood called on the EU and world to send immediate humanitarian relief to Afghanistan, where thousands of lives are in dire jeopardy. [eds: Nationwide famine is a never before seen phenomenon in Afghanistan that has only affected the country since the advent of the Taliban and Pakistan's intensifying interventionist policy.]

Throughout their discussion, the high-ranking national resistance force delegation highlighted the importance of reinforcing, reinvigorating and fortifying national unity among Afghanistan's various ethnic and religious groups. And each asked Afghan expatriates to promote national unity in their own capacity. The gathering, which was peppered with the slogan "Death to Pakistan" forcefully shouted by the audience, ended at 9 in the evening.

On Thursday, Cmdr. Masood and delegation traveled to Strasbourg, where he received a head of state welcome by the European Parliament and its President, Ms. Nicole Fontaine. This was the first time that an Afghan figure was feted by the European Parliament. It is of great pride for our nation that such a reception was afforded to the illustrious and inimitable figure of Ahmad Shah Masood, not just because of his continuing and unsurpassed heroism, but also because it was, in fact, a respect being paid to our entire nation.

As reported in international news agencies, Cmdr. Masood and delegation held discussions with Pres. Fontaine and various high-ranking EP officials and committees. Cmdr. Masood and delegation were also received by another gathering of 400 Afghans in Strasbourg. They next traveled to Brussels for further meetings with Belgian and European officials. Cmdr. Masood's officials visit ended on Friday.

On Saturday, Omaid Weekly has been informed, Cmdr. Masood and delegation returned to Paris. Cmdr. Masood underwent a thorough medical examination in the

French capital, which found the supreme commander to be in complete good health.

Cmdr. Masood and delegation are expected to return to Afghanistan on Monday.

In response to a question by Omaid Weekly, Cmdr. Masood termed his historic first visit to the West a "success." The supreme leader of Afghanistan's national resistance force said the events of the past week succeeded in heightening awareness of Pakistan's direct intervention in Afghanistan, and unmasking their Taliban militia servants.

Appendix 6

Masood to Bush: Help Bring Peace to Afghanistan, Else the U.S. and Other Nations Will Face Dire Consequences

Islamic world's inaction over Afghan tragedy is unfortunate

Concluded from our two previous issues: In continuation of Omaid Weekly's coverage of the early April European tour of Ahmad Shah Masood, generalissimo of Afghanistan's national resistance force, the following is a summarized translation from the original Dar-Persian text, as compiled by our senior correspondent Wais Nassery, of our transcript from the April 4 press conference, held at 11:30 a.m. in Paris.

Q: Have your talks with French officials focused on bringing pressure on Pakistan to end its interference in Afghanistan? ...Can you confirm recent military aid from Iran to the United Front?

A: As I have repeated many times, a major way in which other countries and the international community can help to establish peace in Afghanistan and end the fighting and bloodshed is to bring adequate pressure on Pakistan. This has been mentioned in talks with the French Foreign Ministry, and it will also be mentioned in talks with others. It is then up to these officials to make a decision.

Concerning your second question, we have good and friendly relations with not only Iran, but also other neighboring and Central Asian countries. But recent and previous rumors of military assistance are false.

Q: What is your opinion on terrorist actions in the name of Islam in Algeria? What information do you have on the involvement of Osama bin Laden's organization in this region, and are you in contact with Algerian political forces opposing the terrorists?

A: We are against any sort of [so-called] "Islamic" terrorist actions and "non-Islamic" terrorist actions, and we consider terrorism to be against Islam and against the interests of humanity.

Of course bin Laden has groups elsewhere besides Afghanistan. We have [extensive] information about [bin Laden's group] inside Afghanistan, and to varying degrees in other regions.

There are governmental relations with political group in Algeria, but unfortunately I have no direct personal contacts in this regard.

Q: There is a new administration in Washington, however there is still no visible sign of a distinct U.S. policy on Afghanistan. What do you expect from the new U.S. administration and what is your message to President Bush?

A: As you have said, hitherto the Americans have no clear or distinct policy. My message to Mr. Bush is that if attention is not given to bringing peace in Afghanistan, and the people of Afghanistan are not assisted on the road toward achieving peace, then verily this crisis will continue to plague not just the people of Afghanistan, but also spread to America and other countries.

Q: What is your view of the activities of Zaher Shah and the Loya Jirga initiative?

A: First, this depends on his own decision and what he decides to do in the future. In my opinion, the former King has the ability to play a major and axial role in bringing peace to Afghanistan. But it is up to him as to the extent of his activities. With regard to his future role, that is for the people to decide – it depends on the will and mandate of the people.

Q: How do you make sense of the Islamic world's silence on the un-Islamic actions of the Taliban?

A: It is regretful that Islamic countries are not taking requisite measures with regard to the tragic situation in Afghanistan.

We were hopeful that Islamic countries working through the Organization of the Islamic Conference would serve to help bring peace to Afghanistan – unfortunately, hitherto no appropriate steps have been taken.

Unfortunately, in the past, some Islamic countries, like Saudi Arabia, without considering dangerous future consequences, not only did not oppose the Taliban, but took part in creating them, gave them money, and encouraged them.

Now that the Taliban's face has been completely exposed, we are hopeful that Islamic countries will take responsibility with regard to Afghanistan, and take steps toward establishing peace in Afghanistan.

Q: Do you believe that Afghans will continue to support you if you receive aid from Russia?

A: We have very good and friendly relations with regional countries, and it is Pakistan that wants to incite the people's opinion against us through propaganda.

But from another standpoint, when there is a blatant invasion, such as Pakistan's current ongoing incursion into Afghanistan and its [Regular Army] troop presence [in Afghanistan], I give myself the right to seek assistance from anywhere in defense of my homeland, my people's honor, and my country's independence. (Passionate and intense reaction from approving audience.)

Q: You have severely chastised Pakistan... What about Saudi Arabia, the Taliban's bankrollers?
A: It is Pakistan that has a strategic plan for Afghanistan and Central Asia. It is Pakistan that seeks "strategic depth" and "Islamic depth" in Afghanistan and Central Asia. It is Pakistan that, in the past, deceived and used the Saudis and other countries to further its own goals.

Appendix 7

President George W. Bush's Address to a Joint Session of Congress and the American People, 20 September 2001, Declaring War Against Terrorism

The White House Office of the Press Secretary
September 20, 2001
Address to a Joint Session of Congress
and the American People

Mr. Speaker, Mr. President pro tempore, Members of Congress, and fellow Americans:

In the normal course of events, Presidents come to this chamber to report on the state of the Union. Tonight, no such report is needed. It has already been delivered by the American people.

We have seen it in the courage of passengers, who rushed terrorists to save others on the ground – passengers like an exceptional man named Todd Beamer. Please help me to welcome his wife, Lisa Beamer, here tonight.

We have seen the state of our Union in the endurance of rescuers, working past exhaustion. We have seen the unfurling of flags, the lighting of candles, the giving of blood, the saying of prayers – in English, Hebrew, and Arabic. We have seen the decency of a loving and giving people, who have made the grief of strangers their own.

Appendix 7

My fellow citizens, for the last nine days, the entire world has seen for itself the state of our Union – and it is strong.

Tonight we are a country awakened to danger and called to defend freedom. Our grief has turned to anger, and anger to resolution. Whether we bring our enemies to justice, or bring justice to our enemies, justice will be done.

I thank the Congress for its leadership at such an important time. All of America was touched on the evening of the tragedy to see Republicans and Democrats, joined together on the steps of this Capitol, singing "God Bless America." And you did more than sing, you acted, by delivering forty billion dollars to rebuild our communities and meet the needs of our military.

Speaker Hastert and Minority Leader Gephardt – Majority Leader Daschle and Senator Lott – I thank you for your friendship and your leadership and your service to our country.

And on behalf of the American people, I thank the world for its outpouring of support. America will never forget the sounds of our National Anthem playing at Buckingham Palace, and on the streets of Paris, and at Berlin's Brandenburg Gate. We will not forget South Korean children gathering to pray outside our embassy in Seoul, or the prayers of sympathy offered at a mosque in Cairo. We will not forget moments of silence and days of mourning in Australia and Africa and Latin America.

Nor will we forget the citizens of eighty other nations who died with our own. Dozens of Pakistanis. More than 130 Israelis. More than 250 citizens of India. Men and women from El Salvador, Iran, Mexico, and Japan. And hundreds of British citizens. America has no truer friend than Great Britain. Once again, we are joined together in a great cause. The British Prime Minister has crossed an ocean to show his unity of purpose with America, and tonight we welcome Tony Blair.

On September the eleventh, enemies of freedom committed an act of war against our country. Americans have known wars – but for the past 136 years, they have been wars on foreign soil, except for one Sunday in 1941. Americans have known the casualties of war – but not at the center of a great city on a peaceful morning. Americans have known surprise attacks – but never before on thousands of civilians. All of this was brought upon us in a single day – and night fell on a different world, a world where freedom itself is under attack.

Americans have many questions tonight. Americans are asking: Who attacked our country?

The evidence we have gathered all points to a collection of loosely affiliated terrorist organizations known as al-Qaida. They are the same murderers indicted for bombing American embassies in Tanzania and Kenya, and responsible for the bombing of the U.S.S. Cole.

Al-Qaida is to terror what the mafia is to crime. But its goal is not making money; its goal is remaking the world – and imposing its radical beliefs on people everywhere.

The terrorists practice a fringe form of Islamic extremism that has been rejected by Muslim scholars and the vast majority of Muslim clerics – a fringe movement that perverts the peaceful teachings of Islam. The terrorists' directive commands them to kill Christians and Jews, to kill all Americans, and make no distinctions among military and civilians, including women and children.

This group and its leader – a person named Usama bin Ladin – are linked to many other organizations in different countries, including the Egyptian Islamic Jihad and the Islamic Movement of Uzbekistan.

There are thousands of these terrorists in more than sixty countries. They are recruited from their own nations and neighborhoods, and brought to camps in places like Afghanistan where they are trained in the tactics of terror. They are sent back to their homes or sent to hide in countries around the world to plot evil and destruction.

Appendix 7

The leadership of al-Qaida has great influence in Afghanistan, and supports the Taliban regime in controlling most of that country. In Afghanistan, we see al-Qaida's vision for the world.

Afghanistan's people have been brutalized – many are starving and many have fled. Women are not allowed to attend school. You can be jailed for owning a television. Religion can be practiced only as their leaders dictate. A man can be jailed in Afghanistan if his beard is not long enough.

The United States respects the people of Afghanistan – after all, we are currently its largest source of humanitarian aid – but we condemn the Taliban regime. It is not only repressing its own people, it is threatening people everywhere by sponsoring and sheltering and supplying terrorists. By aiding and abetting murder, the Taliban regime is committing murder. And tonight, the United States of America makes the following demands on the Taliban:

Deliver to United States authorities all the leaders of al-Qaida who hide in your land.

Release all foreign nationals – including American citizens – you have unjustly imprisoned, and protect foreign journalists, diplomats, and aid workers in your country.

Close immediately and permanently every terrorist training camp in Afghanistan and hand over every terrorist, and every person in their support structure, to appropriate authorities.

Give the United States full access to terrorist training camps, so we can make sure they are no longer operating.

These demands are not open to negotiation or discussion. The Taliban must act and act immediately. They will hand over the terrorists, or they will share in their fate.

I also want to speak tonight directly to Muslims throughout the world: We respect your faith. It is practiced freely by many millions of Americans, and by millions more in countries that

America counts as friends. Its teachings are good and peaceful, and those who commit evil in the name of Allah blaspheme the name of Allah. The terrorists are traitors to their own faith, trying, in effect, to hijack Islam itself. The enemy of America is not our many Muslim friends; it is not our many Arab friends. Our enemy is a radical network of terrorists, and every government that supports them.

Our war on terror begins with al-Qaida, but it does not end there. It will not end until every terrorist group of global reach has been found, stopped and defeated.

Americans are asking: Why do they hate us?

They hate what we see right here in this chamber – a democratically elected government. Their leaders are self-appointed. They hate our freedoms – our freedom of religion, our freedom of speech, our freedom to vote and assemble and disagree with each other.

They want to overthrow existing governments in many Muslim countries, such as Egypt, Saudi Arabia, and Jordan. They want to drive Israel out of the Middle East. They want to drive Christians and Jews out of vast regions of Asia and Africa.

These terrorists kill not merely to end lives, but to disrupt and end a way of life. With every atrocity, they hope that America grows fearful, retreating from the world and forsaking our friends. They stand against us, because we stand in their way.

We are not deceived by their pretenses to piety. We have seen their kind before. They are the heirs of all the murderous ideologies of the twentieth century. By sacrificing human life to serve their radical visions – by abandoning every value except the will to power – they follow in the path of fascism, and Nazism, and totalitarianism. And they will follow that path all the way, to where it ends: in history's unmarked grave of discarded lies.

Americans are asking: How will we fight and win this war?

We will direct every resource at our command – every means of diplomacy, every tool of intelligence, every instrument of law enforcement, every financial influence, and every necessary weapon of war – to the disruption and defeat of the global terror network.

This war will not be like the war against Iraq a decade ago, with its decisive liberation of territory and its swift conclusion. It will not look like the air war above Kosovo two years ago, where no ground troops were used and not a single American was lost in combat.

Our response involves far more than instant retaliation and isolated strikes. Americans should not expect one battle, but a lengthy campaign, unlike any other we have seen. It may include dramatic strikes, visible on television, and covert operations, secret even in success. We will starve terrorists of funding, turn them one against another, drive them from place to place, until there is no refuge or rest. And we will pursue nations that provide aid or safe haven to terrorism. Every nation, in every region, now has a decision to make. Either you are with us, or you are with the terrorists. From this day forward, any nation that continues to harbor or support terrorism will be regarded by the United States as a hostile regime.

Our Nation has been put on notice: We are not immune from attack. We will take defensive measures against terrorism to protect Americans.

Today, dozens of federal departments and agencies, as well as state and local governments, have responsibilities affecting homeland security. These efforts must be coordinated at the highest level. So tonight I announce the creation of a Cabinet-level position reporting directly to me – the Office of Homeland Security.

These measures are essential. But the only way to defeat terrorism as a threat to our way of life is to stop it, eliminate it, and destroy it where it grows.

Many will be involved in this effort, from FBI agents to intelligence operatives to the reservists we have called to active duty. All deserve our thanks, and all have our prayers. And tonight, a few miles from the damaged Pentagon, I have a message for our military: Be ready. I have called the armed forces to alert, and there is a reason. The hour is coming when America will act, and you will make us proud.

This is not, however, just America's fight. And what is at stake is not just America's freedom. This is the world's fight. This is civilization's fight. This is the fight of all who believe in progress and pluralism, tolerance and freedom.

We ask every nation to join us. We will ask, and we will need, the help of police forces, intelligence services, and banking systems around the world. The United States is grateful that many nations and many international organizations have already responded – with sympathy and with support. Nations from Latin America, to Asia, to Africa, to Europe, to the Islamic world. Perhaps the NATO Charter reflects best the attitude of the world: an attack on one is an attack on all.

The civilized world is rallying to America's side. They understand that if this terror goes unpunished, their own cities, their own citizens may be next. Terror, unanswered, can not only bring down buildings, it can threaten the stability of legitimate governments. And we will not allow it.

Americans are asking: What is expected of us?

I ask you to live your lives and hug your children. I know many citizens have fears tonight, and I ask you to be calm and resolute, even in the face of a continuing threat.

I ask you to uphold the values of America, and remember why so many have come here. We are in a fight for our principles, and our first responsibility is to live by them. No one should be singled out for unfair treatment or unkind words because of their ethnic background or religious faith.

I ask you to continue to support the victims of this tragedy with your contributions. Those who want to give can go to a central source of information, libertyunites.org, to find the names of groups providing direct help in New York, Pennsylvania, and Virginia.

The thousands of FBI agents who are now at work in this investigation may need your cooperation, and I ask you to give it.

I ask for your patience, with the delays and inconveniences that may accompany tighter security – and for your patience in what will be a long struggle.

I ask your continued participation and confidence in the American economy. Terrorists attacked a symbol of American prosperity. They did not touch its source. America is successful because of the hard work, and creativity, and enterprise of our people. These were the true strengths of our economy before September eleventh, and they are our strengths today.

Finally, please continue praying for the victims of terror and their families, for those in uniform, and for our great country. Prayer has comforted us in sorrow, and will help strengthen us for the journey ahead.

Tonight I thank my fellow Americans for what you have already done and for what you will do. And ladies and gentlemen of the Congress, I thank you, their representatives, for what you have already done, and for what we will do together.

Tonight, we face new and sudden national challenges. We will come together to improve air safety, to dramatically expand the number of air marshals on domestic flights, and take new measures to prevent hijacking. We will come together to promote stability and keep our airlines flying with direct assistance during this emergency.

We will come together to give law enforcement the additional tools it needs to track down terror here at home. We will come together to strengthen our intelligence capabilities to know the plans of terrorists before they act, and find them before they strike.

We will come together to take active steps that strengthen America's economy, and put our people back to work.

Tonight we welcome here two leaders who embody the extraordinary spirit of all New Yorkers: Governor George Pataki, and Mayor Rudy Giuliani. As a symbol of America's resolve, my Administraion will work with the Congress, and these two leaders, to show the world that we will rebuild New York City.

After all that has just passed – all the lives taken, and all the possibilities and hopes that died with them – it is natural to wonder if America's future is one of fear. Some speak of an age of terror. I know there are struggles ahead, and dangers to face. But this country will define our times, not be defined by them. As long as the United States of America is determined and strong, this will not be an age of terror; this will be an age of liberty, here and across the world.

Great harm has been done to us. We have suffered great loss. And in our grief and anger we have found our mission and our moment. Freedom and fear are at war. The advance of human freedom – the great achievement of our time, and the great hope of every time – now depends on us. Our Nation – this generation – will lift a dark threat of violence from our people and our future. We will rally the world to this cause, by our efforts and by our courage. We will not tire, we will not falter, and we will not fail.

Appendix 7

It is my hope that in the months and years ahead, life will return almost to normal. We'll go back to our lives and routines, and that is good. Even grief recedes with time and grace. But our resolve must not pass. Each of us will remember what happened that day, and to whom it happened. We will remember the moment the news came – where we were and what we were doing. Some will remember an image of fire, or a story of rescue. Some will carry memories of a face and a voice gone forever.

And I will carry this. It is the police shield of a man named George Howard, who died at the World Trade Center trying to save others. It was given to me by his mom, Arlene, as a proud memorial to her son. This is my reminder of lives that ended, and a task that does not end.

I will not forget this wound to our country, or those who inflicted it. I will not yield – I will not rest – I will not relent in waging this struggle for the freedom and security of the American people.

The course of this conflict is not known, yet its outcome is certain. Freedom and fear, justice and cruelty, have always been at war, and we know that God is not neutral between them.

Fellow citizens, we will meet violence with patient justice – assured of the rightness of our cause, and confident of the victories to come. In all that lies before us, may God grant us wisdom, and may He watch over the United States of America.

Thank You.

Index

ABC-TV, 173
AC-130, 170-172, 173
AFP, 39, 198
AIM Television, 50
Abbas, Mullah Mohammed, 76
Abdel Rahman, 1
Abdul Majid, 73
Abdul Qadeer, Haji, 2, 13, 32, 92, 156, 238
Abdul Rasul, 8
Abdul Razaq, Mullah, 93, 117
Abdul Sattar, Mullah, 146
Abdul Wahib, 42
Abdul Wali, 238
Abdullah, Dr Abdullah, 15, 28, 32, 33, 57, 215, 237, 238
Abdurraham, 28
Achakzai, Mansur, 82
Ackerman, Gary, 137-138
Aden, 194
Afghan Islamic Press, 148
Afghan NGO, 25
Afghanistan-Tajikistan border, 180, 200
Africa, North, 154
Afghan Transit Trade Agreement, 25 (*see also* Drugs)
Agriculture, 133
Ahmadzai, Ashraf Ghani, 42, 57
Ahmadzai, Shahpur, 93
  : execution of, 93-94, 107
Ahmed Salim, 128
Aid, foreign (*see also* Economy), 74
Akhtar, Qari Saifullah, 167

Akhunzadah, Gaffar, 87
Al-Ali, Sulaiman, 165
Al-Qaeda (*see also* Taleban-al-Qaeda), 19, 36, 43, 49, 153-154, 157, 165, 168, 174, 175, 180-181, 183-184, 195, 197, 199, 202, 206-210, 220, 224, 225, 227, 238, 240
  : terrorist network, 153-154, 165-166, 202, 225
al-Zawahiri, Ayman, 184
al-Zumur, Abdul, 184
Alexander the Great, 225
Algeria (Algerians), 97, 127, 194
America (*see also* USA)
  : north, 154
Amir-ul Mumineen, 77
Amnesty International, 135
Amu Dariya, 7
Anachronism, 36
Anarchy, 58
Anderson, Jon Lee, 181, 195, 196, 197
Andishman, Rajab Ali, 42-43
Andrew H. Card Jr., 201
Annan, Kofi, 124, 131
Arab (Arabs) (nations), 49, 96-98, 128, 158, 164-167, 184, 193, 195, 196, 197, 214, 216, 238
  : extremists, 129
  : fundamentalists, 96
  : Islamism, 162
  : Islamist groups, 184
  : mercenaries, 128
  : militants, 158

: mujahideen, 155, 163, 164
: nationals' activities, 127
: terrorist training camps in Pakistan, 97
Ariana, 197
Armed Islamic Movement, 95
Armitage, Richard, 193, 202-203
Ashkabad, 80, 81, 82
Asia, 64, 154
   : central, 23, 25, 53, 57, 59, 65, 80, 81, 82, 85, 86, 115, 118, 131, 148-149, 151, 181, 217, 227
   : South, 53, 137, 138
   : Southwest, 57, 59
Asia Society, blown off, 103
Assassinations, 2, 28-29
Atta Mohammad, 226, 238
Azerbaijan, 97, 125
Azzam, Sheikh Abdallah Yussuf, 158-159, 163
   : killing of, 163

BBC, 19-20, 149, 210, 215, 228
Babar, Naseerullah, 70, 80, 82, 83, 84
Bacha Khan, 31
Badakhstan, 20
Badghis, 29, 122, 136
Bagh-i-Bala, 167
Bagh Zakheera, 141
Baghdadi scholars, 38
Bagram airfield, 3, 92, 100, 119, 129, 135, 212, 225, 235
Bagram Collection, 65
Baig, Mirza Aslam, 193
Bakhtar News Agency, Taleban-run, 101
Balkans, 57, 97, 98
Balkh, 29, 30, 117, 129
   : Balkh University, 116
Baluchistan, 83, 85, 192, 217-218
   : Baluchi tribes, 85
Bamiyan Valley (*see also* Buddhas), 4, 30, 101-106, 118, 124, 141, 142
   : Buddhas, 101-106

   : caves, Buddhas' statues demolished in, 101-106
   : massacre, 104
   : studies, 105
Bana, Hassan-ul, 72
Bandsarda, 156
Bangladesh, 127
Batuta, Ibn, 159
   : on sufism, 159
Bayh, Evan, 32
Bed Mushkin, 146
Belgium, 216
Bharat Bhusan, 61
Bhutto, Benazir, 70, 81, 85-86, 96-97
Bhutto, Zulfiqar Ali, 70, 72
bin Laden (*see* Osama bin Laden)
Bismillah Khan, 195, 199
Blair, Tony, 19, 235
Bodansky, Yossef, 84-85, 95, 96-98, 127, 159, 162-163, 184
Bonn Agreement (accord), 9, 14, 15, 28, 46, 51, 132, 239-240
Borjan, 82
Boucher, Richard, 213
Brahimi, Lakhdar, 12-14, 76, 130, 239
Britain (*see also* UK), 18, 19, 46, 80, 223, 235, 236
   : Islamic Observation Centre, London, 196
Buddhas (*see also* Bamiyan Valley), 101-106, 109
   : Bamiyan Buddhas, destruction of statues of, 101-106, 109
   : India condemned destruction, 106
   : larger, representing Vairocana "Light Shining throughout the Universe of Buddha", 103-104
Buddhism, 104
   : Buddhists, 104
Bulgarians, 168
Bureaucracy, 52, 59
   : bureaucrats, 71
Bush, George W. (Bush administration) (*see also* USA), 31-32, 190, 194, 201-204, 206, 207, 208-209, 211,

Index

212, 219-220, 221, 222, 228, 229, 233, 239

C-4 sophisticated explosives, 95-96
CJTF-180, 172
CIA (*see* USA)
CNN, 20
CNRS (Centre National des Recherches' Scientifiques), France
 : summed situation in war-devastated country, 150-151
Canada, 194
Central Asia (*see* Asia)
Chahar-Asiab, 96
Chal, 193
Chaman, 80, 81, 192
Charasyab, 87, 88, 168
Charikar, 100, 119, 135
Chechens, 49, 167, 168, 238 (*see also* Russia)
Chehle-Tan, 127
Cherat, 192
Children, 10, 30, 36, 119, 132, 208
 : killings of, 148
 : Taleban's measures abolishing completely individual freedom to live normal life, 107-108
 : treatment to, 140
China, 80, 168, 183
 : Uighurs from Xinjiang, 168
Chirac, Jacques, 186, 187-188
Christians, 104, 208
 : Christian missionary non-governmental organisation, destruction of, Ghazni, 156
Chossuovsky, Michel, 21
Ciriello, A. Raffaele, 50
Civil liberties, 175
Civil war, 65, 80, 96, 102, 186, 189
Clinton, Bill, 125, 126, 182
Cold War allies, 51
Commonwealth of Independent States, conference, 148
Communism, 66
 : Communists, 66

Congressional India Caucus, 137
Constitution (1964), 36-38, 39, 43
Cooley, John K., 23, 91
Corruption, 137
Crimes, 11
 : criminals, 140
 : organised, 11
Cross-border terrorism (*see* Terrorism)
Cyprus process, 132
Czechs, 168

Daga, 144
Dagestan, 131
Daoud, 147
Daoud Khan, 238
Daoud Mohammad, 73
Daoud, Sardar Mohammad, 37-38
Dara-e-Suf, 129
Dar-es-Salaam, 175, 182, 194
Dar-i-Ali, 144, 146, 147
Daschle, Tom, 32
Dash-te-Laili desert, 121, 141-142
Dashty, Fahim, 197
Death (punishment) (*see also* Punishment), 14, 24, 133, 134, 174
 : stonings to, 24, 134
Deh Rawod, 169-170
Deh Surkh, 144
Delhi (New Delhi), 94, 130, 196, 198, 199, 205, 206-207, 237
De-miners, ambushed, killed and burned in Badghis, 136
Democracy, 15, 33-35, 36, 58, 138
 : parliamentary, 34-35, 36
Deobandism, 162
Depredation, twenty-three years of, 3-4
Destruction, 14, 174
Dilaram, 90
Diplomacy, international, 216-217
Displaced persons (refugees) (*see also* Pakistan, Refugees), 10, 13, 29, 30, 120
Dobbins, James, 234

Donor countries, 12, 14, 57-59 (*see also* Economy)
: International conference of donor countries (January 2002), Tokyo, 12, 14

Dost Mohammad Mullah, 192

Dostum, Abdul Rashid, 8, 56, 67, 81, 87, 90, 115-116, 120, 121, 238

Drought, 132-133, 186

Drugs, 11, 17-26, 52-57, 69, 96, 132-133, 136, 143, 212 (*see also* Narcotics, Poppy)
: Afghan Golden Crescent drug trade, 21
: Afghan Transit Trade Agreement, 25
: Asian drug trade, 22
: counter-narcotics capacity, 19
: dealers, 124
: Drugscope, British charity, 18-19
: European Conference on Drug Trafficking and Law Enforcement, second annual (September 2002), 18
: European drug markets, 21
: illicit, 69
: Illicit Crop Monitoring Programme (ICMP), 17-18
: international drug control treaties, 21
: International Narcotics Control Board, 20-21
: Latin American drug trade, 22
: mafia, 25
: merchants, 96
: narcotics production, 17
: narcotics trade, 17
: opium poppy cultivation, production, trade, 17-26, 53-55, 132-133, 137
: routes, 21-22
: smuggling, 25, 53-57, 80, 115, 133, 136, 140, 154-155
: trade, 17-18, 21-22, 25, 26, 52-57, 124, 132-133, 136
: trafficking, 52, 55, 56
: UN Drug Control Programme (UNDCP), 17-18, 54
: UN Office for Drugs Control and Crime Prevention, 20
: warlords, 143

Dudaru, 30

Dupree, Louis, 5, 6, 34-35, 37-39, 43

Durranis, 74

Dushanbe, 148, 149, 192, 198, 212, 219
: conference at, 50

Ecevit, Bulent, 216-217

Economy, 17, 26, 57, 132-133, 140-141
: donor countries, 12, 14, 57-59
: Economic Cooperation Organisation, 7th summit of 10-member (October 2002), Istanbul, 174-175
: economic incentives, 55-56
: foreign aid, 57-59, 74
: International conference of donor countries (January 2002), Tokyo, 12, 14
: nation-building, 57-62

Education, 134-135

Egypt, 65, 97, 127, 168, 184
: Egyptian Islamic jihad, 208
: Egyptian Islamists, 158

Ehsanullah, Mullah, 117

Emergency Loya Jirgah (Emergency Grand Council) (Traditional Grand Council), 10-11, 12, 15, 16, 32-34, 36-38, 39, 40, 41-42, 43, 48, 52, 121, 132, 189-190, 213, 215, 220, 239, 240

Environment, 4-7
: pollution, 5
: UNEP, 4, 5, 7

Eshfaq Ahmad, 192

Eshkamish, 193

Ethnicity (ethnic communities) (*see also* Pushtums, Tajiks), 11, 15, 41-42, 121

Index

: affiliations, 28
: conflicts, 52
: groups, 46, 116
: minorities, 28, 29, 36
: Nooristan group, 42
: warlords (warlordism), 30
Europe (Europeans), 54, 57, 59, 154, 185-192
   : European Conference on Drug Trafficking and Law Enforcement, second annual (September 2002), Paris, 18, 19
   : European drug markets, 21
   : European Union, 12, 175, 185, 186, 187, 190, 216
   : Western, 98
Executions (*see also* Punishments), 133, 134, 136, 141-142, 146
   : summary executions, 141, 142, 143, 212
Extremists, Islamic (extremist groups) (*see also* Islamic), 14, 97, 127, 129, 149, 174

Fact Sheet, 139-140
Fahim, Muhammad, 200, 212, 237, 238
Fanaticism, 79, 161
Faqoori, Haji, 146
Farah, 89
Farhadi, Rawan, 238
Farkhar gorge, 193
Farmers, 53-55
Faryab, 29, 30, 117, 122
Fatwa, 68
Fazlur Rahman Maulana, 70
Feroz Bahar, 144
Fidayeen missions, 155-156
Floggings, 24
Foltz, Richard, 104
Foreign aid (*see also* Donor Countries, Economy), 57-59
France, 186-188, 216 (*see also* Paris)
   : CNRS, 150
Franks, Tommy, 226

Freedom, measures abolishing completely individual freedom to live normal life under Taleban, 107-114
Fundamentalism
   : fanatic forces of fundamentalist faith, 138
   : Islamic, 241
   : religious, 14, 75
Fundamentalists, 96, 167
   : group, 95
   : Islamic, 71, 72, 241
   : Islamic organisations, 72
   : militia, 132
   : movements, 71-72
   : Muslims, 104
   : networks, 72
   : rulers, 180
   : Uzbek, 131

Gailani, Pir Sayed Ahmad, 160, 215, 238
Gardez, 56
Geneva, 57, 141
Germany (Germans), 194, 199, 216
Ghaus, Mohammed, 73, 75
Ghaus, Mullah, 83
Ghazni, 133, 156
Ghent, 216
Ghodse, Hamid, 20
Ghosphandi, 142
Ghulam, Harakat-ul-Ansar (Harakat-ul-Mujahideen), 127
Girdbayd, 145
Girls (*see* Women)
Gohar Ayab, 116
Goldenberg, Suzanne, 78
Goodwin, Jan, 109-111
Governance, 13, 15, 17
Greece, 65, 106
Gross, Nasrine (of Negar), woman activist, 121
   : support of women of Afghanistan, 39-41
Guantanamo, 155

Guerilla warfare, 128
Gul, Hamid, 200
Gulbuddin, 8
Gulf War, 226

Haavisto, Pekka, 5
Hagel, Chuck, 32
Haider, Salman, 204
Hajj, 164
Hanafi Shari'a, 37, 39
Haq, Abdul, 218, 220, 221
: death of, 219
Harakat-i-Inquilab-i-Islami Afghanistan (Afghanistan's Movement of Islamic Revolution), 9, 67, 70, 75, 143, 161
Harakat-ul-Ansar, 126
Harakat-ul-Mujahideen, 127, 128
Hazaras, 39, 87, 88-89, 116, 117, 118, 119, 120, 121, 148, 229
: Shia Hazaras, 231 (*see also* Shias)
: tussle between Taleban and, 124
Hazarjat, 102
Health and physical conditions during Taleban rule, 113-114
Hekmatyar, Gulbuddin, 8, 17, 70, 71, 72, 73, 79, 81, 87, 91, 96, 108, 151, 160, 161, 228, 238
Helmand, 17, 87, 90
Herat, 30, 56, 78, 79, 80, 81, 82, 86, 87, 89, 90, 91, 93, 116, 133, 192
: women in, suffering of, 91
Hersh, Seymour, 223
Hijacking, 157
Hindu Kush mountains, 80
Hizb-i-Islami (Islamic Party), 67, 75, 96, 97, 98, 108, 161, 164
Hizb-i-Wahdat, 8, 9, 67, 124, 143, 144, 146, 231
Holl, Norbet, 94
Holy Mosques, two, 164, 165
Howard, Roger, 18-19
Howe, Jonathan, 222
Human endeavour, negative aspects of, 35-36

Human rights, 11, 14, 35, 49, 69, 107-109, 112-113, 114, 133-134, 175, 188
: Country Reports on Human Rights Practices-2000 Afghanistan, 135
: Human Rights Commission report (2001), 141-143
: Human Rights Watch (HRW) report: Crisis of Impurity, New York, 7, 8, 143, 147
: situation, 29, 30
: violations, 11, 12, 30, 142-143, 212
Humanitarian law, international, 11
Hussain Ahmad, Qazi, 97, 98

IHT, 223
ISI (Inter-Services Intelligence (*see also* Pakistan)
Ijtihad, 38
Ikhwan-ul-Muslimeen Leaders, 72, 160, 162
Imam, Colonel, 82
Imarat, 85, 97, 98
India, 55, 59-60, 65, 67, 97, 98, 131, 137-138, 164, 180, 183, 201, 206-207, 234
: assistance of, 59-60
: Atal Behari Vajpayee ordered reappraisal of India's Afghanistan policy, 130
: condemned destruction of statues of Buddhas, 106
: Cross-border terrorism in Jammu and Kashmir, victims of, 137-138, 205
: India-Russia summit, 149
: Indian doctors, 197
: Indo-Pak relations, 124-126
: Islamic University of Deoband, 70
: Islamist terrorists in Kashmir, 127-128
: Kargil war, 124-126, 128, 129, 205
: Kashmir fighters, 126

Index

- : LOC (Line of Control), 124-125
- : offer to bring the surviving Buddhist relics free of cost for preservation, 106
- : Pakistan's armed infiltrations intrusions into Indian territories, 124-126; into Kargil sector, 124-126, 128, 129; into Jammu and Kashmir, 127-128, 204, 237
- : Pakistan's inspired Pakistan-sponsored Islamic Terrorism in Jammu and Kashmir, 96, 127, 204
- : Pakistan-occupied Kashmir, terrorist centres in, 204-205
- : Pakistan's war waged in Jammu and Kashmir, 96
- : President K.R. Narayanan on situation in Afghanistan, 129-130
- : Proxy War by Pakistan in Jammu and Kashmir, 125-126
- : Simla agreement (1972), 124
- : Taleban-al-Qaeda terrorist network in Jammu and Kashmir, 205
- : Taleban-Osama bin Laden's international terrorism nexus, 124, 127-128
- : Terrorist attack (13 December 2001) on Indian Parliament House, 205
- : Terrorists trained in camps in Afghanistan entered Jammu and Kashmir, 230

Indian Ocean, 85
Interim administration (authority), 2 10-12, 15, 16, 21, 25-26, 28, 30-31, 33-34, 53, 54, 88, 105, 130, 200, 240
Iran (Iranians) 45, 67, 84, 85, 90, 118, 132, 150, 151, 164, 175, 183, 196, 231, 233
- : Teheran, 214

Islam, 14, 37, 38, 49, 66, 70, 101, 115, 137, 159, 160, 162, 174, 194, 208, 236

- : traditionalist-radical 160, 184-185

Islamabad (*see* Pakistan)
Islamic centres, 180
Islamic Emirate, 69
Islamic extremists (*see* Extremists)
Islamic fundamentalism, (*see* Fundamentalism)
Islamic fundamentalists (*see* Fundamentalists)
Islamic hejab, 69
Islamic jurisprudence, 38
Islamic militants, foreign, 151 (*see also* militants)
Islamic modernists, 38
Islamic Observation Centre, London, 196
Islamic radicals, 73
Islamic Revolutionary Movement, 71-72, 83, 150-151
Islamic Sharia (*see* Sharia)
Islamic Students (Talaba), 66
Islamic Transitional Government (*see* Transitional Government)
Islamic Ulema, 67
Islamic values, 14
Islamicism, 72
- : radical, 162

Islamist movement, 71-72, 83, 150-151
Islamist nationalist movement, 157
Islamist terrorists 95, 96-97, 98, 127-128 (*see also* Terrorists)
Islamists, 71-72, 75, 83, 98, 127-128, 150-151
Ismael Khan, 56, 79, 80, 81, 87, 89, 90, 238
Israel, 55, 223
Italy, 80, 106, 187, 216
Ittehad-e-Islami, Wahabbi party, 160
Ivanov, Igor, 234

JAMA, 111, 112-113
Jabal-ul-Seraj, 118, 135
Jabba-i-Najat Milli Afghanistan, 160
Jalalabad, 6, 7, 87, 92, 167, 168
- : battle, 162

: bombing of police headquarters in, 164
Jamaat-i-Islami, 70, 72, 160
Jami'at-i-Ulema-i-Islam, (JUI) (Society of Islamic Scholars), 70, 80, 83
: madrassas, 83
: Srinagar, 127
Jamshed, 195-196, 197
Jammu and Kashmir, 98, 151, 155, 156 (*see also* India, Pakistan)
Jan Agha, 145, 146
Japan, 12, 42, 175
: attack on Pearl Harbour, 207
Jews, 104, 208
Jihad (holy war), 9, 49, 66-67, 69, 70, 72, 73, 76, 78, 97, 115, 127, 151, 158-159, 160, 162, 163, 164, 165, 168, 174, 188
: Egyptian Islamic Jihad, 208
: first jihad movement bureaus opened in 1984 by Ayman al-Zawahiri, 184
: funding of, 159-160
: international jihadi movement, 151
: international jihad organisation, 184
: Islamic jihad movement of Abdul al-Zumur, 184
: leaders, 72
: three factors that provided leadership to Afghan Jihad, 159-162
: tribal jihad, 74
Jirgah, Wolesi, 35
Jordan (Jordanians), 194
Jospin, Lionel, 186, 187-188
Jowzjan, 117, 121
Judicial system, 10
: Judicial Commission, 175
Juma Gul, 39

Kabul, 2, 3, 4, 7, 8, 12, 13, 24, 28, 29, 31, 35, 44, 45, 47, 53, 56, 57, 60, 64-65, 68, 73, 76, 79, 80, 86, 87, 88, 89, 91, 92, 93, 94, 95, 97, 98, 100, 101, 105, 111, 112, 113, 115, 116, 118, 119, 120, 127, 128-129, 130, 135, 136, 137, 138, 139, 140, 141, 149, 156, 161, 166, 167, 168, 180, 181, 182, 185, 198, 199, 212, 218, 219, 221, 222, 224, 225, 227, 228, 229, 233, 234, 235, 236, 237, 240
: bomb blast at Pakistan embassy in, 138
: Kabul museum, destruction of statues by Taleban, 64-65
: Old Road and New Road areas, 128-129
Kahmard, 30
Kakkul, 30
Kalafghan, 193
Kalat, 76
Kamal Hossain, 141-143
Kandahar, 18, 54, 74, 75, 76, 78, 80, 81, 82-83, 84, 86, 88, 89, 90, 91, 133, 146, 166, 167, 168, 181, 182, 217, 221, 236, 237, 240
Kanishka, Emperor, destruction of statue of, 65
Karachi, 203, (*see also* Pakistan)
Kargil war (*see also* India, Pakistan) 124-126, 128, 129, 205
Karim, Mohammad, 39
Karzai, Hamid, 1-2, 9, 13, 14, 16, 21, 22, 30-31, 33, 41, 42, 56, 58, 175, 215, 217, 218, 238, 240, 241
: assassination of, 156
: assessment of Afghanistan by, 14-15
Kashmir (*see* Jammu and Kashmir) *see also* India, Pakistan)
Kata Khana, 146
Katju, Vivek, 61
Kayan Valley, 142
Keith, Kenton W., 235
Kenya, 131, 208
Khair Khana, 120
Khaksar, Haji Mullah, 185, 186
Khalili, Karim, 118-119, 124, 146, 238

Index

Khalili, Masood, 47, 106, 122, 179-180, 195, 196, 197, 198, 199
Khalis, Maulvi Mohammed Younis, 67, 75, 97, 161, 164, 238
Khan, Bismillah (*see* Bismillah Khan)
Khan, Ismael (*see* Ismael Khan)
Khan, Riaz Mohammed, 203
Kharazi, Kamal, 148
Khoja Bhauddin, 50, 196, 200
Khost
 : Badr Campin, 127
Khuhisan, 30
Khwaja Ghar, 142, 193
Killings (*see also* Punishment), 133-136, 141-149, 153-154
 : extrajudicial, 135-136
King Abdul Aziz University, Jeddah, 158-159
Koppel, Ted, 230, 232
Koran, 72, 104
 : Koranic slogans, 91
 : pocket Korans, 128
Korea, South, 80
Krakowski, Elie D., 191
Krieken, Jet van, 101, 102, 103
Kuliab airport, 118
Kunar, 18, 92, 97
Kunduz, 117, 119, 120, 122, 127, 129, 135, 141, 205, 206, 207, 235, 236, 237, 238, 239
Kushan fort, 65
Kyrgyzstan, 23, 131

Laden, Osama bin (*see* Osama bin Laden)
Laghman, 39, 72, 92
Lahore (*see also* Pakistan), 97
Lalande, Brice, 186, 187
Lambah, S.K., 237
Lashkar-e-Toiba, 155
Liberalism, 160
 : religious tradition, 159
Libya, 168
Los Angeles
 : terrorist attack on, 194

Loya Jirgah (*see* Emergency Loya Jirgah)
Ludin, Jawed, 46-47

Madrassas (religious schools), 65, 66, 69-70, 75, 76, 78, 81, 83, 85, 86, 92 (*see also* Pakistan)
Magnus, Ralph H., 69-70
Mahaz-e-Milli, 160
Mahmoud Ahmad, 202-203
Maktab Soltan Raziyeh area, 231-232
Malik, Pahlawan, 115, 117, 118-119, 120, 121
 : Taleban-Malik collaboration, 116
Mamayee, 141
Manila, 86
Maoist groups, 71
Ma'sadat Al-ansar, 158
Massacres, 114, 117, 119-120, 121, 141-142, 143, 146
 : counter-massacres, 121
 : in Shamali Valey, 119-120
Massoud, Ahmad Shah, 7, 8, 16-17, 23, 47-51, 72, 73, 87, 89, 90, 91, 92, 93, 95, 100, 101, 104, 109, 116, 117-118, 119, 122, 123, 148, 149, 150, 151, 160, 161, 179, 181, 182, 183, 185-192, 211-212, 220, 228
 : assassination (9 September 2001) by Tunisians (not Moroccans), 45, 107-108, 179-181, 182, 183, 185, 189, 195-196, 198, 199, 200, 210
 : European tour, 185-192
 : International Conference on Massoud Studies, first Kabul (September 2002), 50-51, 200
Massoud, Ahmad Wali, 98, 182, 199, 235
Massouda Jalal, 41
Maulvis (teachers), 70
Mazarai, Abdul Ali, 88
Mazar-i-Sharif, 56, 80, 115-116, 117, 120, 122, 141, 142, 166, 167, 168, 224, 226, 227, 231, 233, 236, 238

: Mazar-i-Sharif, Airport
(Qezelabad), 142
Mehmoud, 92
Mestiri, Mehmoud, 88
Mewand, 78
Middle East, 98, 154
Milan, William, 193
Militant Islamists (groups) (Islamic militants) (terrorists), 96-97, 154, 184
: foreign, 151
Mindayak, 146
Mine Action Centre, 10
Mir Ali, 147
Mirwais, 213
Mishra, Brajesh, 207
Modernisation plans, 38
Modernist Islamic thinkers, 38
Mohammad, Prophet, 72, 76, 115
Mohammad Ghaus, Mullah, 117
Mohammad Omar, Mullah (*see* Omar Mullah, Mohammad)
Mohammedi, Maulvi Mohammed Nabi, 67, 70, 71, 75, 161
Money laundering, 56-57
Moroccans, 179
: terrorists, 50
Moudodi, 72
Muhaqiq, Haji Mohammad, 231, 232, 238
Mujaddedi, Sibgatullah, 160
Mujahideen 8, 9, 11, 49, 61, 65, 66, 71, 74, 75 98, 115, 155, 156, 158, 159, 160, 161, 162, 168, 193
: commanders, 79
: groups, 67, 71, 75-76, 81
: organisations, 72
: parties, 70
Mullah Berader, 169
Mullah Omar (*see* Omar Mullah, Mohammad)
Mullahs, 82, 161
: traditionist, 37
Munich Conference on Security Policy, 207

Murders, 29
Musharraf, Pervez, 138, 157, 199-200, 203-204, 214, 215, 220, 221, 222, 223, 224, 228-232, 235, 236
Mushkin, 147
Muslims, 78, 88, 155, 184-185, 196, 208, 209, 231, 236
: brotherhood, 160
: fundamentalist, 104
: movement of young Muslims (Tehreek Jamiat Muslimeen), 156
: Plight of, 158
: Shia, 9, 115, 163, 231
: Sunnis, 70, 85, 88, 95, 159, 184, (*see also* Sunnis)
: women, 155-166
Mustafa, 192
Mutamain, Abdul Hai, 149
Muttahida-Majlis-e-Amal (MMA), 218, 241
Muttawakil, Wakil Ahmed, 185-186, 194
Myers, Richard, 173

NYT, 222
Naby, Eden, 69-70
Naderi, Sayyid Jaffar, 118
Nahreen, 136
Nairobi, 175, 182, 194
Najibullah, President, 75, 93-85, 130, 219
: execution of, 93-94, 107
: family in safe shelter in New Delhi, 94
Nangarhar, 18, 92, 97, 164
Naquib, Mullah, 82
Narayanan, K. R.
: on situation in Afghanistan, 129-130
Narcotics (*see also* Drugs), 19-22
: cultivation and trafficking of illegal, 49, 188
: International Narcotics Control Board, 20-21
: trade in, 21-22

Index

Nation-building (*see also* Economy), 57-62
: rebuilding, 174-175, 189
: women's instrumental role in, 189
National Mourning Day, 124
National Movement of Afghanistan, Massoudist party, 182
National Unity, 42
Nawaz Sharif (*see* Sharif, Nawaz)
Nayak, 144, 145, 146
Netherlands, 101
Nimrooz, 71, 89
Noori, Noorallah, 238
North West Frontier Province, 218
Northern Alliance (later United Front) (*see also* United Front), 28, 44, 102, 114, 122
Nuristan, 5,6
Nuristani, Nalim, 42

Oakley, Robert, 222
Omar Mullah, Mohammad, 73, 75, 76, 77, 78, 79, 81, 101, 117, 146, 149, 155, 156, 157, 167, 168, 169, 181, 182, 214, 233, 236, 237, 240
Operation Anaconda, 153, 168, 240
Operation Enduring Freedom, 44, 47, 121, 153, 166, 168, 203, 204, 205, 207, 212, 218, 240
: psychology of Taleban under impact of, 166-167
Operation Full Throttle, 170, 172, 173
Opium poppy (*see also* Drugs), 17-26, 53-55, 137
: cultivation (crops) (production) 18-26, 132-133
: smuggling, 53-55 (*see also* smuggling)
: trade (business), 53-54, 137
Organisation of Islamic Conference (OIC), 68, 190, 216
: Tehran summit, 123
Oruzgan, 18, 75, 172
Osama bin Laden, 50, 85, 95, 97, 98, 125, 127-128, 129, 131, 151, 155, 156, 160, 163, 164-168, 175, 181-182, 186, 193, 194, 197, 202, 208, 210, 211, 220, 224, 225, 232, 233, 236
: one of the first Arabs to join jihad in Afghanistan, 158
: involvement with Afghan jihad, 158-159
: survival of, 156-157
: Taleban-Osama bin Laden's is international terrorism nexus to Indian State of Jammu and Kashmir, 124, 127-128
: terrorist network, 127
Osh, 23
Otilie, 49

Pahalwan, Abdul Malik, 238
Pahalwan, Rasul, 115
Pakistan (Pakistanis), 3, 17, 25, 40, 45, 50, 53, 67, 70-72 (*passim*), 75, 79-98 (*passim*), 104-109 (*passim*), 115-120 (*passim*), 123-132 (*passim*), 137-141 (*passim*), 153, 157, 161, 163, 167-168, 175, 180, 183-195 (*passim*), 199, 201-206 (*passim*), 210, 212-224 (*passim*), 227-241 (*passim*).
: AWACS reconnaissance plane, 168
: activities, 164
: Afghan policy, 106
: Afghan refugee camps in, 65, 76, 162
: Afghan refugees in, 9, 42, 70, 72, 112-113, 135,
: bomb blast at Pakistan embassy in Kabul, 138
: bureaucracy, 71
: cricket team of Afghanistan, sent to play to, 107
: embassy raided by mob in Afghanistan, 90-91
: factionalist war in Afghanistan, 96
: forces in Afghanistan, 168

- frontier militia forces from North West Frontier Province, 126
- fundamentalists 71, 167
- game plan, 73
- ISI (Inter-Services Intelligence), 24, 70, 71, 72, 74, 80, 82, 84, 85, 90, 95, 96, 97, 98, 125, 126, 127, 129, 137, 160, 161, 162, 163 199, 200, 219, 220, 221, 230; ISI-CIA nexus, 160
- infiltrators into Indian territories, 124-126
- Islamabad, 73, 79-80, 83, 84, 85, 92, 94, 96, 106, 138, 140, 161, 162, 189, 190, 214, 219, 229, 235, 237, 238
- Islamic fundamentalists, 71
- Islamic Group, 97
- Islamic parties, 162
- Jalalabad, 92
- Jamaat Islami, 72
- Karachi, 193, 203
- Kargil war, 124-126, 128, 129, 205
- Lahore, special terrorist training camps in, 97
- madrassas in, 65, 70, 76, 81, 86, 92; Sunni, 85
- media, 139-140
- militant Islamists (terrorists), 96-97
- military units from Churat and Sahiwal divisions and officers and soldiers from military mostly Punjabis, 126-127
- Musharraf (*see* Musharraf)
- NWF Province, 83, 126
- Pakistan-backed Taleban, 192
- Pakistan-based terrorist group Lashkar-e-Toiba, 155
- Pakistan-inspired terrorism in Indian state of Jammu and Kashmir, 127, 204
- Pakistan-occupied Kashmir, terrorist centres in, 204-205
- Poonch area, 128
- Proxy war, 125-126
- Punjab, 126, 192
- radical parties, 160
- religious movements, 151
- road to Central Asia from, 83
- role in perpetuating Taleban rule, 189
- running nineteen camps, 168
- Simla agreement (1972), 124
- Sipah-e-Sahaba, 126, 192
- Sipah-e- Tayeba, 126
- six Pakistani held senior posts in Taleban military, 168
- smuggling from, 133
- sponsored Islamist terrorism in Kashmir, 127, 204
- sponsorship of international and regional terrorism, 96
- Talebanisation of, 224
- terrorist training camps, 97, 168, 204-205
- terrorist training centres of Arab Afghans in, 97
- terrorists, 127-128, 155
- transport mafia, 83; donations to Mullah Omar, 81-82
- US seven demands to, 202-204

Paktia, 31, 56, 96, 97, 156
Paktiya, 5, 6
Palenbagh, 30
Palestine, 155
Panjsher Valley, 4, 5-6, 8, 72, 73, 92, 100, 115, 135, 197, 200
Parachinar, 192
para-military groups, 126
Paris, 48, 186
- European Conference on Drug Trafficking and Law Enforcement, second annual (September 2002), 18, 19

Peace, 24-25, 58, 174
- efforts, 68

Pearl Harbour, Japanese attack on, 207
Pennsylvania, 201
Pentagon (*see* USA)

Peshawar, 74, 80, 108, 156, 163, 184
Philipines, 168
: Philipinos, 167, 168
Phul Sofiaz, 128
Political inclinations, 159-161
Political parties, 67
Popal, Mohammad Akbar, 60-61
Powell, Colin, 202, 203
Prodi, Romano, 216
Property, destruction of, 29
Provincial authorities, 29, 30
Proxy war, 125-126 (see also India, Pakistan)
Public live burial (by bulldozing layers of rocks into them), punishment, 24 (see also punishment)
Punishment under Taleban administration, 24, 109-112, 133, 134
: amputations of fingers, hands and feet (limbs), 24, 134
: beatings of women and children, 134
: death, 14, 24, 133, 134, 174
: death, stoning to, 24, 134
: deaths in custody, 133
: executions, 133, 134, 136, 141-142, 143, 146, 212
: flogging, 134
: killings, 133-136, 141-149, 153-154 (see also Killings)
: public live burial, 24
: targeted killings, 133
Punjab (Pakistan), 126, 192
: Punjabis, 49
Purdah, 24 (see also Women)
Pushtuns, ethnic community, 15-17, 31, 36, 39, 42, 46, 52, 72, 75, 79, 84, 85, 91, 94, 116, 117, 121, 122, 137, 159, 189 212, 218, 219, 221, 222, 224, 227, 228, 229, 230, 233, 234
: Durrani, 74
: educated scholars, 108
: Ghilzai, 74
: military and political officials, 80

: mujahideen leadership, 75

Qadeer, Haji Abdul, 16, 29
Qala Arbab Hassan, 147
Qala Issa Khan, 145, 146
Qanooni, Mohammad Yunus, 33, 237
Qasim, 147
Qaysar, 142
Quetta, 74, 75, 80, 81, 82, 83, 217
: Quetta-Kandahar-Herat-Ashkabad route, 89
Qutb, Sayed, 72

RPK, 172
Rabbani, Burhanuddin, 8, 23, 47, 48, 49, 67, 68, 71, 72, 79, 80, 85, 86, 88, 89, 95, 118, 119, 120, 123, 125-126, 127, 160, 179, 198, 212, 215, 220, 234, 235, 237, 238
Rabbani, Mullah Mohammed, 75, 79
Radical parties, 160
Rapes, 29
Rashid, Ahmed, 24, 25, 54, 55, 73, 75, 76, 77, 78, 80, 82, 83, 84-85, 89, 90, 94-95, 116, 159, 162
Rathje, W.L. 102, 103, 104
Red Cross
: International Committee of the Red Cross (ICRC), 74, 112
Red Tapism, 58
Reeker, Philip T., 25
Rees-Khor, 127
Refhat, Ahmad Zia, 33
Refugees
: Afghan refugees (camps) in Pakistan, 9, 13, 29, 30, 42, 70, 72, 76, 112-113, 134
: UN High Commissioner for Refugees, 134
Regional cooperation, 174
Rehmani, Mullah Mohammed Hassan, 75
Religious communities, 11
Religious fanaticism, 79 (see also fanaticism)

Religious fundamentalism, 14, 75 (*see also* Fundamentalism, Fundamentalists)
Ressam, Ahmed, 194-195
Rishkhor, 167
Robberies, 29
Rohni, Naseer Ahmed, 156
Rome, 65, 132, 213, 219
  : Rome Group, 28
Roundtable on Afghanistan: Governance Scenarios and Canadian Policy Options, 44
Rowland, B., 102-103
Roy, Olivier, 150, 157
  : Islamist movement in Afghanistan, 150-151
  : summary of war-devastated country, 150-151
Rubin, Barnett R., 23, 24, 25, 55-57, 210
Rumsfeld, Donald H., 211, 218, 221, 224, 226-227
Russia (Russians) (*see also* Soviet Union), 23, 49, 67, 118, 131, 148, 149-150, 183, 188, 196, 212, 234
  : Chechens, 49, 167, 168, 238
  : confidential memo to UN (2001): influence of al-Qaeda and Osama bin Laden on Taleban-ruled Afghanistan, 167-168
  : India-Russia summit, 149
  : invasion (*see* Soviet Union)
  : mafia, 23
  : military support to anti-Taleban forces, 148
  : Russian Federation, 55, 118
  : Russian United Front defence ministers' meeting, 149
Rustaq, 123, 141
SEMTEX, sophisticated explosives, 95-96
SPACH (Society for the Preservation of Afghanistan's Cultural Heritage), 101, 102, 103

Sadar, Anwar
  : assassination of, 184
Saeed, Hafiz Muhammad, 155-156
Saighan, 30
Salang Pass, 118
Salang tunnel, 118
Samangan, 30, 117, 129
Sanan, Said, 217
Sangarmal, Mullah Rahmatullah, 193
Sar-i-Pul, 29, 30, 117, 142
Sarobi, 92, 94
Satellites
  : spy satellites, 157
  : Thuraya satellite phone, 157
Saudi Arabia, 12, 67, 85, 90, 92, 97, 116, 139, 157, 159, 160, 164, 165, 175, 233
Sayyaf, Abdul Rasul, 71, 72, 160, 196, 238
Sayyaf's Ittihad-e-Islami Bara-yi-Azadi Afghanistan, 8
Sayyid Ibrahim, 147
Sayyid Sarwar, 147
Sayyid Talib, 147
Security environment and stability, 2-3, 11, 13, 24-25, 29-32, 52, 56, 68
  : International Security Assistance Force (ISAF), 2-3, 13, 31, 222
  : peace and, 24-25, 58, 68, 174 (*see also* Peace)
Sekandar, Sardar, 192
Sergeyev, Igor, 148, 192
Shahir, Mohammad Rafiq, 39
Shamali Valley (Plains), 7, 8, 119, 135, 142, 195
  : massacres in, 119-120 (*see also* Massacres)
  : transformation of, 100-106
Sharia, Islamic, 69, 72, 86, 91, 140
  : code, 134
  : law, 133
Sharif, Nawaz, 70, 125, 126
Sherzai, Gul Agha, 1, 238
Shias, 88, 115
  : Shia Hazaras, 231

Index

: Shia parties, 9
: Shiaite-Communist Confederation, 163
Shiberghan, 120
Shindand, 89, 90
Sholayees, 71
Sholgara, 30
Shulgara, 129
Silk Road, 104
Silk Route, 101
Simla Agreement (1972), 124 (*see also* India, Pakistan)
Singesar, 78
Sipah-e-Sahaba, extremist religious party, Pakistan, 126, 192 (*see also* Pakistan)
Sipah-e-Tayeba, 126 (*see also* Pakistan)
Smuggling (*see also* Drugs), 53-57, 115, 133, 136, 140, 154-155
: mafia, 80
: organised, 25
Somalia, 222
South Asia (*see* Asia)
South Korea, 80
Soviet Union (Soviets) (*see also* Russia), 66, 83, 162, 168, 190
: airbase at Shindand, 89
: Arabs fighing army of, 151, 158
: era communist parties, 167
: invasion and occupation of Afghanistan (1979), 9, 66, 69, 71, 72, 73, 74, 150-151, 158, 168, 184, 187, 225
: withdrawal (departure, left) from Afghanistan (1989), 67, 131, 212, 228, 230
Spain, 80
Spin Baldak, 81, 83, 236
: battle of, 82
Statues of Buddhas, demolition of (*see* Buddhas) (*see also* Bamiyan Valley)
Straw Jack, 19, 216
Subversive activities, 14, 72
Sudan, 97, 164

Sufism, 159, 160, 162
: Sufis, 162
Sunnis (*see also* Muslims), 88, 95
: Islamists, 184
: madrassas, 85
: orthodoxy, Hanafi, 70, 159

Tagab, 128
Tahsili, 147
Tajikistan, 23, 97, 118, 123, 148, 149-150, 151, 180, 183, 197, 199, 200
: Tajikistan-Afghanistan border, 149-150
Tajiks, ethnic community, 15, 16, 17, 39, 52, 85, 100, 116, 119, 121, 145, 149, 195, 200, 229
Tajuddin, Khokho, 200
Takhar, 117, 122, 123, 141, 142, 192, 193
Taleban (administration, fighters, government, regime, rule), 1-10 (*passim*), 17-26 (*passim*), 35, 36, 40, 41, 44-50, 54, 55, 61, 71-83 (*passim*), 100-156 (*passim*), 159, 161, 162, 174, 175, 182-188 (*passim*), 191-196 (*passim*), 198, 202-226 (*passim*), 230-241 (*passim*)
: acts of atrocities, 141-148
: advent of, 81
: Bakhtar News Agency, Taleban-run, 101
: claimed achievements in (2000), 68-69
: destruction of statues at Kabul Museum by, 64-65, 101-106
: destruction of statues of Buddhas, 64-65, 101-106 (*see also* Bamiyan Valley, Buddhas)
: emergence of rapidly fundamentalist Taleban, 160, 162-163
: entered Jalalabad, 165
: first phase of Taleban mission, 66-67

: five years rule (26 September, 1996-13 November 2001), 114
: geo-political analysis of origin and emergence of, 160, 162-163
: history of, 84-98
: history of control of entire western Afghanistan, 84-90
: influence of al-Qaeda and Osama bin Laden on Taleban-ruled Afghanistan, 167-168
: Islamicist movement, international, 163-164
  leadership, 73-74
: mass killings in course of military offences, 141-148 (*see also* Killings, Punishment)
: measures abolishing completely individual freedom to live normal life, 107-114
: movement, accounts of, 78
: origin of, 65-70, 160, 162-163
: Pakistan-backed Taleban, 192
: Pakistan's role in perpetuating Taleban rule, 189
: Pakistan's six held senior posts in Taleban military, 168
: Pakistani nineteen camps (terrorist), 168
: psychology under impact of Operation Enduring Freedom of, 166-167
: punishment under rule of (*see* Punishment)
: second phase of their holy jihad, 68-69
: Sohaila, young woman: guilty of adultery, punished in Olympic sports stadium, Kabul, 109-110
: Taleban-al-Qaeda, 12, 30, 32, 43, 45, 47, 49, 53-54, 55, 56, 57, 59, 60, 173, 180, 181, 183, 203, 204, 216, 232, 238
: Taleban-al-Qaeda terrorist network, 68, 169, 180, 182, 183, 185, 189, 205, 217, 218, 240, 241

: Taleban-Arab mujahideen relations, 164-167
: Taleban-i-Kashmir organisation: Afghanistan-based Kashmiri Islamist terrorist organisation, 127
: Taleban Islamic Movement of Afghanistan, 68
: Taleban-Malik collaboration, 116
: Taleban-Osama bin Laden's international terrorism nexus to Jammu and Kashmir, 124, 127-128
: Taleban-United Front, 16
: tussle between Hazaras and, 124
Talebanesque hell, 62
Taloqan, 123, 136, 148
Tanzania, 131, 208
Tanzeemha, 67
Tashkent Declaration: Six plus Two contact group-peace talks (Tashkent Declaration on Fundamental Principles for the Peaceful Settlement of the Conflict in Afghanistan, Tashkent (19 July 1999), 7, 80, 129, 150
Taxation, 56
Teheran, 84, 214
: Organisation of Islamic Conference (OIC) at, 123
Tehreek Jamiat Muslimeen (Movement of Young Muslims), 156
Tenet, George, 210-211
Terrorism, 11, 14, 49, 58, 69, 96-97, 131, 137-138, 156, 188, 201, 206, 207, 239 (*see also* Terrorists)
: C-4 and SEMTEX sophisticated explosives, 95-96
: Cross-border terrorism to Jammu and Kashmir, 137-138, 205 (*see also* India)
: global (international) coalition against, US call, 201-202, 204
: House Task on Terrorism and Unconventional Warfare, USA, 84

Index

: international (global) network, 95, 96, 98, 131, 149, 157, 174, 175, 180, 183-184, 236-237
: Pakistan-sponsored Islamic terrorism in Kashmir, 127
: regional, 96
Terrorists (*see also* Terrorism), 43, 85, 124, 125, 131, 202, 208
: activities (acts), 49, 188-194
: Afghan, Pakistani and Arab terrorists (ranks of Kashmiri national liberation forces), 127
: al-Qaeda terrorist network, 153-154, 165-166, 202, 205, 225
: attacks, 2-3, 131, 154; on Indian Parliament House (13 December 2001), 205; on World Trade Centre, USA (11 September 2001) (*see* USA)
: groups, 14, 131, 153, 154
: infrastructure, 95, 97-98, 168-169
: Islamic (Islamist), 95, 96-97, 98, 127-128
: militant Islamists, 96-97
: missions around world, 194-195
: network, 153-154, 165-166, 174, 202, 225
: Taleban-al-Qaeda network, 153-154, 165-166, 202, 205, 225
: Taleban-i-Kashmir organisation: Afghanistan-based Kashmiri Islamist terrorist organisation, 127
: terrorist organisations, 207-208
: terrorist training camps, 168-175
: terrorist training camps for martyrdom operations used for recruits from Arab, Islamic and European countries, 95-96
: terrorist training camps in Afghanistan, 209, 230
: terrorist training centres in Pakistan-occupied Kashmir, 204-205
Tirmez, 80
Toepfer, Klaus, 5

Tokyo, 12, 14, 57
Tolerance, 159, 160
Tomb of Ali, 115
Tomsen, Peter, 59-60, 137
Tora Bora, 155
Torpeka, young woman, 111
Traditionalism, 162
: traditionalists (leadership), 75
Transitional Government (Islamic Transitional Government), 2, 13, 16, 29, 36, 42, 43, 51, 52, 54, 57, 58, 92, 161, 173-174, 240
Tribes (tribal), 224
: affiliations, 28
: conflicts, 52
: elders, 213
: society, 34
: traditional tribal-based parties, 161
: tribal jihad, 74
: tribalism, 108
Tunisia (Tunisians), 168, 179
Turabi, Nuruddin, 73, 82
Turkmenistan, 80, 150, 168
Turkey, 116, 216-217

UK (United Kingdom) (*see also* Britain), 80, 216
UNESCO, 105
UNO (United Nations Organisations), 7-8, 11-12, 17, 21, 28, 48, 51, 52, 58, 68, 69, 76, 87-88, 93, 94-95, 105-106, 117, 120, 121, 122, 130-131, 132, 141, 142, 153-154, 167, 190, 213, 214, 215, 216, 222, 229, 234, 238, 239
: activities, 164
: confidential report (September 2002), 153-155
: framework, 10-12, 15
: General Assembly, 14
: Illicit Crop Monitoring Programme (ICMP), 17-18
: Kofi Annan, 124, 131
: Monitoring Group, 153, 154; report, 174

- sanctions, 59-60, 139, 175
- Security Council, 11-12, 30, 119, 124, 139, 153
- UN Assistance Mission in Afghanistan (UNAMA), 13
- UN Drug Control Programme (UNDCP), 17-18, 22, 23, 54
- UN Environment Programme (UNEP), 4, 5, 7
- UN-funded Organisation for Mine Clearance and Rehabilitation, 138
- UN-mandated force, 12
- UN Office for Drugs Control and Crime Prevention, 20
- UN Special Rapporteur Paik Chong-Hyun, report, 121-131; Rabbani government statement in, 126-127
- UN-sponsored Six-plus-Two contact group meet, Tashkent, 129, 130, 132
- UNEP Afghanistan Task Force, 5
- UNHCR (UN High Commissioner for Refugees), 29 30

USA (United States of America) (America, Americans) (*see also* America), 9-12, 25-26, 44, 46, 51, 52, 55, 57, 67, 80, 96, 125, 126, 131, 139, 151, 155, 164, 166, 167, 168, 173, 175, 182, 190, 191, 193, 207, 208-210, 211, 212, 214, 215, 217, 218, 221-239 (*passim*)
- administration, 31-32, 59, 201-204
- allies, 155, 166
- American-Arab intelligence, activities of, 164
- Association for Peace and Democracy for Afghanistan, seminar: Loya Jirgah and a Political Solution to the Afghan Problem, at Annandale, Virginia (March 2001), 189-190
- attacks (bombing, fight) by allies and (US-led alliance attack), 21-22, 43, 45, 156, 166, 168, 169, 173
- Bush, George W. (*see* Bush)
- CIA (Central Intelligence Agency), 22, 73, 74, 75, 160, 210, 211, 220, 226; CIA-ISI nexus, 160
- global (international) coalition against terrorism, 201-202, 204
- House Task Force on Terrorism and Unconventional Warfare, 84
- Pakistan, seven demands to, by 202-204
- Pentagon, terrorist attack on (*see below* World Trade Centre)
- policy of, 139
- Powell, Colin (*see* Powell)
- retaliation, 182-183
- spy satellites, 157
- trade sanctions, 194
- World Trade Centre and Pentagon, terrorist attack on, 43, 44, 45, 50, 175, 179, 181, 182, 183, 185, 200-202, 207, 210, 211, 231, 236, 239, 241

United Arab Emirates, 116, 139
Uighurs, 49, 195
Ulema, 70, 74
Ummah, 163, 181
Umrah, 164
United Front (earlier Northern Alliance) (*see also* Northern Alliance), 7, 10, 15-16, 20, 22, 44, 45, 46, 47-48, 49, 55, 105, 114, 125, 126, 128, 132, 135, 136, 143, 144, 148, 165, 166, 167, 182, 185, 189, 192, 195, 196-197, 198, 199, 200, 203, 206, 210, 211, 212, 214, 215, 219, 220, 221, 222, 224, 225, 226, 227-228, 229, 231, 233-238 (*passim*)
United Islamic and National Front for the Salvation of Afghanistan, 118
Uzbekistan, 67, 80, 116, 125, 127, 150, 168, 227

Index

: Uzbek Islamic Movement (Islamic Movement of Uzbekistan), 150, 208
: Uzbeks, 39, 85, 115, 116, 119, 120, 121, 150, 195, 229; fundamentalists, 131

Vajpayee, Atal Behari
: re-appraisal of India's Afghanistan policy, ordered by, 130
Vedrine, Hubert, 186, 188, 216
Vendrell, Francis, 214
Violence, 14, 29, 30, 174, 194

Wahabism, 159, 160, 161
: Ittehad-e-Islami, Wahabbi party, 160
Wahib, Abdul, 42
Wakhan, 97
Wakil Ahmad, Mullah, 90
Wali Jan, 54, 182
Warlordism (Warlords), 30-31, 47, 87, 124, 143, 222
West (Western Nations), 191, 216
: allies, 204
: democracies, 138
Wolfowitz, Paul, 231
Women (females, girls), 11, 30, 36, 39-40, 41, 48, 60-61, 78-79, 91, 107-114, 119, 132, 208
: education of, 60-61, 69, 107-109, 134-135, 188-189
: Gross, Nasrine, woman activist of Negar, 121; support of women of Afghanistan, 39-41
: instrumental role in rebuilding country, 189
: killings of, 148
: Loya Jirgah for, 40
: physical and mental health and status of, 111-114
: plight (position, situation) under Taleban exceed all limits of decency and civilisation, 78-79, 109-114
: purdah, 24
: rights of, 107-109, 175
: role of, 49, 189
: safety, dignity and freedom of, 69
: status of, 56, 111-114
: suffering in Herat of, 91
: Taleban's measures abolishing completely individual freedom to live normal life, 107-114
: treatment to, 140
: Women's Health and Human Rights in Afghanistan, report by JAMA, 111-113
World Bank, 133, 134
World Trade Centre (*see* USA)

Yakawlang, 142, 143, 144, 146, 147
: genocide (killings) in, 142, 148
Yemen, 194
Younis Khalis, Maulvi Mohammed, 164, 165
Yousaf, Mohammad, 71
Yusuf Hasan, 29
Yusufzai, Rahimullah, 77

Zabul, 76
Zahir Shah, Mohammad, 11, 44, 48, 132, 189-190, 213, 214, 219, 220, 224, 227, 233, 238
Zaksilwal Omar, 44-46
Zaman, Haji Mohammed, 227
Zarin, 147
Zawahiri, Ayman al (*see* al-Zawahiri)
Zia-ul Haq, 70, 71, 72, 73, 139
Zoroastrians, 104
Zumur, Abdul al (*see* al-Zumur)